Witness in the Holy Land

...Maria's ... reports from that tormented "holy land" shed much needed light into the "real" situation as experienced by Christians. When ... numerous others give the public such a biased account of this "Middle East Problem," Maria's reporting is especially welcome. With her every report, I can only "double-up" my prayers for those poor suffering people, Arabs/Christians and Moslems and Jews... Fr. Athanasios Emmert, Price, Utah.

(letter to the editor, www.orthodoxnews.com site, January 19, 2003)

My deepest appreciation to all who pray for me. I am grateful to all of the internet websites, worthy newspapers, and magazines in many parts of the world that printed my articles. Special thanks to Fr. Raed Abusahlia, former chancellor, Latin Patriarchate of Jerusalem, for giving me a voice in the Olive Branch Newsletter. Special mention should be given to a fellow Greek Ms. Evagelia Alawneh of the Macedonia Greek Cultural Center for being my excellent role model in serving God and through the Palestine Avenir Foundation helping Palestine free from Thalassemia and building the National Center For Blood Diseases "Hippocrates," in Ramallah. Last but not least, my wonderful family for their love and continued encouragement to stay in Palestine.

May all glory be to God!

WITNESS

IN THE HOLY LAND

Maria C. Khoury, Ed. D.

CDK Publications
Holy Land

Scripture Passages are according to the King James Version.

Front and back cover: Oil painting of Jerusalem by Abu Maher, Al Funun, Ramallah.

Photos curtsey of The Jerusalem Times.

Witness in the Holy Land

Printed in the Holy Land.

CDK Publications
P.O. Box 867
Ramallah, Palestine,
Via Israel

For information contact:
khourymaria@hotmail.com
drmariakhoury@yahoo.com
Church website: www.saintgeorgetaybeh.org

This book is lovingly dedicated

to my husband David

who genuinely believes I should spend more time
cooking, cleaning, ironing, dusting, sweeping, mopping …

Contents

Dedication 5

Contents 6

Map of the Holy Land 8

Preface by His Beatitude Michel Sabbah 9

Introduction

Living in the Land of Promise 11

Printing Orthodox Books in the Midst of Violence 17

Roots of Taybeh Traced to Time of Christ 21

Palestinian Beer Brewed in Taybeh 24

Struggling One Day at a Time in the Holy Land 27

The Outbreak of the Palestinian Uprising

The Tragedy in the Holy Land 33

Suffering in the Holy Land 36

This Sunday in the Holy Land 38

Shattered Dreams in Palestine 40

Palestinian Student Voices 42

Christian Voices from the Holy Land 48

Christmas in the Village 51

The True Identity of Taybeh 53

Christmas in Beit Jala 55

The Holiday Nightmare of 11,000 Palestinians 58

Voice of Christian Youth 60

Psychological Affects on Palestinian Students 63

The Memories Will Last Forever 67

The Way to Aboud 69

A Prayer for a Wedding 72

How Many Bombs Can One Home Take? 74

Stuck on Sunday 77

The Voice of Christian Children in Palestine 80

Anxiety and Faith in the Village 83

Do You Believe in Miracles? 86

The Voice of Christian Students in Gaza 89

No Pleasant Stories in the Holy Land 92

Living Under Siege and Closures

Return to the Land of Bloodshed 94

Prayers from the Holy Land: September 11th Letter 96

Enthronement of the Greek Orthodox Patriarch 97

A Checkpoint Away from the Miraculous Icon 100

Occupation Cheats Children from Basic Education 105

This Week in the Holy Land 107
The Challenges Facing the Christian Schools 110
Essays Expressing Faith 114
What's Going on in the Holy Land? 116
Christmas Season in the Holy Land 119
Children's Wishes from Aboud 121
The Distinguishing Character of Taybeh 123
Orthodox Christmas in the Holy Land 126
Epiphany at the Jordan River 128
Nights of Terror in Ramallah 130
On the Way to Beit Jala Today 133
Still Wishing in the Holy Land 135
The Bloodiest Week in the Holy Land 137
The Catastrophe in Ramallah 139
The High Price of Christian Roots 142
The Work of the Church During the Intifada 145
Occupation Will Bring More Terror 147
Ethnic Cleansing in the Land of Christ's Birth 149
Praying Under Israeli Guns 152
Remembering Christ's Visit to Taybeh 155
Orthodox Holy Week in Ramallah 158
School Remains the Only Hope for Palestinian Children 160
Liturgy at the Fourth Century Ruins 164

The Remarkable Experience of the Holy Light 167
Going to School with Gunfire 171
New Leadership for the Latin Schools of Jerusalem 174
The Current Situation in Palestine 177
The Patriarchal Visit to Taybeh 180
Students Speak Out 185
The Humanitarian Fund at a Critical Time 188
Shooting at Children and Teachers at the Checkpoint 190

Living Under Total Military Reoccupation

Greek Women in Ramallah 193
Christian Village Under Curfew 196
Chicago Symposium Speech (Holy Land Christian Ecumenical Foundation) .. 198
Taybeh Glorifies Christ's Birth 207
Orthodox Christmas Silently Passed 209
Preparing for War in the Holy Land 212
The Holy Land Buries Christina 214
Fundraising in the Middle of the Wilderness 217
General Information About the Holy Land 220

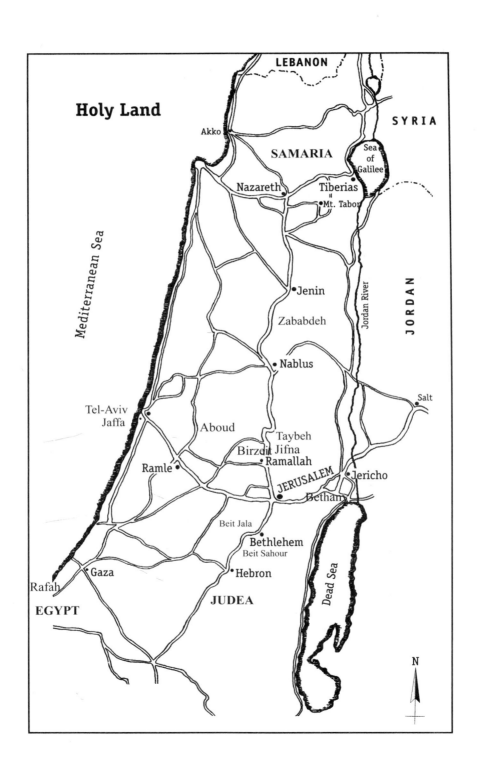

Preface

"But you will receive power when the Holy Spirit has come upon you; and you will be my witnesses in Jerusalem, in all Judea and Samaria, and to the ends of the earth." (Acts 1:8)

More than 2000 years ago a small group of people had gathered in a room in Jerusalem where the Holy Spirit descended upon them. These people become the earliest witnesses to the Gospel of Christ and were well know as the first followers of Jesus that helped develop the Church. It was from Jerusalem that these people went to preach the gospel and spread the good news about the Kingdom of God. Today, descendants of those first Christian witnesses are still to be found in Palestine.

The Palestinians and the Israelis have lived together in conflict for many years and during these difficult times, the Palestinians constantly seek their freedom and dignity. We hope the articles found in this publication that include the voices of teachers and youth from our Latin Patriarchate Schools will give a clear vision for their quest for freedom and peace from a human point of view. We confirm that the first criteria in any society not just the Palestinian and the Israeli society are to live in peace. We hope that the efforts done by Maria Khoury that reflect the realities of the conflict will bring us to stability and give positive sign for peaceful coexistence in the land that has seen too much blood.

The present circumstances under which the Palestinian people live are intolerable from any point of view: legal, political, or human. The narratives of this book are part of what has become a stream of information from Palestine crying out for an international intervention based on a consistent commitment to justice and peace. The Palestinian Christians, to which so many pages in the book are devoted, need hope and a concrete perspective for living. These articles bring awareness of the dramatically diminishing Christian presence in this land where the faith began.

We are called to bear witness to Christ our Lord no matter where we live. The author of these personal experiences reminds us to give glory to Christ our true God with every breath that we take. Maria Khoury attempts to keep the living faith despite the daily suffering and daily trials experienced in the West Bank. As Christians we must carry the Life-giving cross with deep faith, dignity and respect.

May God bless us all to have the eyes to see the glory of His love no matter how much tragedy and loss or joy and abundance we may have in our lives.

+Michel Sabbah
Latin Patriarch of Jerusalem
Jerusalem, April 23, 2003

"...Father, all things are possible unto thee...nevertheless not what I will, but what thou wilt.

Mark 14:36

Living in the Land of Promise

On a bright clear Sunday morning I stared at the beautiful hills and countryside of Biblical Judea and Samaria right outside my huge bay kitchen window. Many Sundays especially during the second Palestinian Uprising and the reoccupation of the Palestinian territories, we had to get ready for church listening to the horrid news that another bomb has gone off in Israel. There was a period of time where Sunday after Sunday an attack would take place that continues to brand the Palestinians as "terrorists." And there's nothing you can do with such news except go to church with a heavy heart and a very sick feeling in your stomach and pray to God for peace to come in the Land of Christ's birth.

I screamed at my children to hurry up since church attendance in our little Christian village of Taybeh is a number one priority and was quite relieved that Hamas (the Islamic Resistance Movement) took a day off. But still the thought crossed my mind that in a land full of violence and bloodshed what kind of future do my children really have as part of the Christian minority?

Little did I know a psychological bomb was about to explode in the Khoury extended family. Every parent's nightmare was about to happen following a Saturday night party in Miami, Florida. Our twenty-one year old cousin Ibrahim George Khoury tragically lost his life to a bullet that ripped through his heart. He was in the wrong place at the wrong time for a nice altar boy born in the village of Taybeh. As Palestine empties out of its Christian population, many families search for the "American Dream" of better education, better living conditions and better job opportunities. But, prosperity and success sometimes have a very high price. This family tragedy and shocking death made us re-evaluate our values, traditions and reasons for returning to the land of promise after twenty-four years of middle-class America.

The current unemployment of over 60% in the village and the awful closure and terrible checkpoints still make every young man want to leave this Biblical town of Ephraim.

A mere ten to fifteen minutes drive from the village to the city of Ramallah takes over two to three hours depending on the checkpoints. I can almost handle one checkpoint with patience but when you stop three times on your way to school to show your identification traveling from a Palestinian village to a Palestinian city, it is frustrating because you are not going anywhere near Israel or threatening the security of Israel. The most aggravating feeling is when the soldiers deny you the right to pass. I JUST WANT TO BLOW UP!!!

The worst I have experienced with the checkpoint phenomenon on more than one occasion is sitting at the Qalandia checkpoint for four hours following a tiring school day in a van with nine children, only three of which are my own. During the whole time, I kept yelling at all the young boys that came to hide behind my van and throw rocks at the Israeli soldiers. I kept screaming "Why do you want to die today, can you please go home." In the mean time my sons were starring out the van window as soldiers were shooting more Palestinian boys hiding behind trashcans.

We watch the violence as we watch a movie and ask for the grace of God to keep us safe. By the time we get home some days, it is completely dark out and we get up the next morning at 6 am to go through the same miserable way because it is the only way to get to school in Palestine. All the main roads have been blocked for such a long time. Money can buy you solutions, so we took an apartment in the city of Ramallah to avoid these checkpoints but when the Israeli tanks invaded the city and the noise of shooting was constant, my children wished to sleep in the village where they had less fear and anxiety.

Following the Oslo Peace Agreement, the picturesque Taybeh village was not a bad place to raise children. We would avoid the Saturday night parties because everyone just visits their grandmother. We would not have teenage peer pressure for drugs because they were simply not available in a little village on the West Bank. We would avoid the malls and being spoiled with too much materialism because we would see so many people that don't even have food to eat. We would easily go to church on Sundays because there would be no hockey conflicts or soccer games at the same time.

Raising children in a small Christian village in the Holy Land appeared like an innocent and wholesome upbringing. There was only one small problem. As an American of Greek descent, I did not have any connection to this land. However, with time and with personal and psychological suffering, the land of Christ's birth gave me a deep spiritual awakening as an Orthodox Christian.

I felt it was the legacy of my children to experience their Palestinian Christian roots since their father, a Palestinian Orthodox Christian had grown up in this tiny village where everyone is related. I thought my children would know themselves deeply if they developed a strong sense of cultural identity and experienced the richness of the Palestinian culture. I even firmly believed the love of a close-knit extended family would help my children be good human beings.

When I met my husband at Hellenic College in Boston in the late 70's, I must admit I did not know anything about Palestinians and truthfully speaking I did not even know there were any Christians in the Holy Land. However, being an obedient wife, I followed him to the land of promise. His personal promises that it was the best place in the world to raise responsible children. It has been a long, painful and rewarding learning adventure.

My husband had a dream to return to his homeland, to be an obedient son who travels to the West for education and money and brings back the skills and the knowledge to help Palestine. It's the ultimate dream of every Palestinian father. It's sort of a noble thing to do and being an entrepreneur, he talked the family into building a microbrewery in the village of Taybeh that would boost the Palestinian economy. The Oslo Peace Agreement gave many people a false promise of peace and prosperity that led into over five years of frozen negotiations where people continued to invest in Palestine.

"Taybeh Beer" was launched in the market in the summer of 1995 as the first Palestinian beer and the only microbrewery in the Middle East. We also spent five years out of suitcases building a huge stone mansion that now we pray the apache helicopters will not see if they decide to bomb Taybeh. The new beer was so successful that it made history in Palestine by being the first and only Palestinian product to be franchised and brewed in Germany under the Taybeh Beer license.

Hundreds of newspapers articles were written because reporters were so curious who are these people who invest millions of dollars to produce beer in a 98% Muslim population. These brave and loyal men are my husband David C. Khoury and my ingenious brother-in-law Nadim. They invested their heart, soul and money to help build Palestine. Receiving Arafat's blessing for the brewery was also a test when there would be a democratic Palestinian state, there would be a place for the Christian minority.

Then came Ariel Sharon and September 28, 2000 and all the dreams of Palestinians that had returned to their homeland following the Oslo Peace Agreement were shattered. Slowly but surely, destruction took place each day with bombings, shootings, assassinations and outright massacres of unarmed civilians. The Israelis have destroyed lives, houses, businesses, roads, olive trees, the economy and education. Everything that was built following Oslo and any progress made was completely ruined. The list of destruction is far too long.

There is nothing left to destroy except the peoples' will power to be free and to seek their human rights and independence. We watched as many families picked up their belongings and returned to their previous lives. They all gave up the hotels they built, the battery factories they created, the health clinics they established. These Palestinians tried to invest and live in Palestine but could not handle the harsh conditions imposed by the Israeli army. They gave up the dream to help their homeland and to live in the land of promise.

Sometimes I just can't understand my husband's decision to stay especially when the imported bottles that he needs so desperately to fill with "Taybeh Beer" are stuck at the Israeli port due to red tape. The fees and storage costs are far beyond what the bottles are worth themselves. I feel it is such a high price to pay, financially and psychologically, to be a Palestinian businessman. Not to mention a 40% production tax that basically cripples you as a new business. The war against the Palestinian economy is an entire story by itself.

When the Second Palestinian Uprising (Intifada) first broke out, we would usually wake up every morning not knowing if we were going to school or not. You must get up, get dressed and try to go to school before you discover the road situation. There is nothing more frustrating than going through all the preparations and not being able to have a school day. Sometimes the road was open, sometimes the road was closed. Sometimes you make it all the way to school passing many checkpoints just to find the school was cancelled because of a funeral or protest. Sometimes while in school, a bomb would go off in Israel and we couldn't get back home. This anxiety was unbearable and drove me crazy. Not knowing day to day what will happen.

In the fall of 2000, it was so common to hear "they're bombing Ramallah." I would drop everything, try to get my children out of school as fast as possible and get back to the village where it was perceived safer. So, you have hundreds of parents doing the same thing. There was panic in the streets and in the schools. The constant fear was very nerve racking.

To top off this instability, constant attacks were happening on the roads because we have hundreds of illegal Israeli settlements choking us up in the West Bank. Israeli settlers killing Palestinians and Palestinian gunman killing Israeli settlers back and forth until the violence escalates so much that it's totally out of control and takes on a life by itself. Then we would observe an abnormal kind of quiet, which is the type of quiet before a heavy storm. There is so much anxiety and confusion, you can't decide what scares you the most, the violence itself or the silence before the bloodshed occurs.

Driving down these roads where innocent people were killed every day was not the easiest thing in the world. The only comfort I could possibly give my children was explaining to them that if it was God's Will for us to die, we would die no matter where we live. For the first three months, I would physically shake driving to school every day. Now, I have somewhat adjusted myself. I just do my cross and say my prayers. I have gained a type of inner peace that allows me to live here and see devastation all around me. I must admit, I owe this inner peace to each and every person that prays for me. May God be with you and bless you.

What really amazes me the most is day in and day out, I see and experience the suffering of the Palestinian people and the world continues to support Israel and allow them to get away with human right violations. I am amazed at how people survive on such low incomes and under such awful conditions. Any human being living under these harsh conditions of Israeli Military Occupation would turn into a terrorist because you reach a mental point of either "freedom or death."

My children keep reminding me of the license plate they saw in New Hampshire on their summer vacation stating "live free or die." I can't remember this plate myself because they say I have lived four decades. But my children insist that if Americans can make such statements why can't Palestinians have the same rights. The struggle for freedom has taken more than fifty years. In this new millennium we must give Palestinians their full human rights and treat them as part of humanity not creatures of a lesser God. For the love of humanity, peace should come to this region where the Prince of Peace lived.

It is important to keep a Christian presence in the Holy Land because it is the land of Christ's Birth. The Holy Land being the "mother church" of Western Christianity stands proud to have so many brothers and sisters in Christ. Together we can work for a great awareness of the Palestinian struggle so that congress can have real names and real faces of how the American support to Israel affects over three million Palestinians in a negative way and cheats them from their basic rights.

We need many prayers to live together as Christians, Muslims and Jews in this precious land. We need people to make their government officials aware of the atrocities that occur in the Holy Land. We need people who can see the human suffering that the Zionist movement created since 1948. We need the occupation to end. We need the world to see the suffering and humiliation the Palestinians face every day. We need the world to understand the cause of terrorism is the Israeli occupation itself and America's policy in the Middle East.

Living in the land of promise may be full of bloodshed, violence and deep anxiety but also it has been the place where I have grown very close to God. I literally must live each day as if it is the last day of my life. Praying more, going to confession and fasting help me realize our final destiny is the kingdom of God. I truly believe God gives us every blessing and every suffering so that we may come to know Him who gives us eternal life. All the riches and the materialism in this world will not provide a place for us in God's kingdom. It is only our good works on earth that will count and the firm belief that Christ is our Savior. When Christ is in your heart you do love your neighbor as yourself and forgiveness becomes essential.

As Christians our ultimate goal is to give glory to God. We are called to see God in each and every human being. Let us pray these Christian values and principles can be practiced in the land of promise, in the land of Canaan as is my first born son's name who as a young Palestinian Christian proudly carries his late grandfather's name "Canaan," indicating the land of Palestine, the land that continues to include the living stones, the Palestinian Christians of the Holy Land.   **Written February 19, 2002**

Printing Orthodox Books in the Midst of Violence

In the middle of bloodshed and violence, the Lord, Christ our Savior is in our midst to give us inner peace since obviously peace is not in our world and specifically not in the Holy Land. For all Palestinians, both Christians and Muslims, it has been almost two years of total destruction and devastation in the land of Christ's birth. The war on terror and getting the terrorists with American tax dollars has brought tremendous collective punishment and has made most of us living in the Holy Land virtual prisoners in our homes. The current curfews since June 2002 deprive millions of people from their basic human rights. The school year began with two regular school days under Israeli guns and four days of total curfew with half of the schoolbooks missing due to the roadblocks.

Having seen the Greek Culture Center "Macedonia" in Ramallah and educational institutions such the ministry of education bombed, it seems that each and every one of us living here are terrorists because the international community is doing nothing to stop Israel from its brutal and cruel occupation of the Palestinian territories. Both on the Palestinian and Israeli side, innocent people continue to die in a catastrophic cycle of violence with the military occupation as the root cause. Living here, I feel Israel is trying to wipe out an entire culture and an entire nation from the face of the earth.

I escaped for the summer to promote my new Orthodox children's book "Christina's Favorite Saints," featuring the lives of holy people to help young readers grow closer to God and grow spiritually as they learn more about their Orthodox faith. Fr. George Alexson and the parish board were generous to allow me to introduce the new saints' book at the Greek Orthodox Cathedral of the Annunciation in Atlanta and to listen to the plight of Christians in the Holy Land during early August. I am truly appreciative and grateful for the solidarity and financial support they have shown to our struggle.

Publishing books in Jerusalem has never been easy for me but since September 28, 2000 it has become almost impossible. I always looked at printing Orthodox literature as my service to Christ. I firmly believed that it was my responsibility to educate my own children and help preserve the Orthodox values, traditions and symbolism since I was born in a Greek Orthodox Christian family in Tripoli, Greece and immigrated to the United

States at a very young age. I can almost say that I spent many years of my childhood in Denver, Colorado trying to be "American" so that I can become more assimilated and acculturated into the American mainstream. Then, I sort of had a cultural awakening and made every effort to be "Greek" and maintain my ethnic values and traditions so I can truly be unique in the world and specifically in the American melting pot. Marrying an Orthodox Palestinian Christian while attending Hellenic College added another culture and challenge to my life.

I had to convince my relatives that my husband David was not Jewish and not Muslim. For some reason it was hard to believe that some Arabs are Christians. My husband was indeed an Orthodox Christian from birth. This was very shocking news to my family because they could not believe his Christian roots dated back to the time of Christ in the land even of Christ's birth. His particular family tree specifically dates back at least five hundred years and is a beautiful piece of art although females are not included on the chart.

Living in the Holy Land the last eight years, I entered a new spiritual phase of making every effort to just be Christian. I could have never guessed the struggle, pain and suffering that would follow this identity. Many people believe that we spend our whole lifetime trying to get to know who we are when all the time our identity is giving to us at birth as being created in the image and likeness of God. Something must go terribly wrong as we live in the world because we could not possibly kill each other like we do if we see God in the other.

My new children's Orthodox book printed in the Holy Land (2002) entitled *Christina's Favorite Saints* presents stories about holy people in children's language with colorful illustrations featuring a saint per month including St. Anthony, St. George, St. Sophia, and St. Katherine. This book helps teach children that we can learn how to live our life better by reading how the saints lived and loved God. Many saints help us to have stronger faith in God because of the hard work they did to preserve the Christian faith not to mention that many of them died for Christ as martyrs because they lived in the early centuries when Christianity was not legal.

I made a great effort to select a variety of saints in terms of their contributions to the Church and balance among male, female, martyrs, some from the monastic tradition, etc. I have been thinking about doing a book about saints for over five years but could never find the right artist for the illustrations until I met Ms. Fotini Dedousi one of the thirty Greek women in the West Bank who is married to a Palestinian.

Twelve illustrations were completed by Fotini, a Greek artist living in the Holy Land and having the desire to draw saints from kindergarten. She is the mother of two boys and works at the Greek Cultural Center in Ramallah. She received a two-year certificate in design from the Veloudakis Workshop of Free Studies in Athens, Greece. Her family comes from Sparta, Greece. Ms. Vasiliki Zarbala, an iconographer from my hometown Tripoli, Greece illustrated the cover of *Christina's Favorite Saints* depicting St. George.

In the early 80's with the help of Antonia Marshal, we created "Christina," an ideal Orthodox character that children could identify to help validate their Orthodox identity. In this first book, *Christina Goes to Church*, Orthodox young children get all of their questions answered about icons, candles, etc., and try to have a deeper understanding of their church experience. It was truly a success and I have continued to publish books on my own ever since because I just can't seem to get an Orthodox publisher to invest in the artistic fees up front.

I have made efforts in the last decade to produce children's Orthodox literature that preserves and documents precious traditions, values and the rich symbolism of the Orthodox faith. All books promote spiritual development at a young age. Light and Life Publishing, St. Vladimir's Bookstore, Conciliar Press, Holy Cross Bookstore and the Department of Religious Education of both the Greek and Antiochian Archdiocese make it possible for me to distribute the books I print in the Holy Land which in a small way contribute to the local economy.

Christina's Favorite Saints is an ideal Orthodox gift for elementary children and I would hope that every godparent would purchase one to help children with their Orthodox identification and spiritual growth. If your godchild is thirty years old, never feel too shy to buy a child's Orthodox book because there is a child in each and every one of us. You never know at their age they might appreciate *Christina's Favorite Saints* the most and keep it in their collection of Orthodox literature as a treasure. May all of God's blessings be yours from this precious land of Christ's birth. Thank you for the prayers.

Written September 11, 2002

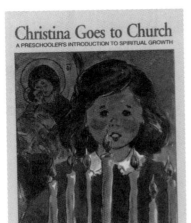

Christina Goes to Church

A PRESCHOOLER'S INTRODUCTION TO SPIRITUAL GROWTH

By Maria C. Khoury, Ed. D.
Illustrated by Antonia Mellen

YOU ARE SPECIAL

an alphabet book for children
By Maria C. Khoury, Ed. D.

Christina's Favorite Saints

By Maria C. Khoury, Ed. D.

MY ORTHODOX COUNTING BOOK

A MULTI CULTURAL WAY TO STIMULATE CURIOSITY ABOUT FAITH

By Maria C. Khoury, Ed. D.

Christina Learns the Sacraments

By Maria C. Khoury, Ed. D.
Illustrated by Antonia Marshall

Roots of Taybeh Traced to Time of Christ

The Christian roots in Taybeh are traced to our Lord and Savior Christ Himself as stated in the New Testament. Jesus came to the village of Taybeh with his disciples after the decision was taken by the Sanhedrin to prosecute him. *"Jesus therefore walked no more openly among the Jews; but went thence unto a country near the wilderness, into a city called Ephraim..."* (John 11:54).

The village of Taybeh had the biblical name Ephraim. The biblical name was changed to the modern name Taybeh by the Islamic leader Salahdin around 1187. The folktale states that Salahdin visited the village Ephraim and found its people very hospitable and generous thus he made a statement that they are "Taybehn" people in Arabic meaning "good and kind," thereby since that day Biblical Ephraim took the modern name "Taybeh." However, there are three places called "Taybeh" in this region. One is "Taybeh Zaman" (original Taybeh) in Jordan, the other is "Taybeh", north of Israel and close to Jenin.

Our village of Taybeh is the only all Christian village that remains in Palestine twenty minutes outside Jerusalem before Jericho with 1300 residents all of whom are Christian and the majority is Greek Orthodox. All residents are Palestinians with a handful of outsiders. Following the 1967 Israeli invasion of the West Bank approximately ten thousand people from Taybeh have emigrated to Australia, America and Europe due to the politics, bad economic situation and daily suffering faced under military occupation. The village is located between Jerusalem and Jericho in the biblical land of Judea known as the West Bank of Jordan and unfortunately does not exist on any modern map.

The village does exist here however since the time of Christ and it sits on the highest mountain region of Biblical Judea and Samaria called Mount Asur. On a clear day from the highest hill in Taybeh you can see the magnificent Dead Sea, the Jordan valley, the mountains of Samaria, the mountainous desert of Judea and also Jerusalem. It is really amazing and spiritually rewarding to stare down at the same valley where St. Mary of Egypt is said to have spent over forty years of her life in solitude.

The village has five places of worship including the original St. George Greek Orthodox Church in ruins (built in the 4th century by St. Constantine and St. Helen), the new St. George Greek Orthodox Church (rebuild in 1929-1932), the Melkite Church (called Catholic and build in 1964 but Melkite worship was founded in the village in 1869), the Roman Catholic Church (called Latin) dedicated to "The Last Retreat of Jesus" (inaugurated 1971) and a small monastery build by a French monk Brother Jack Frant in 1990.

We are identified as area C and have technically remained under Israeli military occupation even throughout the Oslo Peace Agreement. The settlements are a big obstacle to peace because Palestinians suffer trying to get between ABC areas for work, school and hospitals. It is impossible to get anywhere when the Israelis control all the roads and they just gave the Palestinians the center of towns to control. Our area was never turned over to the Palestinian Authority because we have hundreds of illegal settlements all around us. The largest settlement in the West Bank "Ofra" is next to our village. Ofra is the Hebrew name for the village of Ephraim.

The village also has one clinic sponsored by the CARITAS organization directed by Dr. Riayd Muaddi, one pharmacy and many mini-markets. Since 1956 the village was one of the first in the area to receive water, electricity and phone lines. The majority of the residents are unskilled workers with a few professionals. Traditionally, the residents of Taybeh have earned their living from the land especially cultivating olive trees. The village was put on the map in modern times because the Canaan Khoury family established The Taybeh Brewing Company making "Taybeh Beer" following the Oslo Peace Agreement of 1993. The brewery is the only factory in Taybeh and the only microbrewery in the Middle East.

Taybeh has good relationships with its neighboring Muslim villages. The village of Reimon is on one side and the village of Deir Ejrear on the other side. Taybeh village has no communication with the neighboring Israeli settlements that are constantly depriving the village of water and stealing more and more Palestinian land to build illegal Israeli settlements.

The residents of Taybeh share the same language, food, music and cultural values with the neighboring Muslim villages thus an exchange of invitations for weddings can often be found. However, there is no intermarriage among Muslims and Christians and it is almost forbidden. The few times that such marriages might take place their families disown the married couple. Muslims and Christians are somehow united by their Palestinian identity and their fight for independence and freedom but are obviously very different in their ways of worship and how they celebrate their holy days.

The Taybeh village has always been under the protection of our patron Saint George ever since Constantine the great emperor built the first church to be named after St. George in the Holy Land right in our little village. We have been blessed not to have seen the destruction and bombings that have happened in nearby Ramallah and other parts of Palestine. For two thousand years this tiny little village has had the blessing to maintain a Christian presence in the Holy Land. When the village was placed under curfew for only one day in April most people waited with faith in God for the Israelis soldiers to approach.

Does it sound strange to have seen so much bloodshed and terror that you can actually transcend beyond fear and anxiety and wait with faith in God? At the end, our final destiny is the Kingdom of God so we pray for God's mercy as we live under Israeli guns. In the mean time we must walk with the cross that God offered us and preserve our Christian roots in the land of Christ's birth. This is the legacy of the living stones, the Palestinian Christians of the Holy Land.

Written October 28, 2002

The village of Taybeh, Biblical Ephraim

Palestinian Beer Brewed in Taybeh

In the middle of Biblical Judea and Samaria, "Taybeh Beer" is still being brewed following the German purity law of producing an all-natural product and the only micro-brewed beer in the entire Middle East region in the spectacular rocky hill village of Taybeh.

The first and only Palestinian beer, "Taybeh Beer" was launched in 1995 following the Oslo Peace Agreement which gave great hope to many Palestinians living in the Diaspora to return and invest in their country and boost the economy. My husband, David C. Khoury and his brother Nadim Khoury returned to Palestine after twenty years in Boston and founded the new microbrewery operating The Taybeh Brewing Company, in their home village of Taybeh, near Ramallah, approximately twenty minutes from Jerusalem.

This investment and homecoming fulfilled the life long dream of their late father, Mr. Canaan Khoury, who like every Palestinian father hoped his sons would get the skills and knowledge from the West and return to their homeland to maintain their roots and pass on their values and traditions to their children. A dream of passing on to the next generation the beauty and richness of the Palestinian culture which has been overshadowed by the Israeli occupation of the West Bank since 1967.

Taybeh Beer is produced according to the German purity law with no preservatives and no additives. The ingredients are all healthy and top quality: malted barley, imported from Belgium; hops, imported from the best place in the world to obtain hops Bavaria and Czechoslovakia; yeast, and pure water, from the local natural spring Ein Samia. Taybeh Beer is all natural and 100% Palestinian. The word "Taybeh" in Arabic means delicious, thus not only named after the small Christian village of 1300 inhabitants that date their roots to the time of Christ.

The current reoccupation of the Palestinian territories and the general closure on all West Bank towns and villages has decreased Taybeh Beer sales by 80%. However, the Khourys are staying committed to producing the first and only premium quality Palestinian Beer and have great hope to overcome the current political and economic crisis in their area. They have faith in a new future in Palestine and Nadim, the master brewer states their aim is "to try to trade people up from drinking good to drinking best." All is possible if Palestine has freedom and independence believes David. They will continue to brew Taybeh Beer even if it is in small batches and especially for loyal costumers who are great supports and request Taybeh Beer at popular spots like the American Colony, Ambassador Hotel and Jerusalem Hotel.

Hope is good but lately the Taybeh Beer employees have been shrinking down from twelve to three people working in the brewery. They have experienced the worst of the worst with delivering beer to most locations due to the siege. For only a twenty minute ride, sometimes it takes up to four hours with the checkpoints and having to unload from a Palestinian registered plate truck to an Israeli registered plate truck and at times opening each and every single case for inspection. These procedures cause long delays and extra expenses in running the brewery, which imports all of its raw products through the Israeli port. Prior to September 2000, the markets for Taybeh Beer were in Palestine, Israel and Jordan.

Taybeh Beer is the first Palestinian product to receive franchise and be produced in Germany under the Taybeh Beer license from Palestine. The Khourys feel this fact alone helped them make history and great proof of the high quality of their product. Part of the reason Taybeh Beer gave franchise to Germany is to avoid the Israeli port that always has red tape for Palestinians using it.

This fall, the imported bottles from Portugal were held at the Israeli port for over three weeks costing excessively high port charges and fines. These difficulties living and working under Israeli occupation and also the decrease in the tourist industry because of the political instability has made the company suffer substantial losses. However, the Khourys remain hopeful for a better future and are willing to continue to produce the Palestinian beer in small batches.

Taybeh Beer is produced in three different flavors. The original brand, which is golden, is produced in bottles and draft for bars and hotels having 5% alcohol. The Taybeh Beer Dark was introduced to celebrate the new millennium in the Holy Land. It follows a classic style of the way monks brewed beer in the Middle Ages in order to fortify themselves during their fasting. It is a rich smooth dark beer. Also introduced for the 2000 celebrations in the Holy Land was Taybeh Beer Light, on the lighter side with flavor and character that can compete with the imported beers with less than 4% alcohol.

The microbrewery started as a small family investment project with over a million dollars in state-of-the-art equipment imported from Canada and semi automatic bottling line imported from Europe. Prior to the current crisis the brewery was producing 24,000 bottles of beer a week. As a service to the community, the left-over grain is given to the local farmers to be used as cattle feed. But all of the efforts and dreams of producing a Palestinian beer still remain at the mercy of Israel's military policy.

Written May 29, 2002

President Yasser Arafat congratulating Mr. David Khoury.

Mr. Nadim C. Khoury

Struggling One Day at a Time in the Holy Land

The Islamic call to prayer wakes me daily at 4 am or sometimes at 4:20 am. I don't complain when it is an extra 20 minutes later but than again after eight years of listening to the loud speakers' blasting in Arabic "God is great" from the two Muslim villages that sandwich our little Christian village there is no point in complaining about traditions and customs in a land that is sacred to Christians, Muslims and Jews.

We don't have a government, we don't have a police department, and we don't have law and order, just total military occupation to protect the hundreds of illegal Israeli settlements that surround our small village of Taybeh. However, what we do have here in the land of Christ's birth is the responsibility and the moral obligation to keep our Christian presence. Unfortunately, the mere existence of only 2% Christians among three million Palestinians is a number constantly dwindling due to the awful military occupation that deprives people of their basic human rights and human dignity.

It is too dark and I can't get up so early in the morning. The minute I will look out my kitchen window I will see the new expansion of the Israeli settlement of Ofra, the largest settlement in the West Bank that has just practically reached my front door. Finally when the sunlight hits my room, I will get up and stare out my bay window at the beautiful hills and valley of biblical Judea and recall this is the village that Christ visited before his crucifixion. Each and every day I feel I truly live in a sacred and holy place. But I believe there is a high price to pay as a Christian living in the Holy Land under Israeli guns and struggling to teach my children their Palestinian Christian roots.

After a little screaming and yelling at the boys to try and leave the house on time by 7 am, we finally pass up the Latin Church (Roman Catholic) in the village center and the Orthodox Church down on the right while the Melkite Church is on the left as we pray to arrive to school safe for another day.

However, the magnificent site of all is the extraordinary ruins of St. George Church built by St. Constantine and St. Helen. And daily as I see this historic site, I am reminded of the great faith and deep commitment these two great saints had to help preserve the Christian faith and value the spots that Christ walked by building shrines and churches all over the Holy Land. As a matter of fact, it was Constantine the Great that called Palestine the "Holy Land." At every Christian event and holiday we are reminded that this land was indeed made holy by Christ Himself because He walked among the people teaching salvation and He is the truth, the way and the Light in this world of darkness. *"In him was life; and the life was the light of men. And the light shineth in darkness; and the darkness comprehended it not."* (John 1:4).

It has never been darker in the Holy Land than today following two years of state sponsored terrorism against the Palestinian people who are desperately seeking a homeland, freedom and independence from Israeli occupation and brutality that has almost totally destroyed the land of Christ's birth along with several precious Christian sites.

We need to travel out of the village to go to school in the city but the only two main roads have been technically blocked for over two years by large concrete cement blocks and piles of dirt so that no one passes. Constantly the young men from the village move these blocks a little to the side so at least one car can squeeze by at a time and sneak on to the Israeli settlement roads to get out of the village at least for those that have foreign passports and Israeli registered vehicles. You can just count these people on one hand. The rest of the thirteen hundred residents are practically prisoners in the village. Sometimes they walk the mountains and the valley when absolutely necessary but they often get caught in the middle of shooting or get detained for many hours.

Many times I return home to the village to find the same road I used in the morning completely blocked and can't get back home after a very tiring and hot day. Thus the children get out of the car and walk over the dirt piles with those heavy back packs that feel like rocks and I call my husband to meet me at the checkpoint and drive the car through the valley because he will hit fewer rocks than me. At least if he damages the car there is less screaming and yelling at home.

After climbing over a dirt bump on this bright autumn morning we drive for at least 45 minutes on the settlement roads listening to church tapes that Fr. Bill Chiganos records in the Holy Apostles Church in Chicago. Taped and emailed sermons have kept my sanity the last few years. I must mention that prayers from others have also saved me and given me inner peace. If suicide was not forbidden by my religion, I would have taken my own life years ago. Now I have placed my life in God's hands and pray daily for a peaceful passing without suffering and without pain. By the time I finish this prayer, I have passed up two empty checkpoints that have been uplifted from the main road and the soldiers stand on the mountain tops with their full gear and American paid weapons ever since June when seven soldiers were killed at a nearby checkpoint on a Sunday morning.

As the sun shines in my face and I can barely see the road, I do notice the soldiers holding their guns on top of the mountain and right next to them is an Israeli settler draped with a white towel or robe on his head holding his book and praying next to the Israeli flag by swinging himself back and forth. If you need guns and soldiers to protect you while praying than there is a great injustice somewhere. This is not a normal thing.

People should pray in peace and freedom. But not of course if you have confiscated land that belongs to another nation and you deprive the local people from their human rights and cage them in their villages like animals. Obviously some type of misery will follow this great injustice that was initiated with the creation of Israel in 1948 and the massacre of thousands of Palestinians and millions of refugees with the total destruction and disappearance of whole villages in one day.

Finally I reach another major checkpoint blocking the main road called Beit El before entering Ramallah. On the mountain tops and the valleys there are many students and teachers walking through the weeds, dirt and rocks to avoid the checkpoint so that they might pass and go to school or work in the city of Ramallah. On the bottom of the mountain, off the road is an Israeli jeep with a least six soldiers all out of the jeep, fully armed and holding a group of ten or fifteen Palestinians at gun point, mostly young men. This is a daily scene.

It is customary that Israeli soldiers stop people at random for no reason whatsoever and harass and hassle them. Just the other day, Lui, a twenty year old neighbor in my village was detained from 9 am until 3 pm when the soldier finally returned his identification card to him to pass after a boiling hot day in the sun. He is one of the few who has work in the small gold factory but can not get a salary when soldiers deprive him from moving around. It is so unbelievable. It is so unreal that this would happen to innocent human beings. What is more frustrating is that these are people going between Palestinian villages and cities. They are not trying to enter Israel proper before the 1967 boarders. These are people hassled and harassed on the West Bank where the Israelis invaded in 1967 and refuse to leave by building illegal settlements and continuing their heavy army presence that initiates violence because of the daily tortures and ordeals that are totally inhuman.

The minute I reached the checkpoint in order to pass, the soldier signals me with his hand to turn around and not even approach him. I drive up anyway and make him angrier by just saying "good morning." He responds harshly: "curfew, go back." I beg him to pass and that to my knowledge there is no curfew because all the people are walking by the mountain side to reach the city and I need to send my children to school. It was terrible to have had only nine school days in September because the Israeli army imposes curfew as they wish. If there is school today, we want to get there and learn. The soldier responded again with a fierce voice and look: "I told you Ramallah is closed, now go back."

Well, frustrated and angry I backed up my car a few meters away and called Fr. Jack our religion teacher from Taybeh to see if he had passed up the checkpoint and if truly the school was open. I just absolutely hate it when priests have more privileges than me. Because I am willing to serve Christ in this manner but my religion will not allow women to be priests. Now I am angrier than ever because the soldiers allowed Fr. Jack to pass and not me. I called up my husband for help but his advice is always the same, come back home and don't go to school today.

Feeling helpless and totally disappointed at this crazy system I approached the soldier again and showed him my Greek passport with a valid visitor's visa and demanded my internationally right to pass at my own risk and die inside Ramallah. He responded: "Do I have to damage or shoot your car so you can go back?" Having had my car damaged by soldiers before I didn't want this expense so I finally turned around went to the closest valley side and let the children walk across the weeds and dirt to catch a taxi on the other side to take them to school. This is not the safest thing in the world with tanks and armored jeeps flocking the area. As the children got out of the car my heart began to beat a little faster.

I continued to be very worried and fearful something would happen to them so I kept calling every five minutes until I knew they had reached the school safe. Over two thousand Palestinians have been killed since Sept 2000 and a great number have been children going to school. My two boys are becoming young men now of sixteen years of age and fourteen years of age and when the Israelis start rounding up Palestinians, they pick up boys as young as fifteen.

Speaking to many mothers in Ramallah in April, it was the scariest thing for families to wait for their sons to come back home safe after being interrogated by the Israeli army with the house to house invasions carried out by the democratic country of Israel as they were telling the world "they were getting the terrorists," they were actually terrorizing us to death with their tanks, armored jeeps, apache helicopters, F-16 war planes, destructive assassination campaigns and endless bombings and shooting of every neighborhood in Palestine. Although international regulations forbid such weapons to be used against unarmed civilians, the Israelis are above all laws.

My struggle for the day is not over because I still have to pick up the children from their school in a city that is totally under siege, so I must try another checkpoint. I opted for the famous three to four hours wait. As I reached the Qalandia checkpoint during this beautiful hot day I decided to just cheat and pass up the countless trucks and cars waiting because I find it bizarre to wait many hours when I can just drive by at the risk of being shot. It is so chaotic and confusing at these checkpoints that if I don't cheat someone else will come and cheat the checkpoint line and I will be seating there for many hours wishing it was me.

There is so much disorder, mess and delay that when my mother was visiting me she said: "there is no way they would keep me in this country even if they tied me up with chains." During the nightly bombings in Beit Jala, a very prominent bishop from the Greek Orthodox Archdiocese instructed me to pick up my children and leave because he felt it's not necessary to have a Christian presence in the Holy Land. Ariel Sharon is doing such a great job at making all of us want to leave which I would assume in some places this forced emigration is called ethnic cleansing.

The true meaning of serving Christ is to sacrifice our life so that we may gain eternal life in God's kingdom. If truly we accept God as our savior, we must accept the cross he hands us to carry. No one can understand how Christians and Muslims possibly live under such horrible and awful daily conditions while most of them have known the freedom and life in the western world. However, as a Christian living in the Holy Land, the challenge is to see God in each and every human being under these tragic and brutal conditions and at any risk to give witness to Christ our Savior in the land of His birth by believing and practicing peaceful resolutions.

Truly Christ is in our midst and we are one body because the prayers of people everywhere are powerful and justice will one day prevail in the Holy Land. If we can not have peace in our world right now, let us at least have peace in our souls: *"Peace I leave with you, my peace I give unto you: not as the world giveth, give I unto you. Let not your heart be troubled, neither let it be afraid."* (John 14:27).

Written October 24, 2002

People walking in the valley to get to school and work.
In the winter they become full of mud.
In the rain season they become soaking wet.

The Tragedy in the Holy Land
October 30, 2000

The tragedies that have taken place in the Holy Land this month are atrocities of the worst type that will affect the heart and soul of Palestinian children for generations to come. Life as usual has stopped especially for a month now since Ariel Sharon sparked a violence of the worst type that resulted in the Palestinian Massacre of hundreds of innocent children seeking their freedom, human rights and basic right to a homeland. The complete closure of the West Bank and curfews imposed by the occupying power Israel has resulted in the loss of one school month and it paralyzed the already poor economy.

During these dark days in the Holy Land everything was completely shut down. It is during such violent moments seeing thousands of people being brutally injured that one needs great faith. The words of Edith Stein greatly comforted me: "The darker it grows around us here on earth, the wider must we open our hearts to the light from above". These dark days were the worst I have seen in the Holy Land in the last five years since our investment with the only microbrewery in the Middle East in my husband's home village of Taybeh. We left the comfortable middle-class life of Boston to offer our children a chance to love and be loved by the extended family, know their roots that go back 500 years in a Christian family, learn the Arabic language, experience a different culture and boost the economy in Palestine. This violence and continued brutality from the Israelis makes it seem like a very high price to pay to shape a Palestinian Christian identity. The same situation seems to be true for families like ours that have tried to return to Palestine after the Oslo Agreement. Following twelve years in the state of Iowa, Dr. Nedal Harb, a well know heart specialist in Ramallah brought his four children and wife to their Christian roots, in order to be well rooted in the Palestinian values and traditions. The Roukab family, famous for their ice cream in Ramallah also returned with their son and two daughters after living in Florida for many years. Most Christian families are the first to immigrate seeking better education, housing and career opportunities thus this Israeli occupation and current massacre against Palestinians will deplete the Holy Land from its Christian population. In the land where our Lord and Savior established our roots, this is certainly a depressing phenomenon.

On Thursday, October 12th, Israel once again showed its great might and power with American tax dollars and bombed the police station next to my children's school in addition to multiple bombings that brutally took place throughout Ramallah and other West Bank cities. Imagine what it's like to try to get back to a regular school day after ten days under siege in your home from the cruel Israeli military occupation. During the math lesson in the third period your child is suppose to evacuate the school immediately because a public announcement states that Israel will bomb Ramallah due to the death of two Israelis. In the mean time, over a hundred Palestinian children had been brutally murdered and no human rights organization even opened their eyes to make a statement against Israel. Why is the life of two Israelis worth bombing a city and the life of hundreds of Palestinians not worth even a reaction from the world?

The whole city went into a panic as Israeli helicopters; sirens and military tanks overshadowed Ramallah. Hundreds of parents were trying to desperately pick up their children from a dozen schools all at the same time, the younger children were crying and feeling lost in this cataclysm. Some people were being evacuated from their homes near dangerous points and some foreigners like our volunteers from England at the Birzeit School went straight to the airport. It was a traumatic experience of the worst kind. Israel has been aggressive by using excessive force and has taking the opportunity to kill as many Palestinians as possible. The American public is not aware of the atrocities that take place against Palestinians. Fr. Ibrahim Hajazin, a local priest and the principal at the Latin school in Ramallah, was stopped by Israeli settlers traveling from Nablus where he officiated at an engagement to his home parish in Ramallah. Settlers in the West Bank are allowed to carry weapons but Palestinians are not. They brutally starting beating him with their clubs and throwing stones at his car, he was able to escape, stay alive and have a much damaged automobile. However, the American public cannot know dozens of such attacks that have even resulted in the death of Palestinians because it will change their image of Israel.

The two nights of October 22 and 23, the Beit Jala community mostly a Christian majority has seen the worst of the bombings and heavy artillery. These terrible bombings are taking place fifty meters away from the Beit Jala Latin Church, and the Orthodox Christian club building was also directly hit by a rocket. This week, the children arrived to the Beit Jala Latin School traumatized, not having slept all night from the bombings and the sirens, not able to do their homework because the electricity got cut off. Furthermore, there is a high rate of absence in the school due to fear and for the young children that do show up, they spend their day crying, being frightened and not knowing what will happen tomorrow. Surely, too scared to concentrate on a lesson when outside their classroom window processions and marches are taking place for the funerals of the day.

Two homes were destroyed on the same block that our first grade teacher Dolly Mitwasi lives with her husband and baby girl. All the windows were shattered in her home along with other homes in a hundred-meter circular area surrounding the explosions. The third home damaged that same evening included the rocket falling in a young child's bedroom leaving black debris everywhere and the icon of the Virgin Mary collapsed on the floor before the child escaped to another room. This first hand trauma that Palestinian children experience will surely affect them for a lifetime. The atrocities they see daily perpetrated by Israeli soldiers will affect their thinking and well being. Quality education cannot take place unless these crimes against humanity stop.

Education and good schooling is the foundation for the future state of Palestine. Children deserve their international right to education and their basic human right to a Palestinian homeland. They deserve to have a regular education that will allow them to be active and powerful members of the society. Once again during this terrible and long thirty three (33) year occupation of the West Bank, children are being cheated from their basic right to learn. The Israeli closure, imposed curfews and checkpoints make it difficult and impossible for some children to travel from their villages to our schools. Many students and teachers have not made it to their schools in a month. All of our special programs aimed at educating the whole person such as the Hearts and Hands program, the sports activities and the English Language training have come to a stand still. The few steps we have taken forward in academic excellence have now gone backwards. Furthermore, all of the Palestinian Universities have been closed since September 27th. This will certainly result in the loss of a full semester for university students.

Thousands of Palestinians that work in the West Bank cannot get to their jobs. Over one hundred thousand Palestinian workers that provide labor inside Israel are under siege. These tragedies in the Holy Land cannot continue anymore. The American government needs to ask Israel to stop the massacre of Palestinian children and end the occupation now. Military occupation should not be tolerable anywhere in this new millennium.

Suffering in the Holy Land
November 10, 2000

As thousands of children across America wait for the tooth fairy to arrive this weekend, thousands of Palestinian children wait for the Israeli soldiers to go away and uplift a severe curfew that has left the Holy Land under siege. In the Hebron area, 44,000 Palestinians are prisoners in their own homes. As a result of the curfew, thirty-four schools are closed and three of the schools have been taken over by the Israeli soldiers and turned into military zones. Palestinian children are somehow being cheated out of their childhood and of their basic right to education.

The prolonged curfew imposed by the Israeli Occupation harms all aspects of life and constitutes a collective punishment, forbidden under international law. However, the curfew does not apply to the hundreds of Jewish settlers living in the same area. Thousands of Palestinians suffer from: a shortage of food and other essential supplies, health services and ambulances, loss of employment and source of income and lack of regular garbage collection. In Hares, cement blocks since the 2nd of October have blocked all entry points to this village. The main water line has been cut off for a week with no running water in the village.

For several weeks now in the Bethlehem area, the Beit Jala and Beit Sahour communities with a Christian residential majority have seen the worst of heavy bombings from tanks and missile attacks damaging many homes. The Orthodox Christian club building was hit with a missile and survived without severe damage as well as many bullets received at St. Nicholas Church. The Bethlehem University building and nearby monastery were hit by alive ammunition. In the city of Nablus, the Israelis bombed Arafat's headquarters, which is only 120 yards away from the Anglican Church and across the street from the Sisters of Mercy Hospice (Mother Theresa's order). Although these churches were not harmed, in the Ramallah area when Arafat's headquarters were bombed the same day, residential housing was destroyed and civilians were injured.

Members of all the churches in Ramallah participated in a peaceful demonstration last Sunday seeking for the bloodshed to stop in this sacred land. His Beatitude Michel Sabbah, Latin Patriarch of Jerusalem visited many damaged homes in the Bethlehem area and the nearby refugee camp to console people who have sustained property damage and loss of loved ones. Many church leaders offered prayers that both the Israelis and Palestinians find ways for reconciliation and stop the current bloodshed that has left over 200 dead and thousands severely wounded. The Palestinian Ministry of Health reports 18% of all wounded are in a state of clinical death, paraplegic or quadriplegic; 20% of all the wounded are likely to remain saddled with a permanent disability. The psychological scars people will endure from the present slaughter are incalculable.

Finally, we have children that cannot go to school at all and in the Bethlehem area we have children that do go to school terrorized because of the all night bombings and shootings in their neighborhoods. These children arrive to school not knowing what will happen day to day and being traumatized by the missiles that have fallen in their neighborhoods and the helicopters with sirens that overshadow their homes nightly. The electricity gets cut off many evenings so they are not able to accomplish a basic activity like their homework. Teachers and students are too frightened to concentrate on lessons. This first hand trauma that these children experience will affect them for a lifetime. Not just children, but everyone has been terrified by these brutal and cruel bombings that we pray will stop.

Thousands of Palestinians that work in the West Bank cannot get to their jobs. Over one hundred thousand Palestinian workers that provide labor inside Israel are under siege for over a month. They are penniless and cannot feed their families. These tragedies in the Holy Land cannot continue. Children are brutally injured and murdered daily by bullets manufactured in the United States. The rockets that have damaged so many Christian homes are given to Israel by the American government. Are American tax dollars well spent in this massacre of Palestinian children?

Military occupation should not be tolerable anywhere in this new millennium especially in the sacred land where Christ carried out His ministry. In general, most Christian families are the first to immigrate seeking better education, housing and career opportunities. Thus, this Israeli occupation will definitely deplete the Holy Land from its Christian population, which at present is less than 2% of the total three million Palestinians in the West Bank and Gaza. However, according to the Latin Patriarchate, in 1922, the Christian population was 51% in the Holy City of Jerusalem.

This Sunday in the Holy Land
November 18, 2000

As Christians we glorify God unceasingly but especially on Sunday it's typical to pray in Church. Sunday, Nov. 12th was not going to be a typical Sunday in Bethlehem anyway. The surrounding Beit Sahour and Beit Jala Christian communities have been devastated by nightly shootings, bombings and a total destruction of their homes which in this country is a complete loss of a life savings due to lack of house insurance. It was not going to be a typical Sunday because the Palestinian massacre continues with over 200 dead and more than 7000 severely injured.

Our students in the Christian schools of Beit Sahour and Beit Jala have been traumatized by the brutal Israeli attacks. A great number of children have moved out of their homes because the missiles that American tax dollars send to Israel keep falling in their neighborhoods and terrorizing them. Our Beit Sahour 8th grade student George Hijazeen had his home totally destroyed by Israeli bombs, as have hundreds of other Christians in the area.

Our Beit Jala 8th grade student Jadallah Emil Khamamshta tried to escape the missile attacks by moving with his family to his uncle's house. However, on Sunday as he was walking home after attending church services he was seriously injured when a missile suddenly exploded near St. Nicholas' Church. He sustained head trauma as the shrapnel hit his head. Jadallah, in Arabic meaning, "as God gives" lies in the intensive care unit at Hadassah Hospital in Jerusalem after a major operation to save his life. His Uncle Sammy survived the missile attack and was also shot in the shoulder. Nine innocent civilians were reported wounded in this broad daylight attack after Sunday worship.

The next day in school who will concentrate on math? English? Science? Certainly none of the children that were walking home after church and were lucky enough to survive the brutal and unnecessary explosion that took place near St. Nicholas Church. Certainly not the children that listened to the all night bombing in their neighborhoods that lasted until 3am. Did these children even sleep enough to concentrate on any lesson? They did not have electricity to do their homework or review any of their studies.

Jadallah's brother, sixth grader Jimmy says that these bombings are not fair and he is so scared that the Israelis "just want to kill us all." He also said that he can't concentrate on what the teacher says in class. Many children report that they are scared from the night because of the bombings and shelling of homes and they are scared from the day because of the killings of innocent civilians. On October 12th, Jadallah wrote in his English classroom journal: "I feel so angry... the bullets hit the yard and the balcony of our house. The tanks on the mountain surrounded Bethlehem area. The settlers attacked the Palestinian villages and the houses and burn the houses. The helicopters shelled the houses with rockets... this is a catastrophe to Palestinians. I feel angry, I can't sleep or study. All the time I think a missile or a bullet will kill me." And, he is blessed to have survived.

Jadallah's English teacher, Ms Sana Abu Amsha, confirmed that it was not a typical Sunday. She attended Church services in Bethlehem and as she left the church with her children she saw the Beit Jala bombings and houses burning in the explosion. She got stuck not being able to return to her home until 5 p.m. However, she was one of the lucky ones because she did have a home to return too. But not true for her uncle Mr. Nasri Jarayseh, a devout Christian who had his Beit Sahour home burned completely. The Israeli soldiers prevented the fire engine from reaching the home to extinguish the fire. One fireman was shot in the leg and the other injured.

The very beautiful villa and clinic of a prominent Christian Gynecologist was also destroyed. During the week we saw the tragic death of a well-known German physiotherapist Dr. Harry Fisher.

It really was not a typical Sunday in the Holy Land, the peaceful Sunday that we yearn to have as a day of worship. The American government can stop the Israelis from carrying out these atrocities. Please contact your senators and representatives to stop these crimes against humanity. This sacred land where our Lord and Savior established our Christian roots deserves peace and a Christian presence.

Shattered Dreams in Palestine
November 20, 2000

Many in the Palestinian Diaspora dream of possibly returning to their homeland and holding on to their roots of a strong Palestinian Christian identity. Few, however, can actually manage to make such dreams come true. A few families in the Ramallah area, thought to have the best of both worlds. To obtain education, knowledge and skills in the West and return after the Oslo Peace Agreement to contribute to the growth of Palestine, make history, boost the economy with our investments and maintain our Palestinian values and traditions for our children. We were begging other rich expatriate Palestinians to do the same and head home to Palestine.

As Palestinian Americans are achieving cultural assimilation by knowing the English language, values, and other modes of cultural discourse that predominate the American society, they are becoming more and more acculturated. However, to be assimilated into the mainstream American culture does not necessarily mean you have to abandon your Palestinian heritage. You can cherish it and keep it on the priority list with all of the other American ideals. However, this becomes hard to do when you start to lose the Arabic language within the generations. Many experts say that language and culture are intertwined. Thus, to have a strong Palestinian cultural identity one should speak and write Arabic. So, the dream of returning home to Palestine develops.

In order to accomplish such a dream, you leave your middle class home and neighborhood in the West and return to your childhood memories of a beautiful Palestine. However, the Palestine you know and love has changed in reality. Palestine after the Oslo Agreement is not the same innocent virgin country you experienced as a ten-year-old child.

The Palestine in your heart and soul that has made everlasting imprints in you spirit has been affected by the occupation, 1967 Invasion, illegal Israeli settlements, closures and curfews, the Palestinian Uprising, the Palestinian Authority and the general multicultural habits that Palestinians brought with them as they returned to their beloved country with foreign spouses and inter-faith marriages from all over the world.

Palestinians returning from abroad felt they can deal with this multiculturalism that started to emerge in the Palestinian society because the most important thing was to allow their Palestinian identity pattern their thinking, feeling and behavior in obvious and subtle ways for themselves and their children. As long as the home and family were the most important element in life everything else will set in place. Thus far, the dream to preserve and pass on a strong Palestinian identity to your children is worthwhile because you believe these strong roots will give your child a great deal of strength to sustain ones self against the various pressures that occur in everyday life.

Most daily elements after the Oslo Agreement, although not perfect could be worth waiting far in the hopes of peace and prosperity in Palestine. Most positive and negative aspects of life in Palestine could be accepted in the name of establishing a strong Palestinian cultural identity with English and Arabic language skills that would make your child an active and powerful member of the new global economy. After so many years in the frozen peace process the possibility still existed that the sleeping giant of overseas Palestinian wealth and expertise can dream of coming home.

However, such dreams were shattered on September 28, 2000 when Israeli War criminal Ariel Sharon sparked a violence of the worst type. The atrocities and cold-blooded murders of Palestinians were not even immediately broadcasted to the world. This terrible massacre of Palestinian children and brutal bombings are yet another cruel act of the long Israeli occupation. It is unthinkable that in this new millennium military occupation should exist in our world. These terrible crimes against humanity must stop because our children deserve the same rights as all children of the world.

Our dreams of peace and prosperity might be momentarily shattered by this Israeli brutality but our hope and ultimate dream of a free and democratic Palestine with Jerusalem as its capital will reign forever in our hearts, until God, for the sake of our children, makes this dream come true.

Palestinian Student Voices
December 3, 2000

The savage massacre of Palestinians will leave our children traumatized for years to come. Our students currently live in fear from Israeli army attacks and brutal Israeli settlers who at random attack their homes and towns. As educators we are seeking ways to allay their fears and heal their psychological scars. The writing process is very therapeutic. In the Latin Patriarchate Schools under the directorship of Fr. Emil Salayta, we have initiated a writing contest among all of our schools to help students defend their rights and learn to lobby their opinions. The occupation and Israeli brutality should not cheat our children from their international basic right to learn. Quality education can only take place if we know ourselves, our roots and seek our freedom and basic rights to our homeland. It should be noted that our school policy promotes peaceful resolutions and non-violence; however, our students may use certain words that in their context are a genuine expression of anger and frustration to the occupation and understood in metaphoric language. Following are excerpts from student essays:

What does one feel when he sees children killed daily? When he feels that he'll die any moment... What does he feel when he can't sleep? What does he feel when his eyes don't stop crying? What does he feel when he sees a child in the flower age become handicapped or killed?
Sahar Allan, 10th grade, Beit Jala Latin School.

As a Palestinian girl I feel very sad and disappointed. Last month was very sad and painful. We felt that we are alone, no one stands besides us to resist the occupation in spite that the Holy Land especially Jerusalem belongs to everyone in the world. The Israeli soldiers chased us everywhere even in our homes, we can't sleep, and we can't go to our school. We want to learn. Education is our right. We want to live happy and free. They destroyed us. They killed more than 260 persons and most of them were innocent children, Why? Don't we have the right to live as all the children of the world? Maybe what is happening around us is not being broadcasted to you. The Israeli government is trying to change its image to the world by saying that the Palestinians are killing them, but no. Please, we need your help. Our Holy Land is in danger. It is crying and shouting for your help. Please, I beg you, don't let your ears and eyes close, and listen to us.
Sammar Massad, 8th grade, Aboud Latin School.

Palestine is a very important country because it's located in the middle of the Arab world and it's the place where Jesus was born and the place for the "Al-Esra and Al-Mirage of Prophet Mohamed.
Hiba Y. Kailel, 8th grade, Birzeit Latin School.

Al-Aqsa Mosque and Jerusalem are a red line, red with the Palestinian blood. The Palestinian youth will never surrender. Our occupier is very brutal. They kill and torture everyone who is under their control. The Intifada will not stop until the liberation of Palestine with Jerusalem as its capital.
Name withheld at request, 9th grade, Al Ahlieyeh College, Ramallah.

Intifada is a holy word to all Palestinians, which means a lot for every Palestinian heart. It lets us remember all the misery that the Palestinian faced and the blood they gave to have their land back. We waited a ray of hope of having Jerusalem by negotiation but negotiating brought nothing. At last we will do everything to have Jerusalem back.
Maysa Al-Kair, Al-Ahlieyeh College, Ramallah.

The stones are our army to defend our rights, our families, and our land.
Tawfiq Hamdan, 8th grade, St. Josheph's School, Nablus.

We are not afraid of Israel because we are right. This is our land, our father's and grandfather's land. We will have it back.
John Tannous, 9th grade, Al Ahliyyeh College, Ramallah.

The tragic killing of Palestinians is not a human act. It is part of a racist act. What I see now is something terrible and an illegal and severe break of the human rights law.
Mohammed Cahla, 9th grade, Taybeh Latin School.

We are alone in this war and the Arab countries help us by conversation. I want to send a letter to every child in the world to help us, to make a demonstration so we can have hope for change.
Katia Abu Odeh, 8th grade, St. Joseph School, Nablus.

Palestine sacrificed thousands of people to get freedom and peace and force Israel to get out of Palestine. I hope that this Intifada will be the last one and it will stop with peace and all the Palestinian kids can live happy and with no fear. **Diala Burbar**, 8th grade, Birzeit Latin School.

After school I go home, when the shooting starts, my family and I go to the smallest room to hide. My two sisters sleep under beds and the rest sleep on the ground for three hours. We are very afraid to die because the bullets go through our house daily. Because of the shooting we stay without electricity. At night when the shooting stops in the late hours, the electricity comes back. Then my mother goes to the kitchen and brings bread and cheese and water to eat and drink.
Rawan Qumsyeh, 6th grade, Beit Sahour Latin School.

I'm a child but I know what is happening in the world. The Israeli army is killing us, the poor Palestinian people without knowing if we are women, men, old persons, and even children. Of course, it sees us all the same, "Arabs." And the USA is supporting it. I'm so sad, so disappointed. We are losing our rights.
Hanan Abd-Alfattah, 8th grade, Aboud Latin School.

Do you really think America told Israel to stop fighting Palestine. We call upon your communities and youth groups to protest to try to make a difference because every teenager deserves to live freely and determines his or her own fate in his or her own country.
Musa Kahla, 9th grade, Taybeh Latin School.

If you think that I would say I'm scared to death, you're wrong because now I'm full of faith in God who'll never leave us. I'm sure that many people have the same feeling like me, which lets them do very courageous things. Let the Israelis bomb us as they want, kill us, but one thing they can't take from us…the Faith.
Farouk Al Masri, 9th grade, St. Josephs School, Nablus.

Finally…we should also remember that during this struggle, we have to keep in mind the phrase "humanity," even if our enemy forgot, and make the whole world remember it. We ask for international protection to save our children and our people.
Sana' Maher, 10th grade, Zababdeh, Latin School.

Questions Never Answered
By Laila Sameer Daibes, 12th grade
Zababdeh Latin Patriarchate College

The Al-Aqsa Intifada is one of the Intifadas in Palestine that, in my short life, has awoken in me my hidden Palestinian feelings. It made these feelings rise with the sun of every morning when many Palestinians who share with me the love our precious country - which was and still is holding them in her arms - were being killed by the fire of the Israeli occupation. I shared all my feelings with them: love, defense of Jerusalem the eternal capital of Palestine, and the insistence to be a state of our own.

One of these early mornings, specifically the 30th of October, I had just woken up when I heard in the news about the two brothers of Yaa'bad who were killed in the same day while they were fighting against the fire of the Israelis with the stones of dear Palestine. They were planning to have their weddings together and they had the best wedding ever...they were wedded to the soil of Palestine and the wedding gift was their pure blood on her dress. Every Palestinian was invited to this wonderful wedding and I was one of them. I was filled with emotions and I wore silence as a beautiful dress for the wedding.

I dressed up and went to school. I was walking along the street with too many questions as if I was wearing a pair of question marks. Why should Palestinians die like this? Why should we all suffer? Why should we be wounded in that way? Why should we be killed in our towns and homes while asking to recover our shelter, our home, our Palestine?...I fell in a deep gap of sadness and pain.

While arguing with some friends at school, I told them about Mrs. Madeleine Albright who was wearing a pin of the "Seeds of Peace" (a program which was made by the USA to make peace between young people from Palestine and Israel). I wished I was there in that conference where she was wearing that pin to ask her a question that came to my mind: How could someone like her wear a pin like this when one of the martyrs who was killed in Nazareth was a member of the "Seeds of Peace" and when he was killed he was wearing the program's t-shirt? Meanwhile, some young Israeli people like him were shouting "Death to the Arabs," and they're still talking about peace. They killed peace with him and with every martyr in this Intifada.

I returned home carrying many souls and too many questions that I had to wear to keep myself from the cruelty of answers. And, in a moment of emotional absence, I felt myself getting on a train towards more questions...I knew I wouldn't arrive to anything. I didn't know where the answers were leading me...because answers are blind...only questions can see...I was sailing on a boat made of paper and I was raising words as sails in front of logic waiting for answers. But in spite of all this I will build a castle from my hope and the blood of all the martyrs...I will kill anyone with my anger...I will take his body and I will put on him the first brick of our new independent strong country...We will never give up Palestine nor will we part with our dreams...Our steadfastness will continue and so will our defense of our holy country until the sun of freedom shines again.

Give us our Childhood
By Rawan Simon Shomaly, 9th grade
Beit Sahour Latin Patriarchate School

Palestine, my country what happened to you? Are you sad? I know that you are weeping your children. Palestine be happy. They die to defend you, to keep you for us, only for Palestinians. Don't be upset. We will give you our lives. We will offer martyrs for Jerusalem, "your capital." Palestine, see what happened to you! You are suffering a day after another.

I, as a Palestinian have needs and rights. We need to live in peace, to sleep in security not in fear. We are people who live in a small country. We want to live peacefully without curfews or sieges and to sleep enough hours and to have sweet dreams instead of nightmares, to play in our land and to learn in our schools. This is what we need and wish.

Israelis--we will be lions, if we are provoked. We can smash you. Be careful! We will defend our country and our dignity. I appeal to all the Arab countries to be with us. I demand the Arab countries to be united, to be one hand against Israel and to stop buying Israeli products.

Stop This War
By Nicola N. Qabar, 9th grade
Beit Jala Latin Patriarchate School

A child is crying, people are shouting, houses are demolished, many attacks on different places in Palestine, and all this, isn't that enough to stand and say, "stop" to Israel. They are searching for different kinds of monuments to prove that they lived here before, but we, the Palestinian people, haven't we proof that we belong to this Holy Land? Christians and Muslims, no difference…the Jewish army started to attack. Sharon's visit to Al-Aqsa Mosque wasn't just a regular visit. He just wants war, and so it was.

One day going to school, there wasn't anything about war, not even a single word, but the next day, there was the Great War against the Palestinians. It was like the earth was standing and running. Suddenly, they started the shootings and bullets, like rain in a sunny day in summer. They were discussing peace and then they started fighting, first on Rachel's graveyard, then in all Palestine. And what makes me angrier is that Arabs in other countries did not do anything to stop this war.

They are demolishing our country even, Beit Jala, the town of peace, it had never been attacked by even little tiny bullets. How could the Jewish army attack it by rockets? Before this, there were many airplanes and helicopters but we didn't pay attention, but now we are afraid from a little helicopter. The fear is in our heart, and the martyrs and the attacking. Isn't that enough from you, Israeli soldiers? We must stop them from killing us, destroying our civilization, our reason to live, and our dreams.

Palestinian children remembering the 1948 Catastrophe (Al-Nakbeh) which resulted into millions of refugees during the creation of Israel

Christian Voices from the Holy Land
December 12, 2000

In order to reward our students for participating in the writing process, we promised to share their opinions with people from all over the world. From the two hundred entries that were received for the Latin Patriarchate Writing Contest, fifty were given to UNICEF in consideration for a book being published by this organization dealing with the current situation in Palestine. We are very proud to have our student writings represented in this new publication and we are working hard to continue providing excellent English language learning in our schools during these very difficult times in the Holy Land. Furthermore, our student essays will be considered for print in "Youth Times" the local Arabic-English publication for students. Although, our workshops and meetings have come to a halt because of the closure and strict checkpoints, we are doing our best to initiate programs that continue to improve the English language. The following our excerpts from student essays:

This world is like a darkroom. I want to let the light through from a hole in the wall. I want somebody to help me find this hole and let the light through it, not only for one day, but forever. One of the differences that God pointed out, between human beings and animals was that humans should not kill each other in order to get what they want, while animals do so to get food. Thus, I would like to point out that Israelis ignored that difference and cancelled it from their brain...They insult us as Arabs, Christians and Muslims. **Mariana Tams,** 11th grade , Al Ahliayyah College, Ramallah

People in Palestine want the Israeli people to hear the children of Palestine, to know how this affects them. They want to stop this massacre. **Saheer Musallam,** 10th grade, Birzeit Latin Patriarchate School

I think this Holy Land is very religious, precious and holy, full of culture and tradition. In 1948, our country was annexed to the state of Israel. I can't believe how criminal and dangerous they were and they still are. They are killing our children without thinking.
Liza Ibrahim Sayeg, 10th grade, Birzeit Latin Patriarchate School

Jerusalem, the city of peace has turned into a point of struggle between Arabs and Israelis...during demonstrations Israeli security forces caused indiscriminate lethal force which killed hundreds of Palestinians many of whom were children under the age of 18.
Joline Fatouleh, 11th grade, Beit Jala Latin Patriarchate School.

We now have more than 300 martyrs and more than 12,000 casualties because of Israeli gun shots and bombardment...I hope that they will stop killing my people. I feel very sorry about the situation in my homeland.
Laura Sayig, 10th grade, Birzeit Latin Patriarchate School

We wanted the real peace...a lot of houses were destroyed and a lot of families now are homeless living in shelters. We lost a lot but we intend to loose more in order to restore our country and to have our independent state and its capital Jerusalem. **Katie Hodaly**, 11th grade, Beit Jala Latin School.

Will the killing of innocent people end?...hundreds of Palestinians became martyrs in the hands of the cruel soldiers...young men and children are living in fear by hearing the sound of bullets or bombs that are shot at civilian houses, which is very frightening...I hope this cruelty will end as soon as possible. **Georgette Elias Samaan**, 11th grade, Beit Jala Latin School.

The world saw the Israeli soldiers killing the children, using helicopters and tanks against unarmed people, and damaging houses and buildings. So most of the countries support our right to have an independent state, to have a peaceful life with security. I hope that peace will prevail and the Palestinians have their freedom. **Hana Abudayeh**, 10th grade, Birzeit Latin School.

I hope that they will stop killing children. Palestinian children have their rights to live free and to live a good life like other people and other kids all over the world. **Varenal Issa Jasser**, 10th grade, Birzeit Latin Patriarchate School.

The massacre brought sorrow to the Palestinian people, through the destruction of their houses and lands and the big fear that they faced in their hearts, let alone the materialism and economy and trade losses. It did not stop here only. They killed our children in a very criminal way...How do they kill those pure children? They kill them without mercy. They explode their faces and chests and snatch their lives by their mean weapons.
Meerna Jasser, 10th grade, Birzeit Latin Patriarchate School

The population in this Holy Land was living in peace until the Jews came to it and stole this peace. And got our land, houses, etc., certainly we resisted the Jews for over 53 years.
Rawan Jasser, 9th grade, Taybeh Latin Patriarchate School

I hope to live in peace without Jews and without weapons.
Juliana Basem Shadadeh, 10th grade, Birzeit Latin Patriarchate School

At the end, all the Palestinians and I want from the whole world is protection, to help us get rid of Israel. We want to live safely in our country and we want our rights.
Jenny Al Bahu, 9th grade, Beit Sahour Latin Patriarchate School

Christmas in the Village
December 16, 2000

The Nativity of our Lord and Savior is a magnificently celebrated event in our small village of Taybeh as are all of the sacred holidays in the Holy Land. It's popular to combine the spiritual celebration with the cultural heritage, thus every year the boy scouts march to the beat of drums throughout the village announcing the peace, love, and joy of Christmas. Boys and girls with happy faces showing off everything they have been practicing the previous months at the youth club.

These Christmas Eve celebrations happen with the backdrop of beautiful wall murals that depict the birth of Christ painted throughout the village center by our own local young artist Shafik Massis. These paintings reflect the rich Christian heritage our little village can offer pilgrims if only we could live in peace and have our freedom and rights as Palestinians.

These same happy children will later rush to enter the church when they hear the charming bells announcing the Christmas Eve services ringing in the joyous time in remembering Christ's birth two thousand years ago. The children will anxiously wait throughout the prayers to receive beautiful little packages filled with candies, toys and religious books. The nuns have usually prepared these Christmas gifts with generous donations that other Christians from around the world have sent to Taybeh to express their solidarity with the only all-Christian village that is currently in existence not just in the Holy Land but in the entire Middle East region.

Our village in biblical times is know for receiving Jesus and his disciples after the decision was taken by the Sanhedin to prosecute Christ. (John 11-54). And because Taybeh is a biblical site holding a special position as a village of reception and meeting, the Latin Patriarchate built the Charles de Foucauld Reception Center in 1986 within the complex of the Latin parish in remembrance of the French hermit that was in Taybeh during 1889. The center can receive visitors for a single meal, a full day, a weekend and can also lodge groups of pilgrims. This center continues to remain empty because the current atrocities in the Holy Land are too frightening for Pilgrims to encounter.

The easy ride to Bethlehem to venerate the birthplace of our Lord and Savior at the Nativity Church can take up to two hours during this siege on Palestine, although it's a simple 45 minute ride during peaceful times. This Christmas, not only will we be too scared to drive to the Nativity Church, but we are terrorized every time we see the Israeli soldiers in our village pointing their guns at innocent civilians.

Because the Israeli military occupation can not go away for Christmas, they have instead taken away the Christmas celebrations from us. They have stolen the Christmas spirit and peace from each and every child in this village thereby cheating them, one more time, from another childhood experience. There will be no Christmas lights to illuminate the village this year in respect for the martyrs, there will be no Christmas trees to rejoice the birth of Christ because the continued massacre of Palestinians has left a dark shadow in all of our hearts. There will be no boy scouts marching, no choir voices chanting joyous Christmas songs, there will be no beautiful paintings depicting the joy and peace that the Christmas season offers humanity. There will be no little packages with candies and toys for children. There will be no Christmas celebrations in this picturesque Christian village.

When you ask children what Christmas will be like this year, they usually have the same answer: "Depressing and sad." When you ask why? They usually say "because there is no joy, no happiness, no one wants to bake Christmas cookies, nobody can have a party, and everybody is dying. And these children are right because we have entered our Christmas season with heavy hearts due to the killings we see every day, and the thousands of innocent people wounded and paralyzed for life. How can we celebrate when everyone around us is suffering?

But the true Christmas message is suppose to give hope to all mankind and thus we pray for peace in Palestine and for justice to prevail so that Palestinian children can live like all children of the world with peace, love and joy.

The True Identity of Taybeh
December 21, 2000

There are a few beautiful Christian villages in the Middle East, although they are in danger of actually becoming extinct. It would be wonderful to allow Christians in the West to become familiar with each and everyone of these special communities. Furthermore, it would be ideal if the parishes in these villages promote more communication and networking among Christians in this region in order to provide more youth exchanges and spiritual retreats. Especially since the Christian population seems to be depleting in the Holy Land.

In result of this depressing phenomenon, we are blessed to actually be the only Palestinian Christian village in the entire Middle East region. For centuries now, Taybeh continues to have Palestinian Christian residents that own 100% of the land in their village and to have so many churches in one little spot in the middle of biblical Judea and Samaria. This extraordinary witness for Christ should be preserved for generations to come. We need to make a conscious effort to preserve our Christian heritage, values and traditions.

Being a foreigner, I immediately notice the village has many difficulties with water, electricity, trash removal, poor telephone lines, environmental issues, and lack of modern facilities, but the blessing, I feel, God has granted Taybeh is its unique Christian community. Not being of Palestinian ethnicity, the only connection I can feel to this village is its rich and historical Christian heritage. I have written many stories about Taybeh in order to share this beautiful history and culture with others in order to show there is much to appreciate in the Holy Land beyond the clashes and violence we hear on the news.

There is a drastic change children are experiencing with the present tragic and horrifying situation here. Last year, we had a joyous Christmas celebration but as a result of the continuous Israeli attacks and brutality, this joyful celebration will not take place this year in Taybeh. There seems to be a loss of beautiful childhood experiences for our young generation during this Holy Season. A dear friend wrote: "I received your magnificent article about Christmas in your village, past and present, and have forwarded it to The National Herald. I hope they run it because you give us such a remarkable description of how you have celebrated Christmas in contrast to this year's. You also give a good perspective on the other churches in the town. Wish I could visit you and see this special place."

(Marylin Rouvelas, USA)

It is my personal observation that Taybeh is the only village that has maintained a totally Palestinian Christian population in the Middle East. In This Week in Palestine publication (February 2000), Taybeh is referred to as a small all-Christian village. In The Jerusalem Times, December 15, 2000, the editorial staff printed a photo of Taybeh identifying it as "the only all Christian village in the West Bank." In the Jerusalem Diocesan Bulletin of the Latin Patriarchate (Jan-Oct 2000), Taybeh is referred to as "the only entirely Christian locality in the Holy Land." Regardless of our identity, as Christians of the Holy Land and the living stones in this region, we pray to co-exist in peace, prosperity and democracy with Jews and Muslims. However, as the Pope clearly stated during his historic Jubilee pilgrimage to the Holy Land, we should not be afraid to preserve our deep roots in this land of our savior.

**St. George Greek Orthodox Church
built by St. Constantine & St. Helen**

Christmas in Beit Jala
December 23, 2000

"Behold, a virgin shall be with child, and shall bring forth a son, and they shall call his name Emmanuel which means 'God with us.' (Matthew 1:23) And it is this faith and hope that our Lord and Savior abides with us unceasingly allowing us to face this fear that has been brought into our daily lives by the injustices we encounter from Israeli soldiers and military attacks that maintains our lives during these difficult times.

The strong belief that God is with us empowers our students not just in Beit Jala but in all of our schools to go to school each day and learn. Education is especially critical during this Uprising. The teachers in Beit Jala report that the students are depressed and they are not happy at all during this Holy Season. They wish to celebrate but no one is in the mood to rejoice. They just can't celebrate with people being killed every day.

One of the 8th grade students told his English teacher that he will put up his Christmas tree this year but the decorations will not be anything that anyone in the world has ever seen on a Christmas tree before. He has collected all the bullets and the missile fragments from the shelling and rocket-fire in his neighborhood and will adorn the tree with them. Indeed, a different childhood experience and very sad. Since most of this military paraphernalia is engraved with "made in the USA" some of us cannot help but interpret this disaster in the Holy Land as the American government's gift to us. At any rate, during this Christmas Season, the Holy Land remains in mourning. The suffering continues day after day until this brutal Israeli occupation ends once and for all.

One of the teaching methods introduced last year in the Latin Patriarchate Schools is journal writing in the classroom, thus we have taken excerpts from our students' writing about "Christmas," because we feel they reflect the hope and desire most of us have for peace in this region. This student writing expresses that faith in God continues to keep these children optimistic. During these holy days, not only do we pray for peace and happiness for our children but for all mankind. Students from the Beit Jala Latin Patriarchate School say the following about Christmas this year:

Christmas, the season of love and miracles, the impossible happens during this time of the year. So, I wish that a miracle will happen and the dream of Palestinians will come true so they could celebrate Christmas time and the children will smile again, with joy in their hearts and the Christmas tree will be decorated again.
Irena Samaan, 10th grade.

Christmas is my favorite feast because all the family meets together in one place, around the Christmas tree, singing, laughing, talking, and we go to church at midnight to share in the celebration and then we come home without any fear. But, how can we do these things, while the bombing is over our heads? I think this year no one will dare to go out of his house after 5pm. We need to pray to God to have peace.
Jania Qabar, 11th grade.

Every year at Christmas we prepare ourselves for it and when it come you will see the smiling faces of our children, they are waiting patiently for it and say Oh! It's Christmas, and they become the happiest on earth. The scouts march with their drums and many musical instruments. It was the happiest day in the year but now we are not going to celebrate since the martyrs are dying to free Palestine. How can we celebrate with blood covering our happiness? They defended Palestine with their bodies and we celebrate? Definitely, it wont happen, maybe we will say "Merry Christmas" to others but not celebrating. There will not be any happiness and the martyrs, one by one are falling down.
Nicola Qabar, 10th grade.

Maybe there won't be a celebration like every year, but in my heart, Jesus will be born again and I will go to church to pray to God to have peace because Christmas is special. We can not forget it, we must try to open a new page to be happy.
Hany Abu Saad, 9th grade.

What could we say when we go across Bethlehem streets and do not see lights on trees or even beautiful decorations. Instead, we see martyrs pictures. At this time of the year, many children all over the world are celebrating this special birthday, Jesus' birthday. All parts of the world are happy for Jesus coming, we too, are happy for His coming but how could we celebrate while we are in war, how could we while Israeli missiles are killing our people.
Rana Kuncar, 9th grade.

Can we celebrate Christmas? Can we feel there is celebration? In this year, our Christmas is in real war that can't give me that peace and security that I must feel. Being in this situation can't give me the chance to buy Christmas clothes and even decorate the tree. My family can not celebrate, but we must build on hope and peace to start the New Year with new thoughts and wishes.
Wurud Abu Rumman, 10th grade.

Christmas is a very beautiful day but this year we will not celebrate as all the years because of the situation but I want to decorate the Christmas tree because it's the symbol of Christmas. I'm not very happy but I hope peace will happen and be happy. **Hiba Abed Rabbo**, 6th grade.

Santa will bring presents but we are sad because of the Intifada. We want peace and we hope peace will happen. We will not forget the people who died and got injured. **Amanda Mukerker**, 5th grade.

We will go to the Church and Santa will bring presents. I feel happy that Christmas will come and we want peace to be happy. We don't want Intifada. We will not forget the people who died and got injured. I hope next year will be better than this year. **Mariam Abu Amsha**, 5th grade.

At Christmas we make a tree and above the tree there is a bright star, and I want to celebrate and to share with people this happiness that is Jesus. I want to go to the Nativity Church. I think that Christmas in this year is sad because the people are sad. The tree means to me Jesus will come. I want to be happy this year. **Reema Konkor**, 7th grade.

Star marks where Jesus was born; Holy Nativity Church

The Holiday Nightmare of 11,000 Palestinians
January 13, 2001

During the Christmas vacation many teachers and students crossed the bridge from the West Bank to the East Bank of Jordan to visit friends and relatives or in my case to show my children the rich history and Holy Sites of Jordan which gave birth not only to our Christian faith but to other religions as well. The twelve hour bridge adventure crossing over due to the Israeli red-tape and politics was the most miserable experience I can re-call in my travels to over thirty countries in the last twenty years. However, the hassle, misery and inconvenience of crossing over the Jordan River would be nothing compared to the nightmare that was waiting for me and 11,000 other Palestinians that could not return home to the West Bank because of the severe closure imposed by the Israeli government.

The country of Jordan is absolutely stunning and beautiful, one of those dream vacations where you can have the ancient historical and biblical sites as well as McDonalds and Pizza Hut not to mention internet access at the hotels for children. Nothing could have been more magnificent than the ninth century "Red Rose City" called Petra. This spectacular place which is over two thousand years old is carved into rose colored stone and hidden away in the mountains. My children were stunned with the beauty and grandeur of this magnificent city which was lost to the world for over one thousand years and was rediscovered in the early 1800's. A two hour walk into this unique city once you enter only through a narrow crevice in the rock called "the Siq" takes you to the "lofty Dayr" the monastery at the top of the hills. It's such a fantastic archaeological location with the best view of the Jordan valley.

My favorite place in Jordan happened to be located in Madaba the ancient city of mosaics where I saw the oldest preserved ancient mosaic map in St. George Orthodox Church. Also nearby was a wonderful fifth century archaeological park at Mt. Nebo traditionally believed to be the burial place of Prophet Moses. The significant locations of both old and New Testament are far too great to mention but the most important one is in the South region, the biblical "Bethany beyond the Jordan," where St. John baptized Jesus.

The day we completed this fantastic dream vacation and were ready to return home we encountered the bridge nightmare of being refused entry into the West Bank. Although it was totally inconvenient to be with ten other family members, I tried to remain positive and think of it as an extra day of vacation, although unplanned for eleven people can be costly. My extra day was spent worthwhile with a trip to a brand new Christian school in Wasieh near Karak which was a very impressive building with all modern facilities, spacious classroom accommodations and a better teacher-student ratio according to Fr. Emil Salayta, the General Director of the Latin Patriarchate Schools. The only thing that kept going through my mind during the tour of the school was what great things money can accomplish to have such a genuine Christian presence in the middle of what appeared to be the dessert.

All the modern facilities that we dream about in our schools such as adequate classroom space, meetings rooms, auditorium, chapel, library and a beautiful playground were all available right here in a place that is not even on the Jordanian map. Impressive indeed and money well spent. If I could have a wish in the new millennium, I would personally wish that every student can have such a marvelous school to love and respect in order to stimulate better learning and more creativity.

Back to the nightmare, another eight hours the next day on the bridge and I still can't get to my office in Ramallah and my children missing the third school day in the new semester. These many efforts to cross the bridge add up to hundreds of non refundable dollars in bridge transit fees, bus fees on the bridge to the Israelis and the Jordanians, taxi fees and after ten days of extra vacation even rich people run out of money. The Holy Land is owned and controlled by Israelis who have total authority to even keep teachers from teaching this week and students out of classrooms. Although the Red Cross tried to help emergency cases get home, we are far too many stuck on the wrong side during this cruel closure aimed at cleaning out the Holy Land of Palestinians.

The nightmare of 11,000 Palestinians who were not able to get home after their holiday vacation and some actually sleeping in the streets and totally out of money is probably not even perceived as a human rights violation or a terrible and cruel collective punishment. They kicked people out of their homes in 1948 and in 1967, what is happening in 2001? When will justice prevail? When will Palestinians stop being treated like last class citizens in their homeland where they were born and their forefathers were born? Oh, did I mention that all of the Israelis and the Americans with me on the bridge where able to cross over, it was only Palestinians denied the right to return.

Voice of Christian Youth
January 23, 2001

The children of Palestine have been living under horrible circumstances in the last few months and many are suffering from immense psychological terror as a result of the Israeli brutality and the Palestinian massacre of innocent people. In our Christian schools, we try as much as possible to live, work and learn under these atrocities. It's so difficult at this point in time to discuss professional development, personal growth and enriching the English language with teachers, which is my official job with the schools, following these tragic events in our land.

Our professional development program in cooperation with Bethlehem University has stopped to even exist. Teachers are facing daily struggles with closures, roadblocks, and checkpoints not to mention shootings and bombings happening near their homes. Teachers and students can barely concentrate beyond the basics. In light of the tragedy in Palestine, our students attempt to put their faith in God and have a positive attitude. Following are excerpts from 9th and 10th grade student essays among ten schools for the Latin Patriarchate Schools Writing Contest 2000. The British Council generously provided prizes.

I am a Palestinian child, and I want to live like other children in the world, and have the right to live in peace. I want peace, I want freedom to my country. I want to free Jerusalem, and keep it the Capital of Palestine. I want Palestine to be free. **Ra'd Munther Qumsieh (Beit Sahour)**

I agree with the Peace Process, to stop killing the Palestinian people and to get our rights. Then, I become happy for this and I live safe and peaceful. **Amanie Khoury (Taybeh)**

These days in Palestine everybody is in danger and scared. I'm scared too. When I heard the sound of helicopters I felt as if it's the end of my life. **Lina Tannous, (Ramallah)**

Every martyr's mother will feel very sad and every mother will panic when the Israeli soldiers started shooting and her son was not at home. One day, it was Sunday and I was at the Mass. After the Mass when I was coming back home, the Israeli soldiers started shooting in Beit Jala. I saw a woman who was crying and panicking because her child escaped from her because he was afraid from the sound of rockets when they hit the house. I think that all of the Palestinian children must have a childhood as good as possible, because if anyone in the world kills this childhood, God will punish him. But now no one will tell the Israeli army to stop killing children and demolishing houses because 90% of the world has projects with Israel so no one will stop Israel.
Joseph George Nagib Hodali (Beit Jala)

When the Intifada reached Beit Jala, they started using tanks, rockets and bullets over our houses. The Israeli forces did not know that the people in Beit Jala are not guilty for shooting bullets over Gilo Mountain. The sound was horrifying, it was a loud sound. All this made me frightened and I was not sure that I will be rescued from this Intifada, and I had imagined all the people whose houses had been badly damaged, so I thanked God because we were fortunate. **Hany Naji Abu Saad (Beit Jala)**

It is a painful feeling to see children, women, and men dying everyday as a result, of shooting from everywhere. It is fearful when you hear the shooting sounds and bombing rockets. It is the right for every human to live with dignity and freedom and it is the right for all children to live safely to have their childhood as all the children around the world. I believe that it is not fair to see our people especially children killed while they are going to their schools or near their houses…I would like to let everyone in the world know that a human being without freedom is like a fish outside water.
Susan Napoleon Massis (Taybeh)

Israelis kill our children in cold blood with bullets, they bomb our houses and everyone knows that houses can keep us safe and inside their walls we have memories and very beautiful times. Yet they bomb them. The martyrs sacrificed their lives and watered Palestine by their blood. See how mean Israelis are?
Jalal Issa Salame (Beit Sahour)

In these days I hate watching news and see how they kill innocent people and children. I was really confused when Mohammed Al Dura died; I asked myself, Why did they kill him? Why did they kill an innocent child that didn't even have the chance to defend himself?
Waseem Massis (Taybeh)

Israelis put thousands of people in jail behind bars, away from their parents, friend wives, sisters, brothers and children. Prisoners suffer from many diseases because of the unhealthy cells they stay in. The rooms are crowded and they are away from sunlight. Israelis want to hurt their feelings, kill their spirits and end their love to Palestine.
Jenny Al Bahu (Beit Sahour)

One of our demands is the right of return for all Palestinian refugees because it is our country. Therefore it is their right to come back and settle in Palestine.
Rawan George Awwad (Beit Sahour)

Hopefully, someday, the people and everyone around the world will see what's going on over here and not just watch the news...
Nataly Rabah (Ramallah)

Until this moment Israelis are still hitting us with helicopters, and bombing many houses in many cities in Palestine. I wish to go to Jerusalem without sieges. As a Palestinian student, I pray for peace, freedom, and independence in Palestine.
Joseph Farah Ayyad (Beit Sahour)

Due to the present situation my heart bleeds with pain, my eyes are stunned with haziness to see my brothers just shot, tortured and massacred by the cruelty of the Israelis. Our cities, towns and villages are besieged and our economic situation is getting worse.
Hana Emel Turjaman (Ramallah)

Psychological Affects on Palestinian Students
January 30, 2001

The students in the Latin Patriarchate Schools in Palestine have lived under terrible circumstances in the last few months. Along with thousands of Palestinian children they have been suffering immense psychological tension as a result of the Israeli brutality and the Palestinian massacre of innocent people. Mr. Abdallah Gazi, our 6th grade English teacher says that "Everyone in Palestine was affected…even the stones are crying." For almost two months during the siege his students did not have a regular English class because he could not travel from Nablus to the Latin Patriarchate School in Taybeh. Now, the normal 45-minute ride takes him about three hours.

Teachers in the Beit Jala Latin Patriarchate School report that children have suffered from nightmares, fear, depression and lack of focus and concentration during daily lessons. Children also seem to be alarmed and shaken by any loud noise. During the many nights of gun battles and bombings, children have developed persistent fear and worry about their life.

Mr. Sami Qumsiyeh, our senior English teacher in Beit Jala states that students are scared of the night because of the helicopter bombings and scared of the day because of street shootings and the bloody scenes on TV. Hundreds of families in the Beit Sahour area had to flee their homes to escape the shower of bullets and the missiles that dropped in their neighborhoods. The psychological impact children are experiencing also shows up by repeated absence from school.

Many of the children's conversation during lessons reflect the state of fear the children are experiencing as a result of the continuous air raids in their neighborhoods. Most Beit Sahour and Beit Jala children suffer from psychological trauma not because they have seen their peers die in cold blood as in Hebron or have lost their classmates to martyrdom as in Gaza. But most of these children for several months have woken up in the middle of the night to the roar of missiles and have seen fear in their parent's eyes. Most teachers in all of our schools report precisely this problem that students are not able to concentrate as a result of repeated gun assaults and air raids exposing them to a very shocking experience.

Ms. Juliana Wakila, our 5th grade English teacher in Ramallah says that some students appear more hyperactive these days than before. Others that were active and excellent students do not participate in class, do not answer questions and seem to stare into space. Ms. Maha Khalil also sees worry and panic in her students' eyes and can't get them to concentrate on English. When the children hear the slightest noise, it is becoming normal for the teacher to hear, "Are they going to bombs us now?" She feels students lack interest in academic work because their future is so bleak.

Most psychologists' state, in general, children need a comfortable and safe environment filled with love and affection to grow and have a healthy upbringing in order to grow physically, mentally and spiritually. If you substitute safety with fear, it is common sense and we actually don't need psychological research to confirm that the child and the family will suffer from worries and tension. Many psychologists believe that talking, writing or drawings are opportunities for the child to release tension. Our schools lack psychological services and the personnel to follow up on monitoring children who are expressing psychological trauma or psychological tension. Teachers are not trained to provide counseling or to even refer serious cases to professionals.

Ms. Abeer Banura, our 6th grade English teacher in Beit Jala reports that her students appear depressed in their faces. They are not very happy in their general attitude and mood. She feels that their academic performance appears worse than previous years. Her students are more interested in talking about the current brutal situation in Palestine than putting efforts and care into their studies. The students are struggling to make good marks on their tests and it can be noticed that last year, the same students had received better marks during the semester finals. In general, students are not achieving their academic potential due to the instability and insecurity of their home life under constant Israeli attacks and bombings.

Ms. Sana Abu Amsha, another excellent English teacher in Beit Jala reports that several students bring to school missile fragments and bullets they find in their neighborhood. Such war paraphernalia consumes school conversations. Ms. Suheila Slebeh who teaches younger children states that her students pretend to play games shooting at each other as Palestinians and Israelis in gun battle. She says the children talk about weapons and express aggressive behaviors in her second grade class.

Ms. Luma Kalak in Birzeit hears her first graders say it's normal to hit each other because they are living under attack by soldiers. Mr. Nabil Ghanaem, the high school teacher in Birzeit thinks the violence and current closure is making the students lazy and very bored because they don't go out of their houses after school. Ms. Reema Sayej had a student tell her what it was like when he called his uncle at the moment the uncle was under missile attacks in Beit Sahour. The student and family were terrified hearing the bombings and shootings on the phone from their Birzeit home.

Furthermore, Ms. Hanan Aranky, our first grade teacher reminds us that many students who live in villages outside Ramallah continue to be late arriving to school due to the Israeli checkpoints, roadblocks and general closure of main roads. Furthermore, she says many parents are consumed with watching news at home in order to be better informed about the current situation that they don't spend as much time helping their children with homework.

Parents themselves report they are terrified with the ongoing Intifada (Uprising) and want to know the latest happenings thus parents and children stay glued to the TV mainly watching news instead of more pleasant programs like movies and cartoons. The constant bloody scenes on the Palestinian news deeply affect not only the children but the adults too. Mr. Hanna Basir, our senior English teacher in Taybeh confirms that he was forced to stop watching TV because the scenes are so bloody and violent they affect everyone emotionally and psychologically.

Moreover, Palestinian children are repeating revolutionary and national songs that are part of their identity and culture. The revolutionary songs are deeply moving and have surely affected children psychologically. These national songs are being sung by children as young as three years old. Even if you don't understand all of the words like me, one hour in the van with young children on the way home after school everyday brings tears to your eyes because the tone, the rhythm, the sound, the beat just seep into your spirit. Preschoolers sing "The martyrs are God's beloved people" instead of alphabet songs.

A popular song by a famous Lebanese singer Julia Boutros encourages young people to go out and protest the occupation by asking, "Where are the millions of Arabs? Where are the young people? Where is the Arab honor?

The rich people are sitting while the poor are fighting." Another song entitled, "The scream of the rock" remembers the Palestinians killed in Der Yassin (1948) and other refugee camps throughout history. Dozens of songs state "Jerusalem will return to us...we will have our rights." Thus, children are hoping everyday through songs for justice to prevail and sovereignty to come because they are the future of Palestine.

In conclusion, there are indeed grave psychological affects on Palestinian students. Last Thursday, January 25th on his way home after school, Mohammed Abu Hadid, a senior student at the Taybeh Latin Patriarchate School, kicked a bag as he stumbled upon it in the street. Instantly a bomb blow up injuring him and leaving him psychologically, physically and spiritually affected by the current situation in Palestine. We consider this student lucky to have his life. Other students are affected these days because in their household they have one less member. According to Palestinian sources, out of the 383 people killed in the last few months, 145 were children under eighteen years of age. Furthermore, from the total injured of 16,445, over five thousand were children under the age of eighteen. The psychological affects not to mention some injuries will last forever.

The Memories Will Last Forever
February 6, 2001

Reading hundreds of essays these last few months has brought many tears to my eyes. Student material we share in the newspapers has to be corrected and edited but sometimes the feelings and the emotions are so powerful that even with poor English, the students are able to express their genuine thoughts and feelings. Some students provide powerful imagery, personal accounts and very touching early childhood memories having known only occupation since their birth. The memories they have will last forever. However, it is encouraging to see hope and faith in their writing. We pray that time will heal their psychological wounds and God will give them the faith they need to become powerful members in the global community.

One of our goals in the Department of Education is to introduce new teaching methods in the Latin Patriarchate Schools of Jerusalem, introduce the reward system that encourages, motivates and appreciates students and allow for critical thinking skills to take place in the classroom. We are slowly achieving these goals since we initiated the five-year English Language Enrichment plan in September 1999. However, we have been extremely set back with the current tragic situation in our country. Our educational goals were partly addressed with the Latin Patriarchate Schools Writing Contest awarding three trophies to the top winners in each grade among all the schools. The winners were selected by the agreement of three judges. The 9th grade first place-winning essay written in November 2000 by a young Christian teenage girl in the Beit Jala School deeply touched my heart and reflects how childhood memories will last forever.

The Story of our Lives By Rana Rimon Kuncar, 9th grade

Our story had started years ago when there was a little boy who always dreamt about olive trees with blood covering them. He dreamt about a blue sky covered with clouds, but wait, he could see the clouds disappearing. His dream had transmitted to other boys in Palestine, such as Mohammed Al-Durrah; it is a name now for all Palestinian children. One of those children killed on the way to school was probably thinking about his toys or his future as a doctor or engineer or teacher. But suddenly all he could see were the bullets that went through his heart and his dream disappeared as his blood ran down on his books and left a mark on an old wall. Another boy was holding his father with fear in his eyes while the soldiers were shooting from all sides and he was killed; his father couldn't protect him. What could he do when the bullets were all over both of them?

Girls do have dreams too; wonderful dreams about their future life, but some of these dreams may fade away and be replaced by fear of what may happen. When I was a little girl, I remember clearly when Israeli soldiers entered our house searching for some young men, they were holding their guns up, and shot the water reservoirs in case some one was hiding in them. This is cruel, they caught some men on the roof and started hitting them with their clubs making their blood run down on the 5th floor, and then took them to jail. The blood's view is still in my memory. I can't remember anything but blood, guns and pain. This was during the first Intifada. This terrible memory has not been forgotten, yet, new terrible situations were added to it during this Intifada.

Last week, when my parents went to buy us a few things, a battle started in the village near us, my sisters and I watched a helicopter throwing one of its missiles on the houses, and one house was on fire. The sound of bullets and gunshots were very close to us. My sisters were frightened; I tried to calm them down, we phoned the neighbors to see what is going on and their answer was that they were attacking us with rockets and bullets and that we must hide in a safe place. I held my sisters, told them not to worry while tears were in my eyes and we sat on the floor away from the windows. This is not the only fearful memory that I will ever forget. Don't we deserve to have bright and happy memories about our life as teenagers? Don't we deserve to smile, to listen to music, or to go to parties, and to be fee? But how could we? How could we have a future without freedom? How could we be happy while seeing our houses demolished, and seeing homeless people, orphans or widows and children dying every day? What's their fault? Is this the price of freedom? What would you feel when seeing a child asking his mom "why are they killing us?" Another mother was crying…why? Her son went out and didn't come back again! His crippled father was crying and shouting, "I tried to protect him but how could I?" I guess that you all heard these words.

However, what could we do? We are always the guilty ones. The Israeli press is smarter than anybody could imagine but what could we do? All that we have is helicopters buzzing over our heads, voices of bullets and rockets and the cries of widows or mothers who lost their beloved ones. Or sitting in a huge fear in our houses and some of us in camps after their houses were damaged. This is a criminal act planned and carried out by the Israelis who want to demolish Palestinians and to ruin their houses and their lives. But we will not let them, we should carry on dreaming the beautiful dream: a dream about blue skies with no clouds and peaceful olive trees with no blood, and a free country where every one has a dream and works for his dream to come true. And we must always remember that we should work for our dreams to come true.

The Way to Aboud
February 17, 2001

Foolishly thinking the closure is getting better, I set out in the hills and countryside of the West Bank to travel to a small Christian community in Aboud where we offer elementary and junior high school education in the Latin Patriarchate School next to the church where Fr. Aktham Hijazin has been serving for the last three years. A very young and kind priest, Fr. Aktham is proud of the active youth group in the village where he serves about one hundred families. They publish a quarterly youth magazine entitled "The Voice of the City of Flowers," and they maintain a web site at http://www.angelfire.com/pa/aboudyouth

The village is about one hour Northwest from Jerusalem on what might be thought of as the borderline before entering Tel Aviv. The two thousand residents of Aboud are half mixed Christians and Muslims and surrounded by Israeli settlers. Besides the Latin Church, there are two other church communities in this lovely village, the Orthodox, and the Protestant school and parish.

Every road to every single Palestinian village on the way to Aboud had large cement blocks about three feet high at the entrance of the village. About four large blocks prevent the entrance and exit on these small roads. One cement block sometimes is pushed out of the way and allows people to temporarily get in and out of the village. However, anytime the Israelis want to make us prisoners in our own homes, they certainly have the power and the control to cage us in like animals.

These cement blocks have prevented about seventy children according to the headmaster Mr. Ibrahim Hemed from reaching the Aboud School since Sept 28th. By now these children have simply stopped being students at the Aboud School. These students were a great loss for such a small school community.

My intention in visiting the Aboud School was to follow up two of our English programs, the writing contest among all the schools and the spelling competition in the 6th and 7th grade. Also, to set up the Holy Land Correspondence program where Palestinian girls in Aboud can exchange letters with American girls to share ideas about culture, school and traditions.

Now, I have a list of boys that would like to participate in this pen-pal activity but no American boys to match up.

Although it's frightening to see the bad road conditions in the Holy Land, I continued my journey to Aboud. What usually is a very busy road hardly had a soul traveling. And the cars that I did see frightened me even more. An army jeep in the front and an army jeep in the back of the bus now accompany most Israeli buses. It's a very strange site. I saw them pass and thought how safe they are being accompanied by a jeep full of soldiers with heavy-duty guns. The Holy Spirit usually accompanies me so I managed to calm down the adrenaline that began to quickly flow at the sight of these soldiers. The problem with the settlement roads is you never know who might attack you at random. Israeli settlers on the mountaintops attack Arabs with white plated cars while Palestinians throw stones on yellow plated cars.

Having reached Aboud safe and following a successful school visit, I head for home. To my surprise there was a new checkpoint set up at a point that was not there when I had passed in the morning. The soldier stopped me. "Shalom," Shalom." To make a long story short, I was not able to pass from the same road I had traveled in the morning to return to my home. Although I tried to be logical and explain my home was just ten minutes away and my children were waiting for me after school to let them in the house and feed them. I need to go home badly. I'm very good at begging and I have gotten use to waiting but the soldier got sick of my pleading and weaning and said: "If you don't go back, I will shoot." "I have done nothing wrong, I just want to go home, please let me get by". "If you don't go now, I will shoot your car."

Well, I know the grace of God was still with me but I was not going to pass this checkpoint. By now, my children are locked out of the house, they will not eat lunch on time, and I better not show up with bullet holes in my car because my husband will kill me if this soldier misses. Besides, Mercedes parts are too expensive to buy on this side of the world. All of a sudden, I knew what Mr. Barak meant when he said that Palestinians would have limited access to roads. I guess it means in my case, I can go to work in the morning, but I can't go back home. This is the democracy of Israel and the insanity of the Israeli occupation.

Thus, frustrated, angry and mad some people have dealt with these conditions since 1948. I truly believe the world does not know the daily suffering and the lifetime struggle of the Palestinian people. We are not asking for luxuries here like swimming parties, hockey games, Disneyland and field trips. We are asking for the basic right to go to school and work.

If you are an American voter, please contact your senators and representatives today. Organize a petition in your youth group or in your church community and present it to congress to plead for basic human rights in Palestine. Please know that you can make a difference because it is the American government that is giving blind support to Israel and ignoring war-criminal behaviors and the atrocities we have seen in the last five months. The land where our Lord and Savior established our Christian roots deserves a better environment than this current tragedy and bloodshed.

Roads closed by cement blocks

A Prayer for a Wedding
February 24, 2001

Occupied Palestine is increasingly looking like a prison. Entire towns and villages are still virtually under siege-like conditions. It is difficult to plan anything. And most of all it is almost impossible to plan a wedding. We don't know what will happen hour after hour. Due to this unknowing everyone in Palestine has a story. Each and every person has experienced some type of suffering in this awful occupation. Ms. Maha Kahlil, one of the most outstanding English teachers in Ramallah shared the difficulties they experienced with her brother's wedding during this Al Aqsa Intifada (the second Palestinian Uprising).

Her brother being committed and dedicated to his cultural values and traditions returned from Italy where he is a physician to marry a genuine Palestinian girl and start his family in the Diaspora. And, with this marriage, the great possibility exists that with a Palestinian wife, there is a chance to one-day return to Palestine. This is actually the dream of every Palestinian parent who has lost a child to a foreign country. We hope and pray for peace to have the right to return.

This story is amusing because how is one suppose to schedule a wedding during this Intifada when you can't guarantee the bride can arrive from Nablus where she lives to Ramallah where the wedding must take place with family and friends. Initially, the wedding was postponed in October because the Intifada began and the bloodshed spread. But, by January when things in Palestine did not get better but in fact got worse, an effort was made whenever the roads would open between the Palestinian towns and cities, to try and hold the wedding.

Within just a three-day notice that the possibility of travel existed, the wedding was scheduled with no formal invitations, no reception, no singing and dancing which is a customary way to celebrate a wedding in Palestine. The family merely had a hope to have the ceremony in the Latin Patriarchate Church in Ramallah where Fr. Ibrahim Hajazin has been serving as parish priest to nearly 2000 Roman Catholics in the area for over four years. Thus the invitation was by phone to the all guests: "if the bride can come, there will be a wedding."

You can imagine everyone was praying during this three-day period for the bride to come to the ceremony. The mother prayed the Rosary, the nuns in the convent prayed, all the family members were not sure that the wedding would take place. It is the unknowing that is most frustrating at times. Shall you order cake for five hundred people or not? Can the cake even arrive from Bethlehem, which has the best well know bakery in all of Palestine?

Finally, the day of the wedding arrived and a mere 45-minute ride took several hours through the valleys and the back roads, but the bride did make it to Ramallah. Following the simple yet beautiful wedding service most guests instead of saying "congratulation," were saying: "I prayed for you...I lid candles for you...I said two rosaries for you...Thank God the bride came..." Therefore, we are learning to grow strong in our faith and thank God everyday for our safety and for basic things that others might take for granted around the world.

Finally, after many hours of wait to receive permits to travel to the airport and only after the efforts of the Italian Embassy to help them receive these permits which de-humanize and humiliate our personhood in this country, the bride and the groom began their new life in Italy. If everyone needed permits to travel the roads I would not be so angry, but only Palestinians are treated as last class citizens in their own homeland. The Israelis own all the roads.

We have no human rights whatsoever. And, only the Israelis can give us permission to travel to the airport that takes hours and hours of wait. And if your travel plans dare changed you must wait in line again for a different permit because they are only good for the specific day and time.

The activities that others around the world take for granted, such as freedom of movement, simply don't exist here. Life as "normal" does not exist. It is normal to be harassed, interrogated and hassled. Most people are frightened, anxious, worried, not knowing what tomorrow will bring. We basically adjusted to Israeli air strikes, missile attacks and Israeli gunships ready to shoot anyone at anytime. Are the human rights organizations seeing all of these recent assassinations of Palestinians and closing their eyes? How does Israel get away with all of these human right violations and war criminal behaviors?

How Many Bombs Can One Home Take?
March 2, 2001

As the air raids began to destroy Beit Sahour in early October, Mr. Maher Al-Atrash, the Acting General Director of the Latin Patriarchate Schools in Palestine, did not think they will continue to bomb his Beit Sahour home consistently throughout the last five months of this current Intifada. Maher and his wife Jane, who also works for the Beit Jala Latin Patriarchate School administrative office, live only 200 meters away from an Israeli military camp. Their lives are constantly on edge and lately in danger.

Maher was required to attend the schools commission meetings in Jordan headed by Professor Bart McGettrick of the Equestrian Order of the Holy Sepulchre on October 12-14, 2000. It was a pleasant family get-away from the shootings and killings. However, once in Jordan and with the completion of the commission meetings eventually one needs to return home. Getting home was a prolonged experience, full of wait, harassment, hassle and excessive hours and days to cross over the bridge with three small children. The bridge between the East Bank and the West Bank closed for over a week due to the Israeli siege in Palestine. Sometimes, getting stuck out of your home is worse than being stuck inside your home. Either way, it's a denial of one's basic right to movement and freedom.

When Maher and his family did reach home they were not able to stay even one night because heavy shooting and bombing in his neighborhood and an Israeli missile landing directly in his living room forced them to run away. Specifically, they survived unharmed throughout three hours of massive shooting before they left to safety for his sister's house in the middle of the night.

Eventually Maher fixed the damage to the house and in mid January when things were actually not getting any better, the family moved back into the Beit Sahour house along with the other few hundred families that relocated during the months of heavier shooting. However, twenty of these families could not return to their homes at all because of the severe damage and destruction to their properties. The bombings and the shootings have become so "regular," "normal," for us here in Palestine, that we think of them as rain coming down and sometimes the rain goes away only to come back. But this rain is so deadly.

Was it worth returning home? Is it possible in the Holy Land to think "home sweet home?" Last week Maher's house was bombed again and this time unfortunately he can't think of returning home in order to keep his children safe. The house next door, belonging to Fr. Aktham Hajajin's first cousin was destroyed completely from the bombs and intense fire.

Maher's four year old son Maroun keeps asking (in Arabic) "When are we going back to our house? When will we play with our toys again? When will we go down our slide again?" He is one of the thousands of little children that have not had a good night sleep since the beginning of the Intifada when the images of death and the massacre against Palestinians hit their television screens. They have not had a peaceful day since they stopped showing cartoons on TV and broadcasting the killings and shootings. Maroun's sleep is so short that it's not even a quiet sleep. His dad confesses that actually he just can't sleep at night. His sleep is simply too short for a four-year-old. He is also scared to death to be alone so he insists on sleeping with his mother and father.

Maroun started receiving psychological services at the YMCA in the Bethlehem area because at night he constantly speaks about death. His behavior at school and at home has become aggressive. This once polite and happy child, who is one of our preschool students at the Beit Sahour Latin Patriarchate School, damages everything in his site. Also, it's not unusual to wake up at midnight and start screaming out of fear. His father thinks this behavior is a reaction to the constant Israeli brutality, the nightly shootings, the daily images of killings on TV and the fear he probably senses in his parents' eyes.

Beit Sahour with over 15,000 inhabitants and an 85% Christian rate is the largest Christian community in the Holy Land. Four local churches in Beit Sahour represent the Orthodox, Roman Catholic, Greek Catholic and the Protestant denominations. Most people here are frustrated. They have experienced and seen the Israeli occupation and brutality daily since their birth. They see how the Israelis control all the roads, the airport, Jerusalem since 1967, all the natural resources in the area and they directly control their lives too.

"This is not a normal life. Palestinians in the last eight years since the Oslo Peace Agreement have seen nothing implemented on the ground. The situation is very bad," Maher says who has been working in the education office in Ramallah for the last nine years. Many days he can not even travel from his home to his office. When he does come, he spends double the time on the road and shows his identity card sometimes seven times.

Recently at the Patriarchate two special visitors, a major in the U.S. army and a retired colonel, who are members of the Knights of the Holy Sepulchre joined the Pontifical Mission. After visiting Maher's neighborhood, they could not believe that the Israelis were using such weapons of destruction and carrying out such severe attacks in civilian areas. They specifically said that what they saw in Beit Sahour was intense and excessive use of power on civilians. They could not believe their own eyes as they saw the damage in this Beit Sahour community. In the same evening they met with the patriarch to express their condemnation and anger concerning these unjust attacks.

Thus, this very tiny spot on earth where in the Bible is referred to as Shepherds Field because it is here that the angles proclaimed the Good News to the world is suffering terribly from the Israeli injustice and Israeli brutality. And therefore, we pray that the Prince of Peace and the Lord of Love bring about a miracle during this Lenten Season in this sacred land so that peace may prevail for all the little children that cannot sleep at night like Maroun. Because "...*with God all things are possible*," (Matthew 19:26) and we have great faith "...*The Lord blesses His people with peace.*" (Psalm 29:11)

Stuck on Sunday
March 20, 2001

It was meant to be a beautiful sunny day. *"This is the day that the Lord has made; we will rejoice and be glad in it."* (Psalms 116:24). This was the first sunny Sunday we have seen this spring. Many people leave the villages to travel to the city of Ramallah and shop for their basic needs or visit close relatives. Seven teachers from the Aboud Latin School traveled into Ramallah separately with their families to enjoy this glorious Sunday including the headmaster Mr. Ibrahim Hemed with his four children and wife to see their grandmother they had not spent time with in three months due to the Israeli siege.

One of our best English teachers Mr. Boutros Fawadlah also came to Ramallah with many family members to attend the First Communion Service for his cousin at the Ramallah Latin Church where Fr. Ibrahim Hijajin conducted the mass. It was a joyous family gathering and a beautiful service where everyone prayed for peace and after church they went home to celebrate this special occasion with a delicious lunch. The close family unit is what we appreciate most on this side of the world.

The news of the day spread quickly that an Israeli settler was shot dead near Birzeit and the roads would surely close because when anything happens to one Israeli the entire Palestinian population has to pay a high price for it. Collective punishment continues to exist under Israel's so called "democracy."

As soon as Boutros (meaning Peter in Arabic) and the other twelve members of his family arrived at the Taxi station there were hundreds of people waiting to ride the only two cars that were going to his village. They waited from 3p.m. until 6:30 p.m. in the hope of returning home but along with hundreds of people got stuck at the taxi stand while others got stuck between checkpoints. All were "obliged" says Boutros to stay in Ramallah because they were not allowed to return to their homes. It sounds kind of inhuman to me but Palestinians seem to have accepted these hardships and daily sufferings they encounter under Israeli occupation.

For our small Latin Patriarchate School in Aboud this literally meant that about 50% of the school staff would be absent on Monday because they just could not return home on Sunday. What type of quality education can we have on this particular day? Students came to school as usual of course, but it was not a regular day since most of their teachers and headmaster was stuck in the city. Boutros insists that most of the people from the village just wanted "basic needs…a basic right to buy something and go back home safe. What is happening is strange. You don't want to be violent, even ordinary people who don't think about violence…such measures from the Israelis push you to think about it or to just leave the people…leave the land…settlers, occupation, the army, collective punishment, you can't have a normal life. How can you live a normal life in an abnormal situation? This affects you psychologically… and we will go on seeking our freedom and our rights."

Boutros made an effort to explain his feelings during this very frustrating situation of not being able to be with his students in his classroom after such a beautiful family occasion on Sunday. He said: "To go from a village to a city, it's such an ordinary thing to do, something that expresses freedom of movement. But when you can't go back home, you wonder…What is our fault? What is our mistake? Collective punishment is not good."

The headmaster Mr. Ibrahim listening to this monologue agreed with this young and impressionable English teacher: "If a settler got shot… they should go and find the one that did it but to punish all the people for one person or one accident. A whole nation of people equal one man? Where is justice? This is unjust," insisted Mr. Ibrahim on Monday morning in the education office prior to taking an irregular two-hour ride back to Aboud via mountain dirt roads and valleys with rocks that is not necessarily safe. Furthermore, what is frustrating in addition to the bad road conditions is once you managed to get to your destination and damage your car, you might encounter another checkpoint that does not let you pass.

Mr. Ibrahim rushed out of the office with these last words: "These days…the worst days I have faced. They want to pressure us to make us transfer, shift…any movement in our area is controlled by America …if they want to solve our problems they can, easily and quickly."

It is these awful and depressing daily conditions that make wonderful Christian people like Boutros say "my own personal future is unclear, sometimes I am afraid because you think you have no future here…when I think that's what they want us to do, to leave the land. I just decide to stay…you love life, we do not wish death." My heart poured out to these two very dedicated and hardworking men that just could not make it to their job this day. Such a beautiful Sunday ended up being the tip of an iceberg because following this particular closure; Ramallah experienced a severe siege that left thousands of people from about 30 villages desperate to cross-huge deep trenches to get to their schools and work. These deep holes have completely destroyed the streets. Furthermore, if you make an effort to use any other roads, you encounter hundreds of cars, bumper to bumper passing barricades where the Israeli army and boarder police patrols are firing rubber coated bullets and live ammunition which by the way make New York traffic look like paradise.

Tamer Abdallah who also works in our Education Office was hurt by one of these rubber bullets on his way home to Birzeit last week. All bandaged up, he still had a smile on his face but at eighteen years of age besides girls, he only thinks about running away to America like the rest of the young people in this country. If ethnic cleansing is not the agenda of the Israeli government than why are we all experiencing such hardships and torture here in this sacred land where Christ established our roots.

Thinking of running away myself, I found great comfort in the words Fr. Rick from the Jifna Latin Church shared with me today: *"Trust in the Lord with all your heart and lean not on your own understanding. In all your ways acknowledge him and he will direct your paths."* (Proverbs 5:6) May a miracle happen so that we may continue to have a Christian presence in the Holy Land.

The Israeli army damaged many roads to prevent people entering the city of Ramallah

The Voice of Christian Children in Palestine
March 29, 2001

As I was thinking about running away to middle class America something a child wrote in the Beit Jala Latin Patriarchate School made me feel I should seek the wisdom and faith of this twelve year old. "I pray to God to give us the force to stay and wait until peace happens," wrote six-grader Sandra Khader for the second semester Latin Patriarchate Writing Contest. "The force" reminded me of the strength of the Holy Spirit as referred to in Acts 1:8 *"But you shall receive power when the Holy Spirit has come upon you."* Our country is so destroyed; this is the only type of power that can ever help us since the American government has shut their eyes to the atrocities carried out by Israelis. We are trying to survive a school year full of obstacles and uncertainties. Students will receive awards in each grade for the best essay about their families and the current situation in Palestine. Sandra's entry was not the winning essay so I plunged into reading more from ten schools until the winning words sparkled across the pages. The following are excerpts that express the feelings, attitudes and faith of sixth grade students in our schools. Can you share their voices with others concerned about the Christian presence in the Holy Land?

The life in Palestine is not always easy, because of the occupation …sometimes I am afraid, but I hope that the situation will change and we are able to live a normal life without danger. **(Jeries Zarafili, Nablus)**. Since 1948, our people gave thousands and thousands of martyrs …   **(Joseph F. Kaspari, Ramallah).** Palestinian people defend their country and their capital Jerusalem... **(Olivia Odeh, Birzeit).**

In the past, our life was very good. Christmas was very special in Bethlehem; tourists came from everywhere to celebrate this occasion with joy and happiness… but since 29th Sept 2000, everything has changed. **(Sami Bannoura, Beit Sahour).** The joy and happiness we used to have at Christmas were not there. My parents did not buy us any presents because they said food was more important than toys. **(Sana Hijajin, Beit Sahour).**

When the Intifada started we began to feel afraid in our own house…**(Christine Hodali, Beit Jala).** I was afraid of the Israeli soldiers that they would kill us and destroy our house... **(Nabeel Issa Jaser, Birzeit).**

We can't sleep because we are afraid...we dream at night of this war... **(Fadi Ballout, Beit Jala).**

I'm very scared and I can't do my homework because my father turns off the lights during the shooting. **(Rula Farhoud, Beit Sahour).** It was difficult for me and my sisters to do our homework because we were afraid...most nights I hear the sound of bullets... **(Fady Theodory, Ramallah).** When the Jews shoot I become afraid a little and our family leaves the home in the night and went to another place to escape from the bombs. **(Rani Kattan, Beit Jala).**

Every Palestinian family panics in every minute, because the Israeli soldiers shoot their innocent children in cold blood. **(Jihad Remon, Ain Arik).** The Israeli soldiers began to kill people without any mercy, they used many of their mean weapons in killing them, and they bombed their houses and their lands...they killed children in a very savage way. I feel very sorry about this and I hope that this war will stop and live in peace forever. **(George Jasser, Birzeit).** Aren't the Israeli soldiers feeling shame because they are using heavy weapons against us... **(Diana Al Zeeh, Beit Jala).**

Every day we see the soldiers kill children and every night they bomb houses... **(Nardeen Jawareesh, Beit Sahour).**

All the work has stopped and it is hard for the Palestinian people to make a living. **(Maher Bader, Beit Jala)..** My family and I can't go anywhere to buy food or clothes and sometimes my parents can't go to work because the soldiers close the roads ...we pray to God that everything will be better. **(Shatha Yousef Kaileh, Birzeit).** Many people stop working and some families haven't enough money to buy a loaf of bread **(Freda Nakleh, Jifna).** My father couldn't work so he couldn't bring money and my family had to mange with what we had... **(Maged Abu Saa'da, Beit Sahour).** Workers couldn't arrive to their work and as a result the number of the poor families has increased. **(Khael Sayaj, Birzeit).**

I'm not very happy these days...too many people died and too many people don't work. **(Hiba Abed Rabbo, Beit Jala).** I think that what the Jews did was really unfair... **(Sandra Sayej, Birzeit).** Several people die every day by Israeli soldiers. The news always is sad, so I with my family feel sad **(Tamara Khouriyeh, Taybeh).** They destroyed many houses and many people... **(George Awad, Beit Jala).**

Our house was not longer safe...we left everything...we took only some clothes. Mom and Dad go every day to our house to check the damage...we are still afraid of the coming days...**(Rawan Imad Qumsieh, Beit Sahour).**

...but the children of Israel are playing and happy. This is not fair. Each night I can't sleep because I'm afraid. **(Hurriyah Ziada, Ramallah.** You may not believe that I long to see my two married sisters as I have not seen them since the closure. My sister lost her baby (miscarriage) when she tried to come and see us, as she lives in Jerusalem **(Rula Wehbeh, Nablus).**

We are afraid of shootings, we do not go on picnics every weekend. When we come back from school, we stay in the house until the next morning...we can't play with our friends. We are sad and unhappy... **(Ghaida Musleh, Beit Sahour).** And we don't know when this horrible situation will end. And till that time we hope for peace **(Judeh Walid Shahwan, Beit Jala).**

Thousands of Olive trees and orange trees were over thrown and a lot of land was devastated by bulldozers. **(Helweh Majaj, Birzeit).**

The wedding of my cousin was different; we did not dance or invite lots of people. It was calm. **(Ayman Bannourah, Beit Sahour).** I'm so sad because Israelis killed hundreds of people. **(Ammar Khair, Beit Sahour).** The world is looking at us without doing anything... **(Tarez Daibes, Zababdeh).**

I ask God to help us and bring peace to our land. I think one day Israelis and Palestinians can live together in peace. **(Nadeen Musleh, Beit Sahour).** I'm looking now for a hand that draws happiness on our faces...I looked up the sky and prayed to God to help us live a better life...**(Suha Kamal Ghannam, Birzeit).** I wish to have peace in our country because we have lots of problems and we are looking for freedom and a good life with my family and my friends. **(Jeda Jad Jaser, Birzeit).** My dream is to play, to sing, to dance, go to school. **(Sman Musallam, Jifna).** I wish I can live like the other children in the world...for me, I hope I can go to the park or to the sea one day and live normally. **(Samah Bannoura, Beit Sahour).**

Finally, we hope that all of the world hear our voice and stand near us... **(Dalia Awad, Jifna).**

Anxiety and Faith in the Village
April 7, 2001

As the bombs were dropping on the village next to mine at eight in the evening and my curtains and doors were shaking and the house felt a bid strange, I sensed no choice but to continue reading the essays that were given to me from the Aboud village. If I did stop reading, I would be terrified that fear would overcome me. Following six months of Israeli terror in the Holy Land, you don't stop and listen to the shooting anymore, you just try as hard as possible to concentrate and focus on breathing slowly. Lately I have been trying to select students to award and appreciate for their excellent writing skills in the English language. Full of frustration, worry and anxiety myself, I find it very hard to even breathe slowly. Not knowing what tomorrow will bring promotes great anxiety for the young and old in this sacred land. It is this "not knowing" that is frustrating most of all.

Children throughout Palestine cannot feel a stable, safe and peaceful environment. In most cases without your basic needs you are not able to achieve and grow spiritually or emotionally. However, children growing up with tough circumstances have an opportunity to strength their faith in God. It is amazing to see that at a sensitive and young age children can face fear, frustration and anxiety yet express their faith in God. It is this power of faith that will guide Palestinian children for many years to come because our situation looks gloomier day after day. The following excerpts are all taken from Christian children in the village of Aboud where we continue witness for Christ through our Latin Church and Latin Patriarchate School providing education from preschool to grade eight. When it becomes financially possible, we hope to offer high school education too. Please share these voices with others concerned about the Christian presence in the Holy Land.

"My name is Yasser Ibrahim Hmeid. I am fourteen years old. I am in grade eight. I have one sister and two brothers. We all live in a small house in a small and beautiful village called Aboud. My father is my school's headmaster and my mother is a kindergarten teacher in the same school. We all love each other very much and I feel that we are a happy and beautiful family. What makes me feel angry and disappointed is that the Israeli soldiers are shooting, killing and injuring a lot of people in my country."

(Yasser Hmeid, 14 yrs old).

"We were living happily and safely in the past, but now we are unhappy and sad because of the Israeli measures taken since the beginning of the Intifada last September...This Intifada has spread in all the cities and villages of Palestine. Thus life has become more difficult and dangerous. The Israeli soldiers kill people without mercy and this is so terrible."
(Rana Yacoub, 12 yrs old).

"About four hundred people have been killed and more than 18,000 injured by the wild and cruel Israeli soldiers..." **(Ibrahim Shaheen, 12 yrs old)**. "These massacres that the Israelis are committing forbid us from living our normal lives..."**(Sreen Hmeid, 12 yrs old)**.

"My family and I live bad times now. When the soldiers come into my village, young people start throwing stones at them and the soldiers shoot live bullets and tear gas bombs... So my brothers and I feel very afraid. If my parents go to Ramallah we get worried and unhappy because we think something wrong may happen to them." **(Wala Nafe, 13 yrs old)**.

"I think this is not the life we deserve or want...we seek real peace...we are just defending our country..." **(Dalal Sami, 12 yrs old)**. "The goal of the Intifada is to defend Jerusalem and Palestine against the Israeli occupation. We hope we will be able to liberate them soon." **(Shawqi Hmeid, 13 yrs)**.

"My family and I hope that these bad conditions will disappear soon. My family and I love Jerusalem and Palestine and we pray and wish peace for everybody in this land." **(Niveen Salem, 12 yrs old)**. "I feel unhappy and disappointed... Every day I pray and ask God to protect my family..." **(Iyad Nawaf, 12 yrs old)**. "My family and I live in very bad situation in Palestine these days. The Israeli soldiers close the roads between my village and Ramallah, so my father can't go to work every day. My school itself was closed for more than two weeks and I had to stay home. I feel very bad and unhappy." **(Ala Jihad, 12 yrs old)**.

"My father is a worker in Israel and now he has lost his job. One of my brothers is a mechanic in Ramallah and sometimes he manages to arrive to work and sometimes he can't...My eldest sister is in grade 12. Although she learns in a governmental school that is in our village, she can't study as usual because her teachers especially those who are from other villages can't reach

the school. My mother is always worried and afraid because she thinks if we go to school, perhaps we will not come back home safe...
(Samar Massad, 14 yrs old).

"A lot of people don't go to their work because of the closure. The Israeli soldiers killed many people including a great number of children...I get very angry and irritated... I thank God a lot because the soldiers are far away from my family. **(Ala Karam, 13 yrs old).** "My family and I do not feel happy these days because we live very difficult and bad situation..." (**Khalil Zarour, 12 yrs old**). "I always watch TV because I am afraid from the Israeli army and I want to know what is happening around me and what will happen next...I always pray and ask Jesus our Lord to help us and grant us his blessings and peace." **(Youssef Fayez, 14 yrs old).**

"As a family we feel and live in continuous anxiety. Sometimes when my brother and my father go to Ramallah I become afraid and worried.**"**
(Joleen Massa, 14 yrs old).

"I always look at my parents and can easily see how sad they are because of the difficult situations we live in. My mother feels afraid and worried and she always tells me and my brother to take care and come back quickly home after school finishes." **(Ala Abdallah, 14 yrs old).** "My family and I feel sad these days because sometimes I can not go to school... **(Nidal Hmeid, 13 yrs old).** "We feel very unhappy and I get upset when I see on TV people killed and injured in cold blood. I am not sure about my future. I might be killed or injured, too...." **(Khould Saba, 13 yrs old).**

"People all over the world have seen and witnessed how children like Mohammad Al-Durra were killed without any mercy and they didn't say or do anything to stop the killing of the Palestinian people. This is very strange and I ask why nobody cares or listen to us and helps us to liberate our country, the Holy Land, where Jesus Christ was born and lived." **(Ghalieh Maher, 13).**

"Finally, I ask all the western countries and the USA to help us. I'd like to ask every person to pray for real and just peace in our land." (**Ramez Ghaleb, 13 yrs old**). "At the end I'd like to ask America to press on Israel to stop using violent means against the Palestinian Intifada and young people." **(Anan Da'oud, 13 yrs old).** "Thank you God because you always help me and my family..." **(Admon Shaheen, 12 yrs old).**

Do You Believe in Miracles?
May 1, 2001

Many people have scientific explanations for icons that appear to have liquid coming right through the paintings or oil streaming on paintings, something to do with heat and oil. Since I am not an expert in science, I can't enlighten you from this perspective. However, as a Greek Orthodox Christian Educator living in the Holy Land, I want to share with you an eye witness incident that occurred at the Church of the Holy Sepulchre on Great Friday evening during the Greek Orthodox Services at the tomb of Christ.

It was first brought to my attention that an Icon of Christ was bleeding as I was walking in a procession inside the Holy Sepulchre Church at about 1:00 am. The procession stops at different spots in the Church to signify where Jesus was flogged, where he was crowned with thorns, where he was nailed to the cross, where His body had laid before being placed in the tomb where he was buried. Many people were gathered at one particular tiny chapel that is dedicated to the Mocking of Christ, which is maintained by the Greek Orthodox Patriarchate. They were overcrowded, pushing, shoving and starring at the Icon of Christ depicting the Mocking of Christ during his trial. The chapel had three large wall icons and this particular one was the middle icon at the center of the chapel. It depicts Christ seating on a stool with his hands tied and six individuals that appear to be soldiers are pocking and hitting him with thin long sticks.

Initially, I ignored this crowd to my left and continued in the procession until I overheard an elderly lady tell one of the many bishops in Greek, "The Icon of our Lord is pouring blood." Being a person of such little faith I did not rush to stare at the icon myself. The bishop reassured this lady next to me that they would investigate the icon. As I found my husband David in the crowd I did mention to him the reason that particular chapel we just passed up was overcrowded due to an icon with blood. He ignored me as usual.

After an hour of prayers in Greek, Russian and Arabic, in front of the tomb of Christ, the holiest place on earth for Christians with the Coptic Orthodox chanting in the back of the tomb in another language, I had a hard time following my prayer book. The only thought that kept going through my mind is if Christians serve the same Lord why should we have thirteen different denominations? We need unity badly and better coordination during these services, definitely not microphones. All this simultaneous chanting is disturbing for a foreigner like me. I'm sure God was listening to both groups but I could not follow the Greek or the Coptic lamentations. The Greek Consul, however, Mr. Petros Panagotopoulos never has such problems because he can always stand right in front of the tomb.

Confused and baffled at this four-hour service, I turned around looked at my husband who said: "You should go see the icon, it's bleeding." At this point, I quickly ran back to the chapel and since Jerusalem is empty from pilgrims, it was possible to walk very fast because usually its so crowded you can't budge. It was 2:30 am when I starred at the oil painting of the Icon of Christ very high in the middle of the small chapel. I saw four splashes or smears of a red liquid on Christ's right leg and five red smears or spots on the left leg.

While the crowd at the chapel was chanting in Russian, a young tall man in front of this icon would take items from people and wipe the liquid off from the icon. The items I saw given to this young man were candles, small icons, cotton balls, scarves, crosses, tissues, anything that people happen to have in their possession at this moment to receive this oil and see before their very eyes that it was from Christ's Icon.

As I marveled at this site, I gave this thin young man my black cotton scarf and he jumped up to reach and wiped the icon. For as much oil that was wiped from the icon, more oil would appear instantly before our eyes. I smelled my scarf and it had a neutral smell, no special smell and the oil was moist and seeped into the material. At 2:40 am, I witnessed a very thin strip of oil in the color red appear on the inside of the right leg of Christ below the knee on this very same icon.

The gentleman next to me who later told me his name is Costa Kourtalaris, a tour guide from Cyprus, pocked me on my arm and said in Greek: "Did you see that blood, it's new, it was not there ten minutes ago." And, I was indeed amazed to see this new red liquid before my very eyes because it was so unbelievable and it was not there when I initially began to look at the icon. I had specifically counted the red spots because I was interested in telling my children about them and I wanted to be technically accurate at how many splashes I saw. My twelve-year-old usually asks me technical questions as such.

Furthermore, what really amazed me more was that this new strip of oil that appeared in front of my eyes continued to get longer and stream down the leg of Christ before my very eyes. It was as fat as the thinnest spaghetti string. By 3:00 am, the oil strip that began below the knee had reached the ankle. Ten minutes later before I left the Holy Sepulchre, the stream of oil got longer and had reached the toe of Christ on this icon.

I asked this gentleman from Cyprus how long he has been coming to the Holy Land and if he had ever seen such streaks of oil on this icon before. He said he has come to the Holy Land every year for the last twenty-five years and has never seen these spots before on this particular icon. As I asked him, do you think this is a miracle? I overheard Bishop Timothy from the Greek Patriarchate tell the young man wiping the icon to stop taking the oil off of the icon and to leave the icon alone for an investigation of this incident.

I went home needing no one to research it for me because I saw Christ's Icon bleeding with my own eyes and new strips of blood appearing and streaming down Christ's leg as I starred at it for an hour trying to discern what was happening before me. I do not deserve to be a witness to the Glory of God but I feel it is a sacred duty to tell others so that humanity can give Glory to God. I remembered the words of Christ to the Apostles that I heard during the Epistle at the Easter service: *"..and you shall be witnesses for me in Jerusalem and in all Judea and Samaria and even to the very ends of the earth."* (Acts of the Apostles 1:1-8)

As I sat in my living room each evening this week overlooking the beautiful lights of Jerusalem because I live high on a mountain in the middle of Biblical Judea and Samaria and since I had been in Jerusalem on Great Friday, these words took a special meaning for me. Even after hearing the Epistle, I did not rush to write my personal account. I called Bishop Timothy to confirm the red spots on the icon. He said he had seen the spots himself and the Divine Grace appears to those who believe. However, he could not make an official announcement that this was a miraculous icon, although he has never seen these red splashes before during his many years of praying in the Holy Sepulchre.

My friend, Sister Maria Stephanopoulos said this is the Holy Land and such miraculous incidents happen all the time. Do you believe in Miracles?

The Voice of Christian Students in Gaza
May 22, 2001

Day by day we live with bloodshed and death. We have almost made it to the end of a difficult school year. The Israelis make every effort to cheat Palestinian children from their education. We must try everything in our power to keep our schools open and our programs and activities that promote the education of the whole child alive. School is about the only hope left for every Palestinian child. Even the graduation ceremonies this week have to be in the midst of shooting and bombing. It is amazing that world leaders look at what is happening against the Palestinians and no one can stop the Israeli brutality and cold-blooded killings. So many of our students in our Christian schools refer to their faith in such incidents and call out for God to help us.

We have a very small Christian population in Gaza and the Gaza Latin Patriarchate School has played a vital role since it was built in 1974, not only providing high standards in education but also a Christian atmosphere and religion lessons for Christian children. The school has a little over one thousand students with 15% Christians from kindergarten to 12th grade. It is actually considered one of the best schools in Gaza. I personally find the Gaza Christian population very isolated and in need of solidarity. Thus I wanted to share with you the following excerpts from student essays:

Everyday I see blood and killing. I do not know how to live my life. When my mother hears the crash of the bombs she becomes afraid. My little sister begins to cry...I'm very sad and worried. I don't want every minute to hear crashes of bombs. I want peace, freedom and justice. (**Manar Zommo**, 8th grade). The Israeli forces put us under siege; they separated the areas between each other, so that people in Rafah can't move to Khan Younis and the other parts. (**Dalia Dabbagh**, 8th grade). Everything becomes hard and tragic in our life... (**George Fatouleh**, 9th grade).

My life has changed too much. I don't go to the YMCA. I don't go to restaurants, and I am very afraid from the bombs. But I hope God will save all the children and God will help the Palestinians. (**Dana Burbara**, 8th grade).

When we were studying about 7 o'clock in the evening, we heard a bomb sound. We thought it was thunder, but it happened again and again, so we went to see through the window. We saw the Israeli helicopters bombing us with rockets and we saw the explosion here and there, so we became frightened. It was really the scariest time we lived and till now we are watching more martyrs die. For that we ask God to stop this and to spread the peace. (**Ramzi Frangieh**, 8th grade).

You know we are in hard times. My feelings are too bad and I am very sad because not all the students come to the school because the road is closed…but we must not be afraid because God will help us, you know Palestine is our home and we must not leave it. (**Katreen Masoud**, 8th grade). All my holidays were sad. My feeling these days are very sad and angry because these are hard and difficult days in the Intifada. (**Nour Tarazi**, 8th grade).

One of the fearful and hard times was the absence of my father while the Israeli helicopters were bombing. He was on his way home from his pharmacy. I thanked God when he arrived and I'll pray every day because of the continuous attacks of the Israeli armies on the innocent people. More and more the Israeli siege prevented thousands of workers from gaining their daily bread, which caused the grief and poverty to many people. (**Michael Frangieh**, 9th grade). Our Palestinian people don't have any army to defend their country; we use only the stones…(**Elias Manneh**, 8th grade).

For students like me, it is impossible to study in this situation…the only thing we can do is pray to God… (**Waleed Siam**, 9th grade).

My Life in Palestine these Days By Lulu Dabbagh, 8th grade.

Palestine is the flower in my life. It is our mother. It calls me "help me, help me, help me please." In Palestine, my life is difficult and sad, no travel, not enough food, no place to play and no nice time with friends and no happy holidays.

During these days, my family is very sad. My dad doesn't go to his work because he works near Netzarim settlement. My younger sister is afraid from Sharon because he made many massacres like Dier Yassin, Sabra and Shatila. At home we watch the Palestinian channel to see what happens in Palestine. When we see martyrs, the tears come to our eyes. At the beginning of the Intifada, we watched Mohammed Al Durra while he was crying behind his father and then being shot dead by the Israelis in cold blood. This scene shocked the whole world. My parents cried while watching it because they know what these moments mean to a father who could not protect his son.

My youngest brother was afraid very much when the Israelis planes bombed Gaza and every time he hears the noise of planes he is terrified. My friends at school hate the Israelis as I do. We all prayed to God not to let Sharon win the elections. I spend my school days studying hard because the knowledge is our only weapon. I beg the Lord to give us independence to establish the Palestinian State and its capital Jerusalem. Hand in hand to put the corner stone in our Palestinian State, to protect our holy places and to keep our flag high in the sky.

My Family and Life in Palestine By Lina Dabbagh, 7th grade.

Our life in Gaza has changed in many ways and it has become worse since the beginning of the Intifada last September. We are living in fear and tension and always thinking about our destiny.

The Israelis hit Gaza by rockets many times. Their tanks are surrounding our lands and we expect more from them. Everyday I watch, with my family, the news on TV and see our Palestinian brothers and sisters wounded and killed defending our rights and lands. I feel angry while watching these scenes and wish to join them.

The situation is becoming worse especially since a war criminal won the elections in Israel. Each member of my family is suffering in a different way. My little brother and sister are terrified from being attacked or bombed by the Israelis. We are feeling frightened when hearing the roaring of planes in the sky. My father stopped going to his work as it is next to one of the settlements in Gaza.

Every family in Palestine is suffering especially the ones who lost one or more of their members. Others lost their houses as they were demolished and they became homeless. Workers lost their work and their income to feed their children. In spite of all the suffering of the Palestine people, we are willing to sacrifice our souls cheaply defending our dignity and rights.

No Pleasant Stories in the Holy Land
June 16, 2001

As I was about to write a pleasant story about the open day activities at the Taybeh Latin School, the Israeli settlers burned twenty five of our family olive trees as part of over four hundred trees that were burned to the crisp in the village of Taybeh. The family olive trees were so precious and old and passed from generation to generation, my father-in-law believes they date back two thousand years ago according to their trunk size.

As I was about to write a pleasant story...ten new Israeli settlement houses popped up across my kitchen window on the mountain top in Taybeh. I was in total shock and disbelief. The Ofra settlement reaches from one mountain top to the other and continues to grow while we are forbidden to build on our land that is under Israeli military occupation in the outskirts of Taybeh.

As I was about to write a pleasant story...twenty-five settlers with their guns blocked the road to the entrance of my village and demanded I turn around. Very scary savage looking people with guns, I listened and spent two hours getting home although I was five minutes away then they started banging on my car to turn around.

As I was about to write a pleasant story...we experienced the tragic death of twenty-four year old Thaer Basir in Taybeh, who had a fatal truck accident because the main road Nablus to Taybeh is blocked and his heavy truck did not safely make it up the narrow side dirt road. This was a tragic loss of life due to the Israeli closure and siege in our country.

As I was about to write a pleasant story...the most wonderful Christian family that relocated to Palestine six years ago and founded the Harb Heart Center in Ramallah decided to move back to the United States with their four children who initially came to enrich their Palestinian Christian values and roots.

As I was about to write a pleasant story...we finished the most scary and bloody academic year since the 1967 war.

As I was about to write a pleasant story...many Palestinians like Fr. David Khoury, our first cousin could not travel over the bridge to fly out from

Amman, Jordan to raise money for the housing project in our village of Taybeh. The airport is closed for Palestinians and so is the bridge to Jordan. It's just a big prison.

As I was about to write a pleasant story about the open day activities at the Taybeh Latin School, I realized I must do it on my summer vacation because I am in need of a dose of the western culture due to the fear, anxiety and nightmares I have lived through during these tragic days in the Holy Land full of bloodshed and violence. The sacred land of our Lord's birth deserves so much better.

Church groups need to organize and support their brothers and sisters in Christ to gain justice, liberty, and freedom in the land of Christ's birth. The American government needs to stop sending money and weapons to kill Palestinian children. Palestinians need their basic human rights. Please help so there might be a pleasant story in the Holy Land.

The daily routine of homes being bombed

Return to the Land of Bloodshed
September 11, 2001

In such a sacred place where Christ established our Christian roots it certainly takes your breath away to see death all around you and a total escalation of violence and broken promises of peace. Muslims, Christians and Jews cannot seem to share a land that is precious to all three groups. The fear and the unknowing of what will happen day to day, tear up my soul the most. The "shootings and the bombings" are just what most people consider "rain" in other parts of the world. You wait until it goes away and go out again.

Three months of peaceful vacation and no Israeli checkpoints fooled me into thinking I can escape to middle class America. It's good I have wise children because they said if everyone was like me there will be no Palestinians left in Palestine. I must admit, I was totally shocked that they rather stay two hours at a checkpoint going to school in their own country near their extended family rather than become part of the melting pot of America. Of course, if we did not have this severe closure and blockade, this two-hour checkpoint aimed at taking away your human dignity and humiliating you to the maximum degree would instead be a ten minute ride to school on the beautiful hills and country side of the West Bank.

"Checkpoint" actually means very little to people that have not seen the daily suffering and agony of the Palestinian people trying to go to work and school. For me, it is a very loaded word because these checkpoints make my life miserable and I see them as depriving people of a basic right to just earn their daily bread and children's basic right to receive education. One of our first grade teachers, Ms. Luma Khalak in the Latin Birzeit Patriarchate School travels from Beit Hanina near Jerusalem where she lives through two checkpoints to make it to the Birzeit School. A twenty-minute ride turns into a three-hour nightmare.

Luma said to me: "It's a sacred mission to stay here. It's my duty. If every person will think it's horrible and we must leave, who will stay? Somebody has to decide to stay and help this country and develop this country...Jesus, our Lord and Savior came to this land. He suffered here and was crucified...two thousand years of wars, dead people, injuries...and I am waiting for the word 'holy' to come true...we will hope...we will pray...God gave me this mission to stay in this country." Working with such loyal and dedicated human beings should eventually help me stop thinking of running away. Not to mention they inspire and strength my faith. However, young adults like Luma are deprived of everything that others take for granted all around the world. They are adults but are forbidden to live, there is no social life. They can not celebrate birthdays, take trips, go to conferences, and visit family. All activities are cancelled. They suffer just to make it to work, go home and close the door until the routine starts again the next day with those awful checkpoints. Checkpoints make normal people go into a rage.

Returning to Palestine meant a return to fear and anxiety for me. Returning to a place where American money and American weapons have destroyed the Holy Land. Returning to a place where millions of Palestinians want their basic human rights deprived by Israel since 1948. Returning to a place where fear and the grace of God accompany you unceasingly. Returning to a place where some people have not worked for over ten months. Returning to a place where martyrs, killings and daily funerals have not brought freedom and independence to Palestine. Returning to a place where the price to maintain Christian roots and Palestinian identity is far too high to pay. Returning Palestine as our homeland is the answer to peace in the Middle East.

Surda checkpoint to go from Ramallah to Birzeit University

Prayers from the Holy Land

Letter sent to Holy Land Christian Ecumenical Foundation Website

September 12, 2001

From Dr. Maria C. Khoury
    Education Department
    Latin Patriarchate Schools of Jerusalem

As we hear about the tragic attacks happening in America this week, on behalf of the children and the teachers in the Latin Patriarchate Schools of Jerusalem, whom I have worked with very closely the last two years, we send our fervent prayers for peace in America and in our world. We pray these attacks against humanity will stop and the Grace of the Holy Spirit will guide our lives.

We pray that innocent people will stop being killed and hurt regardless of their nationality, ethnicity, color and/or religion. We are deeply saddened in Palestine when others in the world experience the terror, fear and bombs that overshadow are lives everyday. We pray for peace.

As you, our American friends have shown us your solidarity, your support, your very kind emails, your compassion and your prayers during these dreadful and tragic eleven months of our Palestinian uprising, please know that many of us today have you in our prayers for peace and safety in America.

"The Lord bless you and keep you; The Lord make His face shine upon you and be gracious to you."

Enthronement of the Greek Orthodox Patriarch
September 22, 2001

Four checkpoints later, many hours on the road, foreign passports and the grace of God get local Christians into Jerusalem these days. A simple twenty-minute ride under Israeli occupation and military siege is a nightmare. If you use Palestinian roads, the Israeli soldiers detain you, if you use Israeli settlement roads, the snipers might shoot you. But, it was a special day in the history of Orthodox Christianity last Saturday for the enthronement ceremony of the Greek Orthodox Patriarch of Jerusalem, Irineos I. And, as a Greek by birth, I was compelled to see it.

I believe the Greek delegation from Greece including President Stephanopoulos and Greek foreign minister George Papandreou had an easier time making it to the Holy Sepulchre from Athens than local Palestinian Christians coming from their nearby villages. All faiths were present but this was strictly an Orthodox affair involving a beautifully chanted centuries old ecclesiastical ceremony. The choir members even flew in from Greece.

For the first time in the history of Orthodox services in Jerusalem (that I have seen the last twenty years) there was strict and very tight security. And I don't mean just hundreds of policemen and soldiers in every corner of the old city. Not only did you need an invitation card, which by the way I did not have one. Once you arrived at the entrance of the Holy Sepulchre, you must present your card, check your name on the invitation list, receive a sticker with a seat number on it and present the card with your seat number again before entering the church. And as you might know, Orthodox churches do not have seats on this side of the world, so the Greeks went to a lot of trouble to set up and organize this arranged check-in.

It's Jerusalem and miracles of God do happen so I was able to have a nice seat right behind the American Consul general at which time I expressed my deepest sadness for the tragic events that took place in New York and Washington. Most Palestinians expressed their unequivocal condemnation for this catastrophe in America. But unfortunately the media does not like to promote average Palestinians mourning the life of Americans in East Jerusalem so I won't be surprised if you didn't see this candle light vigil on your TV screen. Here in the Holy Land, we live and suffer with such terror, fear, and daily bombings that we do not wish such horrifying attack on anyone. The tragedy in America is a crime against humanity and shocking to all.

As hundreds of priests and dozens of bishops marched in the Cathedral of the Anastasis (Resurrection) right opposite the Holy tomb of Christ everyone started shouting "Axios" (worthy) as the new Patriarch took the throne. His all holiness received a standing ovation and blessed everyone with the cross in his hand. The Archbishop of Athens and All Greece Christodoulos was the first to praise the new Jerusalem Patriarch followed by warmest wishes read from King Abdallah of Jordan and President Yasser Arafat for the historical position Irineos will hold.

All of the major world Orthodox patriarchs sent official decrees read in Greek during the service with the exception of the Russian patriarch who sent his sermon in Russian. A large TV screen outside the Holy Sepulcher allowed everyone to follow the ceremony with translations available. It is very disturbing that the Israeli government did not send a statement of recognition for the new Greek Orthodox patriarch.

The patriarch of Alexandria sent a special cross as a gift to His All Holiness Irineos reminding him to be a strong witness for Christ in this sacred land while the Patriarch of Antioch suggested the Holy Spirit would help the new patriarch maintain this historic continuation of a big mission for God.

According to Sister Maria Stephanopoulos the feeling of most Orthodox Christians is overall enthusiastic that good changes will take place to deal with old conflicts in the Patriarchate. Most people want to stay positive, have faith in a new era and hope the new patriarch will be a "good shepherd" first and a "Greek" second.

It was indeed a special day for Orthodox Christianity in the Holy Land because in this small chapel overcrowded with high profile dignitaries and representatives of non government organizations, representative from thirteen Christian denominations and simple followers of Christ; one deeply feels the essence and power of faith.

No matter where we live on earth perhaps God calls us to maintain a Christian presence and to be a witness for Christ. As Fr. Demetri Tsigas states with an internet letter: "We need to shine the light of God's love in the world...Let us be a blessing to God that He may bless us all." But for those of us that live in the Holy Land, this witness takes on even a more significant meaning because we really do live in the land made holy from the presence of our Lord Jesus Christ himself over two thousand years ago. Except the modern reality of living in this sacred land rips your soul apart at the injustice and destruction you see.

The same evening of the patriarch's enthronement while diplomats were enjoying a spectacular reception at the King David Hotel, the Israeli army was invading the Al Sharayet residential neighborhood in Ramallah with thirteen military tanks surrounding the area with severe bombing. Several heavy armored jeeps patrolled the neighborhood and heavy gunfire coming from Apache helicopters could be heard in the villages all around including mine.

All American money and American weapons killing us and injuring us daily. May God bring peace to the world.

Greek Orthodox Patriarch of Jerusalem
His Beatitude Irineos I

A Checkpoint Away from the Miraculous Icon
October 10, 2001

It was the first day of the Jewish New Year with a very tight closure on Ramallah. More than seventy-five villages were shut off at 10 am from entering or exiting the Ramallah area. People at the checkpoint were frustrated, very angry and upset as they were stopped from passing. I had to wait until all the rocks were thrown, all the shooting stopped, all the gas bomb smells disappeared and then brave or stupid, I drove up to the Israeli soldier and begged to enter Ramallah. "Go back home, it is forbidden to pass," he said. I told him I would love to have a holiday but my children were in school inside Ramallah because they left the house at 6:30 in the morning when it was not forbidden so I must pick them up. As he looked at my foreign passport he suggested it was too dangerous to live here maybe I should leave the country. This gave me the feeling it will take a long time to pass because I was facing concrete blocks in front of my car not just the soldier.

Such concrete blocks have been blocking all entry points to Ramallah since last October. It's a daily suffering that places all of us at the mercy of the Israelis. I turned off the car, got out and rested on the concrete block as the sun gave me an instant headache from the high heat. The view of nature is spectacular on this high hill full of olive trees that haven't yet been destroyed by Jewish settlers. But the checkpoint is a nightmare and takes away your dignity. Admiring God's beauty in the Holy Land, I felt the presence of God and told the soldier I can light a candle for him in church so that God can protect him and keep him safe if he would just call his commander to let me pass this checkpoint.

I must have been the strangest person he met that day. He made the phone call, brought the jeep over and pushed one concrete block so I could sneak my car by. I have waited hours so one more second to turn my head and thank him with relief was easy. Drenched with sweat in his bulletproof vest the Israeli soldier said: "Can you light that candle for me?" I grew up as a child lighting candles in Greece all the time. Candles represent Christ is the light of the world. Lighting candles for me is giving glory to God. Being true to my faith I went straight to the Ramallah Orthodox Church to fulfill my promise. I actually saw the parish priest Fr. Yacoub (Jacob) Khoury who was ordained two years ago. I began to ask him about the weeping icon of the

Virgin Mary that exists here in the Transfiguration Greek Orthodox Church
of Ramallah. Although I have visited this church many times, only last year
did I come to understand this is a miraculous icon from Fr. Yacoub's
explanations.

This icon of the Virgin Mary with the Christ child was hand painted in 1992
by a local iconographer Mr. Gabriel Gaylmantian from the Bethlehem area.
Many icons in the church were glassed up by lay people and framed in order
to preserve and better protect them. On the morning of June 17, 1998, Fr.
Nicola Akal who teaches in the local Orthodox School went in the church to
light candles as usual. The glass of the framed icon fell on the floor. The
priest was a bit scared and left quickly to report the incident to Archimandrite
Dr. Meletios Bassal, the superior at the Transfiguration convent right next to
the church since 1997.

Both Fr. Nicola and Fr. Meletios thought the glass had possibly fallen from
the strong wind blowing from an open window. But, right next to the icon,
the vigil lamp was still lit from the previous day so this was an indication it
could not have been the wind. Both priests were a bit nervous that the glass
broke so they left the church for the local parish priest at that time Fr. Jeries
(George) Marzouka to see it.

Fr. Jeries who is originally from the Bethlehem area returned about five or six
hours later to the church following a visit with relatives. He was asked to
clean up the glass on the floor that had fallen from the frame of the icon but
cut his hand while touching the glass. He screamed for help so Fr. Meletios
came running inside the church and saw his hand bleeding.

The archimandrite ran quickly to the convent to get a piece of cotton and
alcohol to clean the blood. When he returned, Fr. Jeries' hand had stopped
bleeding and the cut closed up. In an instant they noticed something unusual
happened that the blood had fully disappeared from his hand. When they
observed the icon more carefully they noticed the icon had many streaks of
oil. The icon appeared to be in tears represented by oil. The shedding of oil
tears continued as the oil was collected over the years to heal many people.

Fr. Meletios who also holds a doctor of psychology degree from the
University of Athens has seen many miracles and thousands of people passing
through the church to see the icon from all over the world. But after last

September following the Palestinian uprising not many have come. I asked him what did he first see when he looked at this icon. He replied, he saw the icon full of oil and Christ's face was just a shinning light to him. "I don't see Christ's face when I look at the icon, I just see a shinning light," Fr. Meletios explained to me. He means he did not see the details of the face like the eyes, the nose, the mouth, but instead saw a pure flashing light from Christ's face. I asked him why did he initially get scared and leave the glass on the floor for Fr. Jeries to clean up: "I don't know I just got scared…maybe I am not worthy to see a miracle and just inside my inner self I felt a disturbance," he confessed.

From the many miracles, Fr. Meletios told me the story of a Greek woman with skin cancer who had come to the Hadassah hospital in Jerusalem to receive treatment in September 1998. The doctors encouraged her to return to Greece because her cancer had far progressed and nothing could be done to help her condition because she was in a very late stage in her disease. Being a devote Orthodox Christian this woman went to the Holy Sepulchre to venerate the tomb of Christ and during the long wait she heard of the miraculous icon in Ramallah being talked about by two women who were in fact on their way to see the icon. She asked to go with them and venerate this miraculous icon.

When the sick woman arrived to the Ramallah church and witnessed the icon crying and filled with oil she begged Fr. Meletios to be anointed by this oil. The nun in the convent helped the Greek woman anoint all of her body with the oil. One week later the same woman returned with two Jewish doctors from the Hadassah hospital claiming her cancer had completely disappeared and she had been cured. The Hadassah doctor mentioned to Fr. Meletios that Arab people have practical medicines for health conditions such as drinking herbal mountain tea for sore throats, etc, and the doctor wished to have some of what appeared to be a practical medicine from the icon. Fr. Meletios brought to his attention that it would not be possible to have the ointment because as a Jewish doctor he does not do his cross like most Christians would do before using the ointment. The doctor left the church unhappily and quickly.

I asked Fr. Meletios if there was one miracle that stands out in his mind from the last three years. He mentioned to me a Muslim woman who arrived at the church in June 1998 with her husband after hearing the icon is a miraculous one. The Muslim woman could not see from one eye because her black pupil was larger than her other normal pupil. Fr. Meletios remained in the office while Fr. Nicola received this woman who said she believed in the Virgin Mary and her crucified son Christ and wanted oil to be put on her eye. Making this confession, Fr. Nicola had no choice but to let her venerate the icon and give her the oil. It took the woman about two minutes to exit the church and reach the front entrance where her husband was waiting at which time Fr. Meletios heard screaming and yelling "I see, I see...I am well," the woman was shouting. The husband was very upset and did not believe this is a miracle but instead was angry about what type of magic the priest did. The woman answered her husband by saying that 'whatever you want to believe, believe, the significant thing is that I can see and I am well.' Fr. Meletios thought this was an amazing miracle because it involved a Muslim woman.

The Transfiguration Church of Ramallah was build about 150 years ago. It currently serves about 7,000 local Greek Orthodox Christians all of who are of Palestinian descent. However, before the 1967 war there were 38,000 Christians in the area. I asked Fr. Meletios what does he think about the future of the church and he said he is very worried that fifty years from now maybe there will not be any Orthodox Christians left in Ramallah.

The archimandrite said: "I'm scared for the Church, our numbers are going down because of the propaganda people hear from America and from Canada. Basically, false dreams that you can get rich quick, live better and that all opportunities are available to you." Thus, Fr. Meletios thinks it's not just the occupation and the bad politics that force people to move away from this sacred land but the propaganda about a better life in the west.

I asked Fr. Meletios what does he think people in other parts of the world should know about Orthodox Christians in the Ramallah community and he said: " We are Palestinians, Greek (Byzantine) Orthodox and we live in a very religious level, we gather to pray and attend church but we have a very low theological level. Our roots are Christian from the time of Christ and we live and walk the footsteps of Christ but people in our community need to be more educated about the Orthodox faith."

Finally, I asked Archimandrite Dr. Meletios the most current popular question concerning his thoughts about the new Greek patriarch, His All Holiness Patriarch Irineos of Jerusalem and he said: "I think the patriarch will now try to reinstate the trust of the people towards the Patriarchate because we have lost that for many years. It is encouraging the patriarch will provide theological and liturgical training every few months for local priests. These workshops and training are vital to maintain the true faith and worship. And the patriarch promised to take better care of the Greek Orthodox Christian Schools in the Holy Land. So we have great hope for a new era."

At the end we finished this unplanned interview with Fr. Meletios by him stating that the miraculous icon is God's way of communicating with us. Miracles are difficult to understand and they are beyond our logic so we can only have faith. *"That was the true Light, which lighteth every man that cometh into the world."* (John 1:9).

Icon of the Holy Theotokos Weeping

Occupation Cheats Children from Basic Education
October 23, 2001

The Israeli army is cheating us one more time from our basic right to education in this land. The only hope Palestinian children have for any future is a good education to be viable members of their society and of the world community. But unfortunately the Israeli Occupation continues to rob children out of their basic rights to a fundamental education.

The Bethlehem area has not had school for the last four days. Schools cannot open until it is at least safe on the streets. With Israeli military tanks choking up the city of Bethlehem since last Wednesday, gunfire everywhere and the boom of tank shells day and night does not indicate a peaceful and just solution in sight. Teachers in the area report shooting from midnight to six in the morning. It is impossible for children to sleep through the night and the majorities have to leave their beds and sleep in lower areas of the house and away from windows or glass that might shatter in the middle of the night.

The Bethlehem area is suffering and seeing the worst this week but the Ramallah area also has areas under curfew where Israeli military tanks are blocking students from entering Birzeit University. The university has been officially closed since the Israeli Tourist minister was killed last Wednesday. People are denied freedom of movement even for going to work or going to the hospital.

All members of the Palestinian society are punished when Israel feels pain. But who is keeping the score when over 700 Palestinians have been killed this year. Who is punishing the Israelis for the collective punishment they carry out? This collective punishment is absolutely wrong and punishes an entire group of people who most of them want to live in peace and harmony and co-exist side to side with their neighbors.

On Wednesday morning we woke up to a beautiful sunny day and gave glory to God that the two major checkpoints into Ramallah had been finally uplifted so it was not a two-hour drive to school from the village. For the first time this school year we did not have to see children getting out of one taxi at the checkpoint, carrying their heavy backpack which sometimes feels like it has rocks in it from the heavyweight books, walking quickly in front of soldiers, armed jeeps and tanks and picking up another taxi on the opposite side of the checkpoint (after a long wait of course) just to make it to school. The smile on children's faces making it to school that day was like kids being in Disney World for the first time. It was a great sight and a welcomed change. However, quickly throughout the day rumors spread that the Israeli tourist ministry was killed.

There has been no quality education in Ramallah since that day. Even when the children make it to school, the teachers can not because the Israeli army has invaded all Palestinian areas. How sad that even the bullets have reached the Holy Nativity Church in Manger Square. How sad that people continue to die. It is very confusing to me what terrorism the international community is trying to fight these days when I see Palestinian children on a daily basis traumatized by the Israeli army.

It is very confusing to me who the terrorists really are when my own children out of deep fear say "Mama, what if Sharon does like Sabra and Shatilla (the massacre in the refugee camps) again?" It is really confusing to me that an entire nation of people has suffered a catastrophe of the worst type since 1948. It is so confusing to me when small children and university students cannot get their basic rights to education in the Holy Land. I can only take comfort in the words of Reinhold Niebuhr "God grant me the serenity to accept things I cannot change, courage to change things I can, and wisdom to know the difference."

If you are a reader that can make a difference in the Holy Land by contacting your government officials for a just and peaceful resolution, the children of this region are in grave need of your help.

This wall in Jerusalem prevents the little girls of the Bethany School from making the usual short walk to St. Mary Magdalene's Church

This Week in the Holy Land
November 6, 2001

As I was worried about Palestinian education sitting in my Ramallah office on Thursday, October 25th, a bloodbath was taking place twenty minutes away from me. An outright massacre was happening under the orders of Sharon and his army in the village of Beit Rima near Ramallah where they stormed the area with tanks, armored jeeps and heavy military equipment killing ten Palestinians one after the other. The army made an announcement that they only wanted one person in suspicion of the assassination of the Israeli tourist minister but killed all the others in the process and severely injured dozens including women and children. The wounded were lying under olive trees all day because the ambulances were prevented from getting through to the village.

So I thought to myself does it really matter that 115 schools were closed this week in the Holy Land if we can't even keep the students alive to attend them. Sixty kindergarten centers did not operate in the Bethlehem area this week because the Israeli tanks are destroying this historic city. Does it really matter 120 schools have had a direct missile hit during this Palestinian Uprising just like the one that killed the little girl sitting in her classroom in the Jenin School. Do the human rights organizations know that 50,000 students could not get to school this week in the Holy Land? At least four schools have been occupied by Israeli soldiers and turned into military camps. These statistics are from the Palestinian ministry of education whom also reports the Industrial School in Tulkarim was bulldozed by the Israeli army. Does it make sense to worry about the rights of children and protecting the educational process when the Israelis are just slaughtering Palestinians left and right? This bloodshed is all courtesy of American money and weapons. Does anyone else think that "military occupation is terrorism of the worst type" or I am just losing my senses living in the middle of Biblical Judea and Samaria becoming an extinct living stone.

In the beginning of the Intifada last year, I had to make my opinion a little general so that Muslim and Christian groups can share our Holy Land tragedy. I had to make my opinion a little more specific so Christian organizations can print our daily suffering. I had to make my opinion include teachers and students because I work for the Latin Patriarchate Schools. I had to make my opinion include the affects on the Greek community so the

Orthodox could take an interest and bring awareness to this horrible Israeli occupation. Does it really matter anymore whether one is Muslim, Christian or Jew? The respect for human life should be the same. For the love of humanity can readers across the world contact their government officials to help stop these senseless killings? For the sacredness of this Holy Land can the world community please take notice and stop this Israeli aggression.

The sound of bombs all night long in the land where the Prince of Peace was born and died on the cross for our sins seems an irony to the sacredness of this special place. In a land of violence, terror, fear, bloodshed and the daily unknowing, I find it unbearable to be a shinning light for Christ. I have come to the point where I wish to just go to my creator and if He is indeed a God of love to take me away without suffering and pain. I pray for a peaceful passing. Thousands of people that have not died are left behind paralyzed, children without one eye, children without one hand, children without one leg, children badly wounded. And the children that do not have the physical wounds to show have the worst wounds of all. They have the psychological trauma and the psychological effects that will last a life time and the scars of the heart and soul that affect how you perceive life and people. Furthermore, you have the mothers left behind mourning their dead children.

I actually don't blame my boss for not believing in English Language Development in the Christian Schools because when I called to speak with one of my teachers today, Ms. Sana Abu Amsha from Beit Jala, we really could not talk about the speech festival, spelling competition and writing contest or any new strategies for the classroom because she just kept saying: "Now...now...they are shooting outside ..right now." Actually the more we talked; the more I got chills all over my body. She has been stuck inside the house with her three children the last week because it is safer not to go anywhere. "I don't let them go out...I feel someone will kill them," confesses Sana. By the way, she was not stuck inside her own house but living with an aunt because her home was shelled by rockets so she had to escape at least to the other side of Beit Jala where there is electricity and water.

To keep the children busy she encourages them to draw instead of watching Television all day long. There is absolutely nothing to do. It is not as if the children can concentrate and study. She was surprised when her son Nicola (Nicholas) who is seven years old and a student at the Beit Jala Latin Patriarchate School drew a house with a tank right in front of it, two helicopters on top of the house and children hiding behind the chairs. She said: "My husband and I were upset. We don't want our kids to be like this...when I told him to draw I imagined he will draw a house with flowers or a fish, something pleasant or something he use to draw before...really I was shocked." And, Sana's daughter Mariam (Mary) who is eleven years old just keeps wishing to go back to school. She misses her friends.

This wonderful and hardworking teacher is expecting her fourth child and the doctor told her to stay calm because she is at high risk to deliver the baby early from being terrified by this Israeli invasion into Beit Jala. She cannot sleep at nights from the constant shooting. She is so worried she does not know exactly what happened to her house since she was not able to return and check it from the disaster in the streets. She left the day the Israeli tanks forced their way into Aida Camp and her street is so narrow that the tanks did not fit down the little road. Thus, they destroyed the walls of many houses and damaged everything in site as fire broke out from the telephone lines. Many people are still without electricity and water. Still you can feel Sana's faith. She kept telling me: Thanks to God for everything but I don't know what will happen to my house until now...the Israelis destroyed Bethlehem...the hotels, the houses... the streets...Sharon likes blood and killing. I remember Sabra and Shatilla (Sept 16, 1982 massacre of Palestinians in refugee camps in Lebanon under Sharon's orders)...I was just fifteen years old. I remember those days...our life now is like you are watching a film and you are in it. Thank God we left home and we escaped."

As I hung up the phone with a heavy heart I thought that the presence of tanks, armored jeeps and heavily armed soldiers can only have negative psychological affects on children. You face nothing but fear and more fear. Personally, my last dream was inside one of these tanks and the soldiers were giving me a lift through the checkpoint. The dream before that was that the Israeli soldiers shot me to death and I saw them throwing my body inside a huge big trash dumpster. The most frightening dream of all was when I saw our village on fire with a huge explosion and my two children were with me but I could not find my first born son Canaan (Old Testament name meaning the promise land, Palestine). What do you think children are dreaming of in the Holy Land this week? Please make a difference by contacting your government officials to stop Israeli destruction and aggression against Muslims and Christians in the Holy Land. Palestinian children should have a right to have pleasant dreams this week.

The Challenges Facing the Christian Schools
November 27, 2001

There are many challenges that schools in Palestine face to better serve students. Following the reoccupation of Beit Jala for over ten days in October (2001) and the reoccupation of the outskirts of Ramallah at the same time, our Latin Patriarchate Schools experienced the worst of the Intifada during this thirteen month period since the Uprising was sparked on September 28, 2000. The major challenge is being able to hold a regular school day and complete a regular assigned curriculum with the terrible blockade and siege imposed on the Palestinian territories. The many checkpoints frustrate the majority of students and teachers that just can't seem to make it to school smoothly. An additional major challenge for schools in dealing with children under the general exposure to psychological trauma specifically observed in children facing fear, family unbalance, psychological exhaustion of students, children switching schools, an obsession with knowing the news, and exposure to violence daily. Furthermore, it is a challenge to maintain teacher training and deal with parents that cannot pay their school fees.

Maintaining Attendance

One of the major challenges facing our schools is the actual attendance of teachers and students. People need freedom of movement so that teachers and students can reach the actual school location. During the Uprising we had frequent occurrences where when the students show up for a regular school day, the teachers cannot pass the checkpoints to give the lessons. On other occasions when the teachers manage to pass strict checkpoints, the students are stuck at home because of the severe blockade and siege on their towns. The problem with the blockade and attendance leads to not being able to cover the appropriate curriculum for the school year.

Dealing with Psychological Trauma

Another major challenge facing our schools is how to deal with students experiencing the psychological trauma and psychological effects that shooting and bombing and the denial of human rights bring about in their psyche and emotional attitude. The Latin Patriarchate Schools lack social workers, psychologists and funds for any type of training that can better deal with the crisis children are experiencing dealing with fear and anxiety living under Israeli military occupation.

Children Facing Fear Daily

This challenge is noticed by seeing children that face fear daily. Dealing with children that live without knowing what their future holds. Basic questions such as is there a road to school today or not? Is the checkpoint open today or not? Will the soldiers shoot me at the checkpoint? Will the Israelis invade Ramallah tonight or not? At any moment and at any time any violent act can occur that will change the regular routine of the school child or might leave the child stuck at home for several days because the streets are not safe enough for the child to travel to school. This fear effects the student's concentration in the classroom. The teacher is challenged to keep the student focused on the specific subject taught.

Family Balance Changes

The balance has changed in many families because of the roadblocks and siege. In the villages around the Ramallah area, many fathers moved away from their families to live close to their work so the children do not see the father regularly. On the other hand there are a number of mothers with children that have moved out of their regular family home to live close to the school as to avoid the checkpoints. The family situation, unbalance and change affect how children learn in school because the Palestinian family is known to be a very close knit family so the uprooting of the father or the children from their regular environment affects their emotional behavior. Furthermore, many children in the Beit Sahour area have not lived in their regular family home for over a year now because they live in a high-risk area where it is still dangerous to return to their home because of the constant shooting and bombing which continues on and off. Not having a comfortable, secure and safe home environment shows up in children's attitude and behavior in the classroom.

Psychological Exhaustion of Students

The schools face a challenge to deal with students exhausted making it to school. This challenge is noticed by the tiredness and warring down the children experience by spending too much time on the road traveling back and forth to school. When a child from the village leaves his home at 6:30 in the morning just to make it on time to school for an 8:00 am class, it is frustrating. And, half the time he might arrive later than the first period having gone through a hardship and long wait at the checkpoint and many times several checkpoints. The attitude towards learning and concentration will most likely be affected. The student is psychologically tiered and worn out before making it to school. He has concentrated all his energy and effort as how to make it to school safe. Some small children because of the terrible side roads with holes and rocks and being in the car for over an hour on a poor road, vomit daily before making it to school.

Children Switching Schools

Another challenge facing the schools is students that were forced to change their school because of the terrible blockade and siege. We have many students for example that were attending school in the city of Ramallah and because of the closure they were forced to change their school for this current academic year in order to attend a Latin Patriarchate School nearer to their village. There is a lot of resentment that comes from such a change because the students and the parents did not select the change but it was forced upon them because of the Uprising and the difficulty with freedom of movement. Thus, we have many unhappy and very depressed students who are missing their previous school environment. They miss the teachers they liked, the classmates they knew and the principal they admired. This change has affected their academic learning and their concentration inside the new classroom. Such students report that they hate school.

Mania with Knowing the News

Moreover, a challenge worth mentioning is that teachers are faced with students that do not want to do their homework. Everyone during the Uprising is glued to the TV for news that they can not even think or give any of their energy to academic subjects. This obsession with watching the news and violent events that take place daily effect the thinking and the energy of students towards their studies in general and their daily homework in particular. This lack of interest in learning eventually has to be addressed by educators. It is a challenge to motivate and encourage children to achieve academically with the backdrop of violence and daily bloodshed.

Exposure to Violent Acts and Massacres

A serious phenomenon that is effecting our students' mentality can be seen from the way suicide bombers give up their life and also from the on going massacre of Palestinians during certain intense events when the Israeli army kills at random. When students see and perceive that Palestinian life is so cheap how they could sit in a classroom and make math important or the science lesson important. The killing affects their mentality and their attitude towards education. "Why should I bother to learn if I'm just going to die?"

Maintaining Teacher Training

An additional challenge facing our schools is how to maintain teacher training and development in the schools in order to upgrade skills and teaching methods. It is impossible to coordinate meetings, workshops, lectures among the different schools. Teachers have such difficulty making it to the school itself, that it is impossible to ask them for any additional time. They are overburden by the long hours they spend on the road and the extra cost in traveling since most teachers take one taxi to the checkpoint, walk across the checkpoint and pay for an additional taxi or two to their final destination.

Parents Unable to Pay School Fees

A final challenge facing the schools during the Intifada is the parents not able to pay their school fees due to the poor economy and high unemployment. Some parents are forced to take their children out of the private schools and place them in government schools with minimal fees. For Christian families this is a major problem because their children are no longer in a Christian focused environment. Another challenge faced by the schools is the parents constantly complaining because of the high cost of books during such times of hardship. Worst of all is when parents in the village can not pay the tuition, do not want to switch schools and bring large containers of oil, their only valuable possession from the olive harvest to pay for tuition.

In conclusion, the challenges are far too many and the solutions are few. It is unbelievable that the Intifada has created all these different challenges because it was enough of a challenge to change the traditional Palestinian passive education to a more active and dynamic process of learning, but now that is a far fetched vision.

Essays Expressing Faith
December 4, 2001

As the bloodshed continues on both sides of the Israeli Palestinian conflict, we on the Palestinian side are branded terrorists one more time. We are locked up wherever we happen to be during the bombs in Israel. It is not appropriate now to write about resistance movements and freedom fighters because nothing justifies the killing of innocent people. But, in Greece as a child my favorite Greek hero during Independence Day Celebrations was the one that proclaimed to the Turks "Give me freedom or give me death."

After endless years of military occupation and absolutely no future, some of the Palestinian people have reached this mentality either "freedom or death". It seems the world community quickly understands the definition of terrorism, which is such a general term, but no one seems to understand the brutal consequences of Israeli occupation, which has such a specific aim to deny a nation their independence.

The bombs in Israel this week were tragic and the Israelis have imposed a great collective punishment on all of us. For many schools, Monday was the first day of the final semester exams. For the students that can not make it to their schools, the administration faxed their final exams to the nearest school they can travel. This plan also failed to help the students continue their education because all Ramallah schools are closed today as the Israelis have one more time invaded Ramallah, El Bireh and Betunia. We wait in fear, anxiety, and not knowing what all the helicopters flying overhead will do next.

As I am stuck in my husband's village of Taybeh with this strict closure, I had a chance to read essays collected from eleven of our schools throughout Palestine. I thought I give you an insight into some of our students' thinking by sharing one of the essays from the Latin Patriarchate Writing Competition. The essay topic for this fall semester was "If I had one wish my wish would be…."

The English Department staff felt this open topic would be appropriate to see what is on the mind and heart of Palestinian students in our schools following one year of the Intifada. We felt such a topic would help students escape momentarily from the daily closures, siege and terrible checkpoints they face living inside what everyone calls a "big jail." I found the following essay interesting because it gives great hope to know we have students in our schools with great faith and with the promise to coexist with our neighbors in peaceful ways. It also gives great hope to know that students believe in forgiveness and that is the only way to have a new beginning and a new life in the Holy Land.

The following short essay, entitled **"A Peaceful Bird"** is written **by Ileen Sous,** a tenth grade female student at the Birzeit Latin Patriarchate School.

If I had one wish it would be flying like a bird in the high sky. As everybody else, I would like to have my own freedom, liberty "why, where, when, how?" I don't know. But I hope God will help me to achieve my own wish.

I wish to be a bird because I love freedom, liberty and my country. I love to be a good member in my own country, to help and defend it. I love to be a peace bird, who brings happiness to human beings. I love to shout in a very loud voice, with all my love to my country, ask where is our love to our country, or where has freedom gone. We must defend our country. We should study hard and learn to negotiate.

I would like to fly all over the countries that have wars, especially my country "Palestine" because I love it very much and I love to defend it from the enemies, but in peaceful ways. In these days we have a war with the Jews. Their hearts are made of rocks, they don't have any emotions. Their hearts are full of hatred. All that they need is to kill all the Palestinian people even if they are children.

The people who confiscated our land, our liberty are human beings. Why do they do all that to us? What's our guilt? Is it because we are Palestinian and that we should suffer and be killed everyday?

Finally, I love to fly in the high blue sky to get some strength from God who I'm sure will help me to give love, forgiveness and happiness to all humans.

What's Going on in the Holy Land?
December 8, 2001

The strict closure for one week now has paralyzed all facets of society in the Holy Land. There is no movement among villages and cities. People are cut off from living as usual. For 14 months we adjusted to the misery and humiliation of walking across the checkpoints as the only way to get anywhere. But for one week now, even walking is forbidden for Palestinians. The severe siege has prevented most people from going to work, school or hospitals for health care.

Many children are missing school days like the 70 students that can't make it to the Zababdeh Latin Patriarchate School from their surrounding villages. And when all the children do make it to their school because it is within their own village, a great number of teachers in core subjects such as mathematics, Arabic and English teachers are absent. Such is the case in the Taybeh School where six teachers could not make it to school this week. This list goes on and one with basically each school being affected in one way or another with this siege in the Palestinian territories.

Most small villages will even run out of food and medical supplies if this collective punishment continues. Many people depend on the city for their basic daily needs. In my area alone, about 45 villages depend on access to the city of Ramallah.

As the international community stays silent, Ariel Sharon continues to give orders for more and more bombings of Palestinian targets, which sometimes happen to be next to schools injuring and severely wounding innocent children in Gaza. When Palestinian children die, they must somehow be creatures of a lesser God because major world leaders do not call up to express their condolence like they do with Israelis. And major world powers do not send wreaths of condolence and express their sympathy to the grieving families such is done with Israelis. It is such a tragedy to be in the third millennium and not have human equality and view the value of human life the same regardless of ethnicity and religion. Are we not all beings of the same Creator?

Being stuck at home this week, forces me more to stare at the harsh reality of the Holy Land right outside my kitchen window where the illegal settlement of Ofra is getting bigger and bigger right in front of my eyes. Each night I see more and more lights pop up across the mountain indicating their illegal expansion while throughout Palestine the Israeli government continues to demolish Palestinian homes and make it difficult if not impossible for local people to build on their own land. Such rage and anger takes place in my heart because I see no sign of justice in front of me. And, I see no future for my children in the land of their forefathers.

I use to not understand the young Palestinian boys at the checkpoint throwing rocks at the Israeli soldiers and hiding behind my car. I would roll down my car window and scream at them to go home and ask them to go away before the soldiers shoot them. Go home to what? It is not go home to Nintendo, Game boy, Play station, books to read, travel plans to make for vacation, soccer to play on the weekend.

Usually, these boys go to a home where most of them have lost a father or a brother to Israeli guns; where most of them have a father or a brother in Israeli prisons; where most of them can hardly afford their daily bread never mind an education; where most of them can hardly find a job that pays the average monthly salary of $300 even after a college education; where most of them are prisoners in their own town because the Israelis have chopped up Palestine into so many parts the map looks like Swiss cheese from the illegal Israeli settlements.

The Western world thinks that suicide bombers are "terrorists" because they have not seen the humiliation, misery and horrible conditions the majority of Palestinians experience during 34 years of Israeli Military occupation. Such suicide bombers are so desperate facing Israeli soldiers daily that they take innocent lives with their own. Suicide bombers are freedom fighters for some people because they give their life in martyrdom to a noble cause "Free Palestine from Occupation". We have the children that try to fight occupation with the pen but no one listens at least the suicide bombers get their message on the news but because innocent lives are lost their message is so desperately misunderstood. Following are the wishes of Palestinian teenagers in the Al Ahliyyah College in Ramallah from the English Writing Contest:

"The only wish that I think about, is the wish of all Palestinians, that one day we can have our independent state and have our right to live in peace and to bring all refugees back to their homeland Palestine." (**Joseph** Kasseri).

"I wish to live as other children, so I can have the right to education, play and leisure, cultural activities, and freedom of thought..." (**Kanaan** Khalayleh)

"All people have different wishes, but the Palestinians have the same wish, their wish is Independence, liberty and peace. Also my wish is the same." (**Fady** Theodory)

"My wish is to set free Palestine and to live as all children in the world and I am sure that it is not my wish only, it would be the wish for all Palestinian children." (**Liana** Miqdadi)

"Like a Palestinian child my wish is to have my rights, my normal rights that which all children have elsewhere." (**Hadeel** Dalool)

In conclusion, what really saddens my heart the most is that some students cannot even think of making a wish. The daily conditions are so horrid they affect children's thinking and perception of reality. Thus, the children that don't die from Sharon's bombings will suffer a lifetime of psychological affects:

"It is really too hard for me as a Palestinian to have dreams because since now no one knows where we will be and how we will be in the future. I don't know if I will be alive or dead. So I think that the Israeli Occupation has destroyed our future plans." (**Maysa** Alqara).

Christmas Season in the Holy Land
December 15, 2001

As the Holy Land is once again watered by blood, Muslims, Jews and Christians are preparing to celebrate holy days that traditionally bring joy and happiness into our lives. However, following endless days of closure, two weeks of children missing school, three consecutive days of Israeli bombings and brutal aggression, we are experiencing fear, terror and more bloodshed in the land where the Prince of Peace preached the golden rule love your neighbor as yourself.

We remain speechless and shocked as the Israeli army invaded all Palestinian territories and began a major destructive campaign. We have prayed and hoped for so long that the United States and the European Union could force Israel to recognize the human rights of Palestinians in this new millennium. But, this week, the lowest point since the Oslo Peace Agreement, we are left with death and destruction all around us as President Bush gave Ariel Sharon a green light to get the "terrorists." But sometimes the rockets fall on schools like the ones yesterday that destroyed eight classrooms at my children's school in Ramallah, an elite private Arab-American school famous for graduating leaders in the Palestinian community such as Dr. Hanan Ashrawi. Has CNN ever mentioned that over one hundred schools have had a direct missile hit this last year? I'm just grateful my children were stuck at home because of the siege but the little girl in the town of Jenin last month was not so lucky, she was killed sitting in her classroom at her desk as the rocket hit her school.

We are facing a Christmas Season disappointed that the Oslo Peace Agreement failed, frustrated that the Israeli Army continues to bomb us non-stop, angry that innocent people keep dying on both sides, fed up that the Americans keep supplying the missiles, helicopters and F-16's that continue to destroy the Holy Land, aggravated that most of us are prisoners in our own homes, and miserable with curfews enforced by tanks and armored jeeps in Palestinian streets. Rockets and bullets in our neighborhoods replaced the lovely Christmas decorations again this year. The beautiful Christmas music is replaced by constant bombing and shooting that leaves children with sleepless nights. Children are not receiving Christmas gifts because many parents have been without jobs for 14 months. There are no Christmas Day parades especially as is customary in our village of Taybeh where the boy scouts announce the birth of Christ to the beat of their drums. There are no

Christmas murals painted throughout the village to express joy and happiness because too many martyrs have given their life to free Palestine. There is just mourning and sadness, day after day.

The grace of God sustains most people and our faith for a better future in the Holy Land will maintain the inner peace we need to survive since there is absolutely no peace in our world. No matter where we live or who we are, God calls us to serve Him with all of heart, mind and all of our strength. We are called to do good works on earth that give glory to God. "...*I urge you to live a life worthy of the calling you have received.*" (Ephesians 4:1) This calling for me means bringing awareness to the Palestinian struggle for a homeland in the land of Christ's birth.

As we celebrate this Holy Season with so many families having lost loved ones, we beg the international community to put pressure on Israel to end the military occupation of Palestine. For the love of humanity, we urge people to call their senators and representatives to end the bloodshed and tragedy in the Holy Land. The land of our Christian roots deserves better than the current atrocities. Please make a difference in our lives and know the Israeli army is denying three million Palestinians their human rights to self-determination.

A twelve-year-old student in Ramallah for the English Writing Competition has expressed this urgent need well: "As I am a Palestinian child I have my own wish. My wish is to have our rights as any other children who live in a free country. All children all over the world have a safe home, safe school and safe roads, but we have nothing. I wish we had safe roads to travel from place to place with no fear, with no threatening of death, with no guns that are aimed at our little hearts. I wish I could sleep with soft music playing around, not with voices of bombing and shooting. I wish I could wake up on sounds of birds singing happily not on sounds of destroying houses." (Lara Murrar, 6th grade) Another twelve-year-old student in Nablus wrote: "My wish is the wish of all the Palestinians, all the Muslims and the Christians. It's the freedom of Palestine."

In conclusion, during these holy days, please hear these voices in the wilderness crying for freedom and independence and pray with us for peace in the Holy Land. "...*with God all things are possible.*" (Matthew 19:26). May your holidays be filled with all of God's blessings and may peace and eternal love abide in your hearts.

Children's Wishes from Aboud
December 22, 2001

During this holy Christmas holiday if the children in the small village of Aboud knew I was writing about them I am sure they would extend their warmest wishes to people across the globe in celebrating the birth of our Lord and Savior. Since they attend one of the most isolated Christian schools that we have in our Latin Patriarchate School System, I thought it might be interesting to share an insight into their thinking following one year of the Palestinian Uprising. They went to a lot of trouble to send their essays to our education office for the English competition with the nuns that are able to travel the checkpoints since all the Palestinians in Aboud are literally locked up in their village for several weeks now. Aboud does not even have phone lines so the method other schools used by email and fax does not work for them.

Although they don't have these modern technologies, they do have excellent teachers like Mr. Boutros Fawadleh, the hard working English teacher who always cooperates to have successful English language activities in the Aboud School. He encourages his students and gives all his efforts and talents to the school. His dedication and commitment deserves an award. The Aboud Latin Patriarchate School is also blessed to have an outstanding principal Mr. Ibrahim Hemed who for several years now has been implementing a clear educational vision with high standards in this small school. He cares to make a difference in the Aboud community by running an excellent school and demanding professionalism from his teachers. It is helpful when our students have appropriate adult role models. Although isolated, the students in Aboud tend to have wishes like the rest of the students in Palestine. The following quotations are taking from students' English Essays entitled "If I had one wish, my wish would be..."

My wish is to be a journalist in the future. I love this job so much because I know how much the Palestinian people suffer under the Israeli occupation especially these days. Thus I want to help them in a way that shows their pain and agony to people all over the world and to let them see what the Israelis are committing against the Palestinian people. (**Rana Yacoub**, 7th grade).

My wish is to be the president of the Palestinian State in the future. I want to plant peace in the Middle East first and all over the world second. I will change history. I'd like to be like Nelson Mandela who brought peace to his country South Africa. He did what he could. My slogan will be: "Stop the killing and wars in the region." (**Mohammad Mofeed**, 8th grade).

My most important wish is to stop killing and the acts of violence between the Israelis and Palestinians. I feel that I can't live anywhere else than my country as the proverb says: "East or West, Home is Best." So, I believe it's very important to live in safety and stability in my country. (**Khaled Jamal**, 8th grade).

My wish is to be a doctor in the future…as Palestinians we are in need for doctors and nurses because we are living in a war. Everyday many young people are killed and injured and they need help. I want to help them of course. (**Nidal Hmeid**, 8th grade).

The most important wish in my life is to have peace in the world especially in my country Palestine. I pray and ask God to grant us real peace in my country, and to make us strong to force the Israelis to get out of our land forever. I have this wish because I love Palestine very much and I love to help my people and my country always. (**Iyad Nawwaf**, 7th grade).

My wish is to see the Palestinian people free, safe and independent. I want all the Israelis to get out of my country and give the refugees their right of return to their homeland. Israel seized this land by force. We are staying on our land Palestine to learn and struggle against the occupation until we get our freedom and independence. Everyday the Israelis kill children, men, women, and arrest people and put them in prison. But we are determined to liberate our country by the stone… (**Bnan Khalaf**, 7th grade).

As you celebrate a blessed Christmas Day, please keep these children in your prayers because many like twelve-year-old **Ghadeer Sayen** have great faith: "I wish that peace will be born in the Middle East. I hope everybody will get all their wishes and thanks to God for everything He gives us." Another twelve-year-old **Osama Sammy** writes: "I am sure that with God's help, I will be able to get what I wish for the future." Please pray for Palestinian children. God listens to our prayers.

The Distinguishing Character of Taybeh
December 24, 2001

There is nothing more psychologically comforting and spiritually powerful than feeling the presence of God and knowing as a Christian, you walked the same footsteps as Christ himself during his last retreat into the wilderness before his crucifixion. I have been living in the beautiful hills of Judea and Samaria in my husband's village of Taybeh known in Biblical times as "Ephraim" where his grandfather was the village priest. Jesus came to the village of Taybeh with his disciples after the decision was taken by the Sanhedrin to prosecute him. The original name of Ephraim in Hebrew is Ofra and the village is mentioned eleven times in the Old Testament having been established 5000 years ago as one of the first places of ancient Palestine.

Taybeh holds a special place in the Holy Land having been able to maintain its Christian identity under many occupations by foreign powers. As a teenager Eva Micherky confirms "I like living in Taybeh because it's a holy place where Jesus passed through before he was crucified," and Amanie Khoury says "when you hear the bell of the churches ring together you feel an opera…that gives you pleasure.

The village of Taybeh sits next to the highest mountain in Palestine, Mount Tel Asur. On a clear day from the highest hill you can see the full splendor of the Holy Land: the magnificent Dead Sea, the Jordan valley, the mountains of Samaria, the mountainous desert of Judea and also Jerusalem. A ninth grader Waseem Massis says: "If I get to choose where to live, from the whole wide world, I would choose Taybeh."

Fr. Ibrahim Shomali who is the new priest in the Latin Church into his second year also finds that "Taybeh is a beautiful village, people are kind but everyone is tired from the political situation." Ordained in 1996, Fr. Ibrahim came from Beit Sahour and now is proud to lead the Roman Catholic faith with approximately 185 families founded in Taybeh in 1870. The parish is very active with a youth group split in three age categories and a Ladies Society that meet weekly. Dr. Ryad Muaddi, the director of the Caritas Health Center in Taybeh frequently contributes to the groups by providing nutrition lectures and other critical health issues. Fr. Jack Abed, the Melkite parish priest often prays with Fr. Ibrahim and helps him run the youth groups.

Fr. Jack refuses to leave this small village. Three times the patriarch ordered him to relocate and he refused because he said he loves the village as much "as a father likes his first born son." Fr. Jack's family came from Jaffa. He was ordained on Jan 6, 1990 experiencing such a happy event only to face the passing of his father six days later. I asked him what should others know about us in Taybeh? Fr. Jack stated: "We still maintain our Christian faith and exist since the time of Jesus in this country. We are the descendents of the Apostles and the first Christian people in this land. We are staying in our country. We are maintaining and keeping the traditions."

Fr. Jack speaks seven languages and is the spiritual father of fifty families that have membership in the Melkite Church. Although he travels frequently the best thing he likes about Taybeh is "the climate, the people, the ecumenism among the people...when something happens in the village, they are all there." Actually Mr. Hanna Basir, an English teacher and on the local municipality said the same thing "...they live like a big family." Deacon Sami Hijazin, the new comer assigned to Taybeh for his first year from Jordan but having been a student since 1991 in the Beit Jala Latin Seminary thinks there might be some negative effects when the families are too close and they try to know the business of others. But Rawan Jasser, a ninth grade student disagrees with him, "the people love each other."

Fr. David P. Khoury, the principal at the Orthodox School has a positive outlook. He has a membership of over two hundred families in the Orthodox Church along with Fr. Tawfiq Nasser the senior priest. Fr. David runs the school with 300 students and 24 teachers founded in 1770. The school began at an elementary level and in 1990 officially became a high school. Fr. David says: "We have some distinguished things in our village, St. George ruins, great climate, good atmosphere, people help each other and cooperate with each other. Most people are related to each other in the village."

This is correct! His first cousin David C. Khoury (also my husband) launched the first micro brewery in the Middle East (1994) with his brother Nadim. They created the first Palestinian product to be franchised and produced in Germany under the license of "Taybeh Beer" in Taybeh.

Fr. David discovered 4th century mosaics next to the new Orthodox Church and put up columns, build walls and basically created a small chapel in 1987 to preserve this special site. The generosity of Taybeh people in San Francisco made this chapel possible. Generous donors' abroad like Mr. Yousef Newas established the local laboratory for the health clinic. Mr. Newas also provides college scholarships on an annual basis to three Taybeh students at Birzeit University. Also, Fr. Jack helped fundraise money and build a housing complex for sixteen families in his parish. In addition, we have a four family housing unit build by the Latin Patriarchate. Currently, the St. George's Church Housing Committee is seeking funds to help thirty needy families build their first homes on land donated by the Greek Orthodox Patriarch. One million dollars would build thirty skeletal units.

Another special thing in Taybeh is the ancient Palestinian Old House arranged in 1974. Visitors can see objects, which are no longer used today but were very common in the time of Christ depicting the local peasant scene. The house consists of two levels, one on the ground for the animals and the upper level for the family. In such a similar humble setting Christ was born in the Middle East.

Next to the Palestinian Old House you find the Latin School founded in 1869 and with the help of the Knights and Ladies of the Holy Sepulchre officially became a secondary school in 1978. The School head by Mr. Ghaleb Rizeg has 374 students and 24 teachers.

Not bad for a small village, famous in Biblical times for Christ's visit, placed on the map in modern times for its excellent micro-brewed "Taybeh Beer." As a symbol of ancient roots, the people of Taybeh still practice the Old Testament sacrifice unto the Lord as in the example of Abraham. On many occasions you find local Christians fulfilling their promise to God by taking a lamb to the Al Khadder (the ruins of St. George's Church), slaughtering the lamb and distributing the meat to needy families.

Especially when male babies arrive in traditional families they are the most loved and admired so a sacrifice is a must to thank the Lord for a male heir to the family name. However, when baby girls arrive, forget the lamb, you can't even get a smile out of people who usually say to the mother "oh, that's too bad, God willing it will be a boy next time." But do you think these strange old-fashioned customs stop us from loving this little village with glorious sunsets? In the words of fifteen year old Carol Massis: "I feel proud to be one of the inhabitants of this beautiful village and I like to invite every one to visit."

Orthodox Christmas in the Holy Land
January 8, 2002

This week might have been January 7th for the rest of the world but for Orthodox Christians in the Holy Land it was December 25th according to the old Julian Calendar and we have just celebrated the Birth of Christ. *"For unto you is born this day in the city of David a Savior, who is Christ the Lord."* (Luke 2:11). It was truly a beautiful White Christmas in the Holy Land that rarely sees snow. The flakes began falling early in the morning and continued throughout the day until the hills and countryside had a spectacular white coat.

As Palestinian Christians are forbidden to travel to Bethlehem to celebrate Christmas, the ones living within the city of Christ's birth showed up for the midnight liturgy officiated by the new Greek Orthodox Patriarch Irineos I. Personally, I traveled through five checkpoints aimed at humiliating Palestinians and preventing their freedom of movement while stealing their human dignity. These military checkpoints are making average, good human beings think about becoming suicide bombers because during the day they are absolutely unbearable sometimes taking up to four hours to pass.

Living with the Palestinian Uprising has led me to see the worst conditions ever in the Holy Land. The bloodshed, the terror, the fear, the unknowing are so prevalent in this sacred place. I am surprised the international community does not regard 35 years of oppression as enough for the Palestinians, not to mention how recently Israel has humiliated the Palestinian leadership by locking up President Yasser Arafat inside Ramallah. Israel needs to end this occupation.

This was the first year I did not see Arafat at the Orthodox Christmas service. He usually attends the service with His Beatitude Michel Sabbah, the Latin Patriarch and thirteen days later the service with the Greek patriarch. It is very significant that Arafat selects to attend these services because it indicates the cooperation and unity among Muslims and Christians in a Palestinian State. If we are to maintain a Christian presence in the Holy Land it helps when the government validates our existence. However, we need the Israelis to stop their campaign of ethnic cleansing. Deprive people long enough of their human rights and naturally they will be forced to immigrate to any other country to allow for a pure Jewish state. Ariel Sharon killed the idea of co-existence and sharing the land by his constant bombings and shootings.

As I entered Bethlehem, the magic of the 2000 millennium celebrations was missing from the air because it looked like a ghost town compared to the crowds, the music, the lights and the movement two years ago. Maybe some of you know that "Bethlehem" means "house of bread" indicating the large wheat fields that were in the area in the time of Christ. It is also symbolic that our Savior, the "Bread of Life" selected this city as His birthplace. The Israelis wrecked and trashed this holy city during the October Israeli military invasion killing over twenty innocent people. The residents of Bethlehem were terrorized and under virtual house arrest for over ten days. Please make your government officials aware of their blind support to Israel because all the American money and weapons are not being used for security. They are being used for "military occupation" which is terrorism of the worst type.

As I entered the Church of Nativity, originally built in 324 by St. Helen and remodeled by the Emperor Justinian in the mid-6th century, I felt it was not a regular Christmas. Usually, the long lines and the pushing and shoving go all the way to Manger Square and people sometimes forget they are at a holy site when they give each other dirty looks to enter first. This year the church was empty although the Greeks, Syrians, Coptic and Ethiopians were praying at the same time. Three different liturgies take place simultaneously but my favorite liturgy is the one down stairs of the main Church building in the Cave of the Nativity of our Savior. It is usually held in Greek, Arabic and Russian. This is the very spot that gives glory to Christ's birth marked by a marble slab around a large silver star and ringed by numerous oil lamps. The Silver Star with the words engraved in Latin, "Here Jesus Christ was born to the Virgin Mary," was printed by the Latin Church in 1717. Also down in this small area in the cave is a designated spot for the "Place of the Manger" which is actually an altar.

It was a blessing to light candles in this very special spot and it was worth the bitter cold and freezing weather to reach this holy site. I felt deep in my heart the words the Pope said during his historic visit to Bethlehem (2000 millennium celebrations) that in the hearts of Christians, it is Christmas everyday. It is with this spirit and truth in knowing Christ is born for our salvation that we should live. It is this truth that allows us to see God in each and every human being. It is this truth that allows us to do good works on earth that give glory to God. May all of you feel the Christmas spirit revealed in this small cave in Bethlehem during this white Christmas in the Holy Land. Christ is Born!

Epiphany at the Jordan River
January 19, 2002

The precious site where 2000 years ago "...*the heavens were opened unto Him, and He saw the Spirit of God descending like a dove, and lighting upon Him...*" (Matthew 3:13-17), is currently zoned in an area that is under Israeli military occupation since 1967 and landmines surround it. On the Palestinian side, the Israelis allow the faithful to enter and pray only once a year and the rest of the time it is restricted as a military zone.

Here at the Jordan River, the faithful in Palestine pray on the West side of the river and the faithful in Jordan hold the same Epiphany service on the East side of the river. Of course we have the problem of following different calendars but that is a story by itself, at least as Christians we are constantly giving glory to God while we are on earth!

The Monastery of St. John the Baptist next to the Jordan River is usually flocked with pilgrims but yesterday it was suffering to even have local Palestinian Orthodox Christians attend the service with the strict roadblocks and closures of towns and villages. The Epiphany service takes place outside the monastery by the Jordan River with people traveling from long distances to attend.

This usually inaccessible monastery is in the worst shape from any of the Holy sites because it stands in what is considered "no man's land." The property is really in such terrible and appalling condition. The Israelis and the Palestinians have shed plenty of blood for control in this area. But with the support of the American government the Israelis control everything and the entire Palestinian infrastructure is about destroyed but what will not be destroyed is the will of the Palestinian people to have freedom and independence.

Most of the valuable items have been stolen from the monastery years ago. All of the windows and doors are broken, parts of the ceiling are caving in, the walls are peeling and the monastery has not been maintained whatsoever because the Greek patriarch who is technically responsible cannot have access to it. It's really a disgrace for such a holy site to have piles and piles of trash and be boarded up from the Christian world. But this is the obscure result from years of occupation.

The Jordan River flows toward the Dead Sea. Four streams combine to form the Jordan River that enters the Sea of Galilee at its northeastern tip and leaves it at its southwestern corner. It is the most important river in the Holy Land not only because of its spiritual and religious significance but because it's an excellent source of water. Water is a precious resource in this area. In many Palestinian villages like mine, most times the water is turned on only once or twice a week. The rest of the time the water supply is completely shut off.

However, the surrounding illegal Israeli settlements have no water restrictions whatsoever and are able to have running water twenty-four hours a day, seven days a week. I still wonder sometimes, why God sent me to the Palestinian side. Especially seeing that the Baptism of our Lord was celebrated on a beautiful sunny and very dry day, the water situation will not get any better.

David Khoury in front of St. John the Baptist Monastery

Nights of Terror in Ramallah
January 26, 2002

The residents of Ramallah have been living under intense pressure since the tanks and jeeps began rolling in their neighborhoods. The military invasion has been terrorizing everyone especially in the El Teereh area where the Evangelical School operates down the road from the Greek Orthodox School and the Mustaqbal (Future) School, all terribly affected by over fifteen tanks just on one main road. Many children were absent from these schools because their parents don't want them walking in front of tanks to enter school.

At other schools everyday children can only talk about "tonight they will totally reoccupy all Ramallah." The fear and terror stop them from concentrating on lessons. At work all week most adults are predicting maybe the Israelis will totally get rid of the Palestinian Authority. We just can't figure out why these tanks and jeeps continue to patrol the area and provoke Palestinian gunmen to shoot at them causing severe damage to many houses.

Working about two blocks away from this conflict I spent the majority of the week listening to shooting all day long and watching funeral marches go by my window. I must admit it was hard to work, to think, to write, to be productive. I just had an awkward sick feeling in my stomach and I kept thinking the whole time how children are learning their math, English or sciences.

All schools in Ramallah decided to shorten the school day so children can be off the streets and in their homes where it might be safer. But if your home is in front of the tanks how safe can it be? Ms. Maha from the Al Ahliyyah School, a very dedicated and committed English teacher, could not even get inside her house on Wednesday because of the heavy shooting that broke out on her street. She walked in my office frantically saying "they are shooting right now…it's terrible…I can't go home."

Night after Night, Maha, her husband and three children have been terrorized along with thousands of people who woke up last Friday morning to find tanks and jeeps in their neighborhoods. After spending one night stuck inside her home because of the intense shooting right outside her front door, she took her family to her mother's house.

Severe shooting especially occurred between 8 p.m. until 3 a.m. on Saturday night where the water tanks and the water pipes were damaged in her home but no one could dare to go outside and turn off the running water. The family could not eat, could not sleep, could not move from fear and terror and just kept waiting hour after hour for the shooting to stop.

"We were afraid to take off our clothes…we stayed behind the corridor the whole night…It was terrible being in the dark and just listening to the shooting…the water running from the broken pipes and being able to do nothing…there are no other words to describe it except terrifying…just a terror night…we did not want to leave our home…we left because we were terrified…the fear in our children's faces made us leave." said Ms. Maha. Her children were so terrified they kept vomiting and going to the bathroom all night from the anxiety and the fear. Christina who is six years old knew less of what was going on but Mary who is fourteen probably felt the danger more.

The family left their home to go only a few blocks away but walked through hundreds of bullets on the ground and saw countless bullet holes on the house walls. When they reached the grandmother's house, Khalil who is twelve years old finally said to his mother: "I feel safe now… I am hungry." Maha mentioned to me when she saw her neighbor coming home they could not open their car door and properly walk out to enter their home, instead they opened the car door, threw themselves on the ground to crawl to reach the front door of their home.

The other neighbor opened the front door to let her husband inside the house and the bullet bounced off the wall wounding this helpless neighbor in her stomach. Maha repeated: "It was a night of terror…the soldiers went crazy…they had hysteria to just keep shooting…."

After spending two nights out of their house, Maha wanted to take the children back to their own beds, back to take baths, get clean clothes, stop sleeping on couches. "There is nothing like the feeling of your own home and with all this shooting happening this simple wish is impossible…there is nothing we can do…my husband wants to act courageous and save his family but he is helpless…he wants to protect us but you can see from his face…he is terrified." Even excellent teachers like Maha go to work the next day exhausted, so tiered and having a difficult time concentrating on teaching. They are grateful just to be alive.

Night after night as Palestinians continue to bear the shooting and bombing in their areas, as they continue to bear their homes being demolished by Israelis, as they continue to bear their family members assassinated in cold blood, as they continue to suffer from the blockade and the siege on all Palestinian cities and towns, as they continue to beg soldiers to let them pass checkpoints for hospitals and medical care, as they continue to bear curfews and house arrests, as they continue to bear their homes turned into military camps, as they continue to bear the collapsed economy in order to stay in their land, as they continue to bear countless years of poor conditions, no one seems to be telling Ariel Sharon to stop the occupation.

The Americans continue to tell Arafat he should not harbor the terrorists. Doesn't anyone realize that these totally inhumane conditions in the Holy Land are making all of us terrorists! But, revenge is not the answer. We need to seek forgiveness at some point and not respond by violent resistance. Even when soldiers' point guns at me, I try to remember that non-violence is the answer while my blood is boiling and anger overpowers me. The cycle of violence and the killings back and forth have taken us to a blood bath. The American senators and representatives must know that not only Israel needs security but also more than three million Palestinians need their human rights.

The Palestinian Catastrophe of 1948 needs to be addressed. We need to diplomatically negotiate how to exist in this Holy Land because it is so precious to Christians, Muslims and Jews. The only thing that saves me is the prayers of others and Corinthians 13:4 *"Love is patient, love is kind...it bears all things, believes all things, hopes all things, endures all things. Love never fails."*

With Christ's love, please hear the pain and suffering from the Holy Land as we bear witness for Christ here and help maintain our Christian presence by educating your government officials.

On the Way to Beit Jala Today
February 23, 2002

Three young soldiers with machine guns pointed at my chest want to make sure I understand the road is closed today. I insisted I am a foreigner with a legal visa and I should be allowed to pass. The soldiers insisted, with their guns still aiming at me that this particular road is closed to all except of course the illegal Israeli settlers that fly by in their cars without stopping at checkpoints using these roads built especially for them to avoid going through Arab villages.

It is so frustrating not to be able to get to work sometimes. And not being able to use this particular road for me means being locked up in the village because it is the only road out that doesn't have concrete blocks. Although Taybeh is a very beautiful village, days like today, I feel it's like a big jail. Our situation in the Holy Land is deteriorated so badly and the international community still cannot put pressure on Sharon to at least uplift the severe closure.

Normally, these soldiers can handle up to one hour of my begging, nagging, and pleading to pass. However, these are not normal days in the Holy Land. Fifty people have died just this week alone. The violence has escalated to the point of no return. Especially the last few weeks there have been increased attacks on Israeli soldiers and this fact has put all of them on the edge.

I never had so many guns pointed at me pulling up at checkpoint before. You can just sense the soldiers are nervous and tense. The other day one of them literally said to me as I pulled up faster than usual to show him my passport: "You scared me, don't drive so fast." I thought in my mind, just imagine, he has the gun, the bulletproof vest and the armored jeeps and tanks behind him and I scared him just because I am in a hurry to get to Beit Jala.

Since September this year when the education office for the Latin Patriarchate Schools of Jerusalem relocated from Ramallah, always under siege, to the new location in Beit Jala (which is sometimes under siege), it has been a nightmare for me to make it to Beit Jala even once a week. The rest of the education staff is thrilled about this new office under the leadership of Fr. Majdi Siryani, the new general director because they are mostly from the Beit Sahour and Beit Jala area. But for me, it technically means five checkpoints to reach and many hours on the road. Eventually, I am very worried that these horrible checkpoints or Fr. Majdi will force me to give up the work that has brought so much meaning and purpose in my life.

On the way to work what usually disturbs me the most is to see so many Palestinian young men pulled over and detained longer than what is required. Their identification is taken away from them to be examined and their hands up in the air to be searched and just totally humiliated and every piece of dignity stripped from their being.

The problem with this discrimination is that it occurs every single day. It would be so logical for the Israeli army to pull out of the West Bank and take their illegal settlers with them. Millions of Palestinian people pay such a high price with their dignity and their human rights just for these people to occupy Palestinian land since 1967 illegally. It is so unjust.

Even good decent people can turn into terrorists because the conditions in the Holy Land are so horrid, unacceptable, and inhuman. It is a shame that America has more laws for animal rights than we have in Palestine for human beings. It is really a shame that America is financing such occupation, which is denying over three million people their basic human rights.

My superiors, His Beatitude
Patriarch Michel Sabbah,
Latin Patriarch of Jerusalem;
and Fr. Majdi Al-Siryani,
the new director of the
Latin Patriarchate Schools

Still Wishing in the Holy Land
March 1, 2002

As we watch new tragedies unfold at the checkpoints as more soldiers shoot at innocent people that try to get to the hospital, work or school, we are still keeping the faith that one day we might see peace in the land of Christ's birth. I always thought priests and nuns had special privileges at the checkpoints and could easily pass these miserable spots thus I was completely shocked to see the Rosary Sisters School Bus from Beit Hanina parked for the evening on the grounds of the Latin Patriarchate Church in Ramallah. Usually the Director of the Rosary School, Sister Ortans escorts the students to return home to Ramallah daily after their school day in Beit Hanina.

On Tuesday afternoon the school bus which is registered inside Israel and has a special permit to travel and a huge sign in front of it stating "Rosary Sisters School Bus" could not return back to school after dropping the girls in Ramallah. Fr. Ibrahim Hijazin was hospitable to the bus drivers and Sister Ortans while they spent the night in the Ramallah convent. The next day they spent over six hours at checkpoints getting back to school.

One of the worst experiences for children these days is when a checkpoint exists between their house and school because they must deal with the same humiliation every day. Some children are not so lucky to drive through the checkpoint and must walk a great distance down mountainsides and dirty roads to get to school. What is the purpose behind these checkpoints other than total harassment, humiliation, aggravation, and long delays that influence a generation to hate the other side. No matter what discrimination Palestinian students' experience their wishes reflect their hopes and desire for freedom and peace:

My wish is to see the Palestinian people free, safe and independent. I want all the Israelis to get out of my country and give the refugees their right of return to their homeland. Israel seized this land by force. We are staying on our land Palestine to learn and struggle against the occupation until we get our freedom and independence. Everyday they kill children, men, and women, arrest people and put them in prison. But we are very determined to liberate our country… (**Bnan** Khalaf, 7th grade Aboud).

Since 1948, the Palestinians have been living under occupation…the Palestinian children don't live the same life as other children in other free countries. The Israeli army doesn't allow them to continue their life in peace. Their guns, tanks and helicopters are distributing death everywhere in the West Bank and Gaza…Finally, I want to say that my wish is to stop acting in this way, and to stop the discrimination. (**Mohamad** Silawi, 6th grade, Nablus).

I'm like all the Palestinian children who wish to see my country free. Every child in the world has lots of wishes…I wish to have a free country to see it well, lot of people will come and visit my country…(**Jeries** Kort, 7th grade, Tabyeh).

I hope to free Palestine and Jerusalem the capital of Palestine with her leader and president Yaser Arafat. (**Sundos** Shakeeb Abu-zant, 6th grade Nablus) My wish is about Palestine to liberate Palestine and to stop the violence…stop the shooting…stop the martyrs… (**Muna** Sameer, 6th grade, Ein Arik).

…my country is the most beautiful place all over the world and it has very generous and kind people and I think we have the right to get our freedom and we must fight for it. (**Majd** Ammar, 7th grade Taybeh).

It must be remembered that we are brave and our determination will be forever. We will never give up or yield … let's go and fight to be free, to be great, to be honorable nation that history will bear our name everywhere. (**Saleh** Ghannam, 7th grade, Nablus).

The People of the Holy Land have become victims of the absence of peace. If I had a wish, my wish would be to live in peace forever. (**Maha** Jarrar, 7th grade, Zababdeh).

I don't feel that I'm safe. I always feel that I live in fear and I'm disappointed because there's no stability…so I wish peace would be coming one day. (**Mary** Sayez, 6th grade, Birzeit). I wish our life could be better as well as I hope to live peace fully and freely. (**Wala** Bassim, 6th grade, Zababdeh). If I had a wish my wish would be the liberation of Palestine…I ask God to give us peace to live peacefully in this life and each one enjoys his life without occupation (**Manawel** Salameh, 6th grade, Jifna).

The Bloodiest Week in the Holy Land
March 9, 2002

As more Palestinian and Israeli blood waters this precious land, the international community continues their silence while the Israeli forces totally destroy the West Bank and Gaza killing as many innocent people as possible. More than 1400 people have died in the last 18 months because peace does not exist in the land of Christ's Birth. Fifty Palestinians were killed in just 24 hours, it's a massacre, and the worst week (March 9, 2002) we have ever experienced. The Israeli army began attacking the refugee camps and causing more than 150 people to die within approximately one week while denying entry to ambulances to help people that might be saved.

The refugees are already victims of 1948 and it's a disaster to see them die so brutality as if human life has no value. It's a shame to be abused, traumatized and invaded when they are already the poorest of the poor. Fr. Majdi seemed frustrated at the Israelis as the tanks rolled in front of his office and as he heard nightly shooting from his convent. "They are out of their minds...they are not complying with international laws, humanitarian laws, they are no complying with any laws...they are on top of the world, better than most people... they are above the law," he told me as I called to find out if the bombing in his area had stopped. Mindful and thoughtful people across the world today should contact their government officials to help stop this bloodshed and cycle of violence that has its roots in the military occupation of the Palestinian people and the confiscation of Palestinian land.

We thought we could live with the violence and the bloodshed by putting our life in God's hands but this policy of getting the terrorists is getting so many people dead. The fear is so intense sometimes it just keeps me home. I'm so scared to leave my house, if I drive the van registered under the Palestinian Authority holding a white plate, the Israeli settlers might attack in revenge. If I drive the black car registered inside Israel holding a yellow plate, the Palestinian gunmen might shoot at random. Forgiveness and reconciliation is not in anyone's book. Psalm 23 somehow takes a deeper meaning in my life as I drive down the Biblical valley of Judea to take the children to school daily: "The Lord is my Shepherd...though I walk through the valley of the shadow of death, I will fear no evil; for thou art with me; thy rod and thy staff they comfort me." But, then again, it is faith that gets you killed in this country. A young boy was crossing the military checkpoint with his school bag and out of fear or faith cried out: "God is great" in Arabic, the soldiers shot him to death thinking he might be a suicide bomber only to find books when they opened his backpack.

As my children saw the Israeli settler holding a gun to the Palestinian taxi driver's head probably telling him never to use that road again, they asked: "Mom, what gives them more rights to use the roads, why are the roads just for them?" This simple question open's a Pandora's Box of the perplexing democracy of Israel. And I must tell you it is not the same democracy that my Greek culture contributed to humanity. The only thing I understand living in the Holy Land as a witness for Christ is that you can not have peace and occupation at the same time.

Sharon's policy of political assassinations or as he calls them "target killings" blew five children to so many pieces on Monday in Ramallah that their bodies could not be appropriately identified. The first missile hit the mother and her three children and the second missile hit a sixteen year old picking up his small preschool cousin from school. Five children buried in one funeral. The Israeli government declared that it would continue the massive military assault on the Palestinian people as if 54 years of denying them a homeland has not been enough assault and humiliation.

On the Palestinian side, especially the militant groups will continue the suicide bombings that tragically harm innocent civilians as a response to the military invasions. We are stuck with these insane people. The cycle of violence has reached its climax. Mr. Maher Al Atrash, managing the Latin Patriarchate Schools from Beit Jala, informed me that all Bethlehem area schools are closed today until further notice because of the great danger in the streets: "This is the mentality of Sharon…50 people dead in 24 hours, it's never happened…it's a real war…I have been experiencing the Intifada for 18 months…these past few days has been the most bloodshed…we are now entering a real war."

As a concerned human being, show outrage that medical personnel like Dr. Khalil Suleiman would be shot and killed by Israeli tank fire as he tried to enter Jenin camp this week with his ambulance to help the wounded following a massive Israeli invasion and attack. *"Deliver me from mine enemies, O my God. Defend me from them that rise up against me. Deliver me from the workers of iniquity and save me from bloody men* (Psalm 59).

The Catastrophe in Ramallah
March 15, 2002

O Give thanks unto the Lord, for he is good, for his mercy endureth forever (Psalm 107)

The missiles were falling, the tanks were firing rockets, the home invasions were on a rampage, the Italian photographer was shot dead, killed in cold blood in Ramallah and Fr. Ibrahim Hijazin opened his church as usual to pray during the daily Mass. This was not a well-attended service on Wednesday afternoon with the severe curfew in Ramallah and the Israeli snipers high up on buildings shooting at anything and anyone that moves.

Fr. Ibrahim is a firm believer of keeping the faith and teaching his parishioners the eternal joy and peace that comes from accepting Christ as our Savior. He feels praying is a must: "without prayer we are lost" he told me as I call daily to check on him since they are shooting right outside his convent which happens to be where my office is as well.

The catastrophe in Ramallah started on Monday morning where on our way to school we saw dozens of trailers carrying tanks to the outskirts of Ramallah. Something felt a bit strange. After school on the way home, the same trailers were carrying more tanks. By midnight Monday the majority of tanks had surrounded all of Ramallah and by 1 a.m. the Israeli army had complete control of the city with over 150 tanks in the area and 20,000 soldiers in the West Bank. It was one of the worst and major invasions since the war with Lebanon.

The principal at the Ein Arik School with five tanks in front of her house alone told me: "We want them to leave, the situation is very bad. We are just sitting in the house and we are very scared. Four days just sitting home...doing nothing. I just want to open my door and go outside...I want to breath...we need to sleep safely and go to our work safely," said Mervat who keeps her two little girls sleeping with her because they are too frightened to sleep alone.

The sound of bombs and shooting have kept every adult and child awake the last few nights not just in Ramallah, but Bethlehem, Gaza and most Palestinian cities and towns. Mervat has food supplies to last a few more days.

But in other neighborhoods the situation is much worst especially for mothers with very young children who need milk.

With dozens of tanks in front of her house and heavy shooting in her area, Maha, one of our English teachers has been without electricity for two days and most of her food in the refrigerator is beginning to spoil for her three children. "We hope an end will come to this situation, we are just prisoners without electricity inside our homes…it is so dangerous to move…we hope they leave…I can't even look outside of my window because of the snipers, it is like a ghost town." She thinks she can feed the children for about a week with macaroni that she has in the house and then she would have finished everything.

My Greek friend Margarita ran out of bread early because she lives next to many shops and can purchase everything she needs fresh and daily so she was not prepared for a four day prison sentence in her own home. She has been feeding her little girl dried beans and lentils day in and day out until the stores are allowed to open again.

Margarita's mother-in-law, who did have large supplies of food such as large bags of flour, rice, sugar and large containers of oil had it all sabotaged by the Israeli soldiers. As they do in most homes, they locked up the women and children in one room of the house while they took the men outside to torture them and at the same time destroyed everything on the premises. Also the Israeli soldiers took the bags of flour and spilled them out on the floor and on top of it the bag of rice and on top of it the sugar and poured the containers of oil to finish them off. Then, they continued to look for the "terrorists."

Rana who is an assistant principal to Fr. Ibrahim at the Al Ahliyyah School has been sitting in one corner of her house for the majority of the time. All the members of her family sit in one spot because they are too scared to escape as her neighborhood is being bombarded next to Arafat's headquarters. Sometimes, really, we have a hard time understanding why the American government continues to provide Israel with weapons used against civilians. And even more shocking is how the American people don't stop their government from supporting these crimes against humanity in the Holy Land.

Many houses in different locations in Ramallah have been taken over completely by the Israelis and turned into military posts. The Israeli soldiers terrorize the small children in these homes with their guns. Their tanks and jeeps traumatize even adults because the sound of their movement is so loud and agonizing. Life as "normal" has stopped to exist this week and for most people it has been devastating since September 28, 2000.

The worst situation is the way the Israeli army surrounded the Ramallah hospital and will not allow ambulances to come or go within the city. The hospital has been without electricity and water. The medical staff is prevented from helping wounded people. The dialysis patients were prevented from receiving dialysis treatment since this nightmare began on Monday night. Two women that have died in Margarita's neighborhood could not be buried or placed in the hospital to await burial because of this awful curfew. Nikki, another Greek-American living in this land is passed her due date and does not know where or how she will deliver her baby with Ramallah under occupation.

We ask for your prayers and we ask you to contact your government officials to pressure Israel to stop the occupation and the military escalation against the Palestinian people living in the Holy Land. In this third millennium, the Israeli army does not know the difference between a hospital, a school, a church, a university or a "terrorist." They are simply destroying everything in their site while breaking all humanitarian laws and international laws. Is that what it means to be God's chosen people…to be above the law and to deny over three million Palestinians their human rights?

All roads to Ramallah were dug up and damaged by the Israeli army to prevent access to the city

The High Price of Christian Roots
March 23, 2002

Nine terrorized school children less than sixteen years of age lined up like criminals right outside our white van on a regular school day. The machine gun is pointing at them and the heavily armed soldier maintains his finger on the trigger while I hand over their passports to pass this fourth and final checkpoint before entering our Christian Village of Taybeh on the West Bank of the Jordan River.

Never in my twenty years of traveling in and out of this region have I seen the soldiers so frightened and so intense as this current time in the Holy Land. In the back of my mind I was thinking this soldier has absolutely no common sense whatsoever or the violence has scared him so much it has stolen his logic and his common sense from him to treat a mother and children in this dehumanizing way.

I hated to see my three children and my nieces get out of the car and line up one next to the other, shoulder to shoulder like a police line up only three minutes away from our home. We were so close after such a long and hard school day why can't we pass? In the beginning I tried to argue with the soldier, "are you kidding, why do you want the children to get out of the car?" But my children immediately said: "Mom, we are used to this, can you please not argue, he has a gun." The youngest one was shaking so badly she could hardly get out of the van.

If this type of harsh and cruel treatment continues with civilians in the Holy Land it should not surprise the world we produce "terrorists." We are being denied our very basic rights to move and to just go to school. Why does America's position for Arafat get stuck at "stop the violence." The American policy falls short of addressing the root causes of that violence: denial of Palestinian freedom.

We are so grateful the tanks went outside the center of Ramallah. People are feeling it is a blessing not to be prisoners in their own homes. But can't they take their soldiers, armored jeeps and their checkpoints with them and leave the occupied Palestinian territories for once and for all. The ways the Palestinian towns and villages are cut off from each other are physically and psychologically strangling us. Many tanks are parked at the outskirts of

Ramallah ready to reoccupy the city at any moment. That military presence is what is so nerve wrecking.

The weapons and the money the United States send Israel are not only being used for Israel's security but to totally destroy and ethnically clean the Holy Land. The American military aid is being used to deny over three million people their human rights and to carry out a collective punishment of the worst type to the point where children cannot even go to school.

Every single day is a new way to school. Every minute the situation changes in our lives. Sometimes we drive such a long way to get back home after a long and tiring school day just to find a military tank blocking the entrance to an important road that we need. We have to just turn around and drive the same way back seeking some other dirt road or valley way to make it home. I have totally destroyed all the vehicles that I own because the Israelis have closed the main roads for Palestinians since September 28, 2000. The back roads are full of rocks, holes and terrible bombs that ruin the bottom of the car. Thus, although the ride from home to school can take a ten to fifteen minutes ride during peaceful times it has taken up to four hours during the worst violence.

The situation can only improve if Israel ends the 35-year-old Israeli occupation of Palestinian territories. It is not possible to have peace and occupation at the same time. The Palestinian Authority recognized Israel on 78% of historic Palestine. It is Israel that refuses to acknowledge Palestine's right to exist on the remaining 22% of land occupied in 1967. The constant enlargement of illegal Israeli settlements in the West Bank and Gaza will continue to be an obstacle to peace. There are about 250,000 settlers on Palestinian territories and they require the protection of the army that constantly flares up the violence.

The reason I can get home every day from an Arab city to an Arab village is because the Israelis built the biggest settlement on the West Bank right next to our home. This fact alone causes more and more young people to turn into suicide bombers because the Oslo peace process stayed frozen for so many years and the Palestinians did not see a difference in their daily lives. It is clearly not just and not appropriate for Palestinians to be treated like last class citizens on the land of their birth.

It is clearly wrong for the Israeli army to force us to leave our homes and immigrate because they continue to humiliate, degrade and demoralize us daily. Many people are willing to live under Israeli hardships not to leave their land and not to abandon their roots. However, we do have to pay a very high price to maintain our Christian roots.

Here in the Holy Land we have entered the first week of the Orthodox Lenten Period. We open our hearts to Christ to fill us with his love and everlasting hope so that we will not be forced to leave the land of His birth but stay and bare witness in the Name of our Lord. Christians, Muslims and Jews can live and prosper together because there are enough of us that are not fanatics and just want to raise a generation of children knowing their valuable traditions and roots. Many of us on all sides want the hate and the violence to just stop.

Pray that peace will prevail in this sacred land and make your voices heard in appropriate forums urging the immediate withdrawal of all forms of Israeli military presence from the Palestinian territories. And knowing our story, glorify God for all the blessings that you have in your life and seek joy in the presence of the Lord.

Israeli soldiers blocking road and throwing gas bombs

The Work of the Church During the Intifada
April 1, 2002

Many priests at different church communities made a great effort to create temporary jobs for people that are not employed during these tragic times in the Holy Land. The priests had to find ways to give money with dignity. Fr. Majdi Siryani created a new park in the Beit Sahour parish for small children especially to use during the summer months for entertainment, family gatherings, cooking outdoors and having swings and slides available. This park provides several people with temporary jobs in order to care for the playground area and serve the people visiting.

Also, temporary jobs were created during the restoration of the Church of Our Lady of Fatima. Furthermore, the convent had its doors open to people in deep need especially during November when at least two families needed a place to stay because their homes were in dangerous locations during the Israeli invasion into Bethlehem. The convent was hospitable for over ten days. Another way to help people in serious need is by having them select food items from the supermarket themselves and the parish priest will make the payment.

The Beit Sahour parish also provided a social worker during the last six months coming to the parish twice a week to take care of people in need. Ms. Lydia Habash served as a bridge between the Beit Sahour parish and Jerusalem where the Caritas office is located and helps people in need of food and medicine and families with special situations. Many people are in deep need in the Beit Sahour area because their main source of income usually comes from olive wood handicrafts, tourism and mother of pearl items.

Fr. Shawki Batrian, the assistant priest in Beit Sahour reveals: "If you had rich families, in the last year and a half, they spend most of their money." Most of the 270 families amounting to about 1200 members belonging to the Beit Sahour parish, are categorized in need. Fr. Shawki estimates 80% of his parishioners are not working. Also, a new phenomenon is taken place were you have the majority of women working as teachers and secretaries. It is unusual to have women be the only source of income to support large families. The social ramifications of this situation are great.

Fr. Ibrahim Hijazin in Ramallah also confesses that at least two people every day Christian and Muslim come to the church seeking financial help. His parish has 360 families with about 1650 members in the church and 127 families are categorized as very needy. The St. Vincent de Paul Society has twenty-six volunteers helping these families especially at Christmas and Easter with whatever funds they receive from outside. They periodically visit the families, make assessment of the need and provide as much support as possible. Bingo activities raise money for the poor and having bake sales the first Sunday in each month raises local money as well. Many of the needy families have not had work for over a year and a half not only in this parish but also in Palestine in general.

The Taybeh church under the guidance of Fr. Ibrahim Shomali in his second year in this little Christian village sponsored temporary jobs for people by creating a garden on the parish grounds. He had workers take shifts in working on developing the garden in order to provide as a wide opportunity as possible for people to receive an income. A handful of people started the work and a different group of workers completed it. The Latin Church in Taybeh has 185 families with about 600 members. The village itself has about forty families in serious need but at least twenty of these families are not able to survive at all without help from the church.

Fr. Iyad Twal admits that with the 300 families in the Birzeit Latin Church he feels responsible to help more than just financially but to help all Christians and Muslims in their pastoral needs as well morally and educationally. He has over 45 families that are very needy and poor. He helps them find jobs if he can or provides them with food and money. In his parish he estimates 50% of the people do not have work. The worst of the Intifada, Fr. Iyad feels, is the high unemployment that has devastating affects in caring for large families.

Occupation Will Bring More Terror
April 3, 2002

The War on terror has never terrorized so many of us as currently in the Holy Land. There is nothing more terrifying than hearing the Israeli fighter jets above your head and you just don't know exactly where they will drop the bomb. It seems like it will drop right now above your head and as the sound whooshes away there is a great sign of relief some other place will be bombed instead. This week it was mostly Ramallah, the city I spend three hours trying to get out of last Thursday.

It's difficult to even find the right words to describe the panic, the fear, and the anxiety in the streets among the people. There is nothing like thousands of people looking for taxis at the same time to get home as soon as possible because the Israeli Army is about to totally reoccupy the city. This means military tanks and armored jeeps on almost every street, house invasions and thousands of men between 16-45 years of age collected and detained. There are a few exceptions, however, some are just shot dead in cold blood, and maybe they are on Israel's most wanted list. I am sure there is some good reason for the democracy of Israel to execute these people right on the spot.

Each time the Israelis assassinate people, like the five generals, all in their 50's, in Arafat's compound all shot in the head in close range and found without weapons, these men are someone's father. They are someone's brother. They are someone's husband. Hate and revenge continue. Thus, a brand new generation of "terrorists" will be born in Ramallah following these brutal killings which also included four young men shot to death at the Islamic youth club. I am losing my English on this side of the world because I use to think these things were massacres and war crimes. But I try to keep in mind what the Israeli government says, these Palestinians were terrorists so of course Israel has a right to defend itself. In three days alone, twenty-five bodies lie dead in the Ramallah hospital because no one can even bury the dead since Ramallah has been closed off as a military zone and everyone is under virtual house arrest.

Please pray for Ramallah because actually the people can not even go to church and pray on Sunday. Fr. Ibrahim Hijazin prayed alone with the sisters at the Latin Church because not a single soul was willing to risk walking the streets of Ramallah with snipers on most buildings ready to shoot anyone in site. Fr. Iacoub (Jacob) Khoury conducted the liturgy just with Fr. Meletios at the Greek Orthodox Church. For many years I use to think it is terrible that people are not allowed to enter Jerusalem and pray at the Holy Sepulchre, but now people can't even get out of their house and attend their local church. Most of the neighborhoods in Ramallah have been without electricity and without water for the last four days. Some neighborhoods have the electricity turned on for a few hours in the afternoon.

The building that has the office for the Greek Cultural Center in the middle of Ramallah received ten rockets and went on fire. No one can actually go and access the damage because we can't move from our present locations. Many buildings were bombed and destroyed but the only thing that personally bothers me about this particular destruction is that ten out of the twelve illustrations that a Greek artist Fotini had completed for me where at the cultural center. Beautiful illustrations for a new children's book I was working on called "My Favorite Saints" for elementary ages featuring one saint for each month. I suppose this building had some terrorists in it also.

But the horrid conditions the Israeli army creates for us breads terrorism. The total humiliation and dehumanization of the Palestinian people is worse than the Nazi's did to the Jews in concentration camps. How can these people that have suffered so much in history turn around and conduct worse atrocities towards another group of people. And how can the United States continue to blindly support Israel with billions of dollars each year.

We have lived for the last 18 months with terror. For us terror means apache helicopters dropping bombs in our neighborhoods, F-16 jets dropping bombs and assassinating Palestinian leaders, Israeli soldiers invading homes and destroying everything in their site while looting, tanks firing rockets into schools, Israeli soldiers with machine guns preventing people from going to work and school, checkpoints in all the Palestinian cities and villages that cut them off from each other. Terror is when the ambulances cannot get to injured people and take them to the hospital. Terror is when the Israeli army continues to demolish Palestinian homes leaving thousands of people homeless. For us living in the Holy Land, terror means the occupation that we feel and experience daily not having independence or any basic human rights. Terror to me means when the world is silent and allows Israel to be above all international laws and United Nation Resolutions. What does terror mean to you?

Ethnic Cleansing in the Land of Christ's Birth
April 9, 2002

The slaughter of Palestinian people continues this week especially in the refugee camps in Jenin where Sharon is not willing to listen to the president of the United States and get out of the Palestinian territories. Sharon continues his campaign against terror by terrorizing over three million Palestinians with his brutal and inhuman tactics. Sharon is trying to clean out the Holy Land of all Christians and of all Muslims to make sure he not only guarantees a Jewish state inside Israel created in 1948 but also in the Palestinian territories occupied in 1967. The Oslo Peace Agreement that promised the Palestinians a homeland is absolutely dead.

Many people have a heard time understanding why Arafat gave up such a "generous offer." That is all you hear in the international media, the Israelis are so generous and Arafat is the terrorist. Personally, the last six years I have been living here I just like to give you an idea what type of Palestinian state was giving to Arafat. I live in the village of Taybeh, it is marked area C, it will stay under the total control and occupation of the Israeli army because of the illegal settlements all around me although it is part of the territories occupied by Israel in 1967. I need to go to school in Ramallah (ten minutes away), marked as area A, turned over to Palestinians when the Palestinian Authority was given this generous offer following the 1993 Oslo Peace Agreement.

In order for me to travel from a Palestinian village under Israeli control to a Palestinian city under Palestinian control I must go through four checkpoints that means facing soldiers with guns daily and armored jeeps and tanks. The point is that the Israelis gave the Palestinians a bunch of different cities instead of a Palestinian homeland with Israel controlling the major roads in and out of those cities. Not to mention they control the airport and the seaport for import and export purposes.

This might sound absurd to you, but please believe me it is easier for me to go to Athens roundtrip than to go to school and work everyday. I am about to lose my mind so I went to Athens this weekend to prove my point. I couldn't go to school anyway because currently it is a military zone.

The Israelis never intended to turn over East Jerusalem to the Palestinians either, which was occupied in 1967. What does this mean? For me as a

Christian, if I want to travel from my Palestinian village to the occupied old city of Jerusalem to pray on Sundays in the Holy Sepulchre, I am not allowed. And also, if Muslims wish to go and pray on Fridays at their religious Holy site, it is forbidden.

The generous offer the Israelis gave Arafat was not practical at all because they wish to keep the 250,000 illegal settlers in the West Bank at their comfortable settlements that look like a suburb in Texas. While the settlers have the best of everything, the rest of us, for example, especially in the summer time, can go four days in a row, no running water while the settlements have water running twenty four hours a day, seven days a week.

The other generous offer that Arafat was so foolish not to accept is each and every single time we need to travel out of the country we must have a piece of paper called a permit to travel to the airport to visit our family and friends in other countries. To get a permit is a nightmare and extremely time consuming. The last trip to Boston, took my father-in-law exactly three days in a row, from 8 am to 3 pm to obtain his permission to travel from our village to the airport at 74 years of age. Of course you never know anyone at anytime can really turn into a terrorist because actually we can't handle the prejudice, the racism and the injustice imposed by Israel on Palestinians.

The other "generous offer" Arafat refused to accept is all the Palestinian refugees that were forced out of their homes and their lands in 1948 and 1967 did not have a right to return. While please bear in mind that any Jewish person living anywhere in the world has a right to return to Israel even if they never had a home there at all. Does this sound fair to you? Is this just?

Why can Jewish people return to Israel and the Palestinian people forced out of their home in 1948 in Jaffa and still holding the key to their front doors do not have a right to return. Why are the Israelis above the law? Don't both Israelis and Palestinians have a right to exist? Why do the Israelis get extra privileges? Are we not all part of the human race?

Do you understand the difference between September 11th and resistance to occupation? September 11th was a pure act of violence, a total crime against humanity. The seventeen year old Palestinian girl that blew her self up in Jerusalem, killing innocent people (that we do not condone and we are strictly against such suicide bombs) is in fact giving a desperate message to the world.

She does not have apache helicopters and tanks and guns to ask for her freedom and independence thus she gives the only precious gift God gave her, life itself to resist occupation and seek freedom and independence for her country. If people had a homeland and future they would not go and blow themselves up. But they are deprived of each and every single right that the rest of us take for granted. Occupation is the root cause of this terrible violence happening in Israel.

In this great and holy Orthodox lent, my point is not to help you understand suicide bombers, maybe you can't unless you live with them and see their suffering and their daily struggle. I would like to leave you with the message that God calls each and every one of us to serve Him and give glory to Him while we live here on earth. If God gave you power, use it to help the unfortunate. If God gave you education, use it to help others understand. If God gave you money, help the poor. If God gave you great wealth and materialism, feed the hungry. God asks us to use our gifts and talents to bring Glory to Him who gives us eternal life.

As ethnic cleansing takes place in the Holy Land, pray for God to show His mercy and pray that we may have strength to bear witness for Christ in the Land of His birth. I give up asking you to contact your government officials because we are experiencing a massacre of the worst type and no one seems to be able to stop it. I only ask for your prayers. God will listen and peace will come to the Holy Land.

The daily routine of demolishing Palestinian homes

Praying Under Israeli Guns
April 15, 2002

"Give ear to my word, O Lord, consider my meditation. Hearken unto the voice of my cry, my King, and my God: for unto thee will I pray (Psalm 5) While everyone is rushing to buy bread in Ramallah during the four hours the military curfew is uplifted, Fr. Ibrahim Hijazin is rushing to visit as many elderly and sick parishioners as possible giving them the "Bread of Life" by offering Holy Communion in their homes. He doesn't have much time on his hands, because at exactly 2 p.m. when the curfew is reinforced one more time, the Israeli soldiers begin to shoot at anyone moving in the streets. Thus, Fr. Ibrahim rushes back to conduct a quick Mass for the rest of the parishioners at the Holy Family Parish. During the last three times the curfew was uplifted, a handful of parishioners would come to pray. Today (4/15/02), the church was nearly full.

My cousin Fr. Iacoub Khoury also conducts services daily with Fr. Meletios at the Greek Orthodox Church especially now for the Lenten season. Since they live right next to the church they can hold the services but the faithful cannot attend for fear Israeli snipers reinforcing the strict curfew now in its third week will shoot them. Ms. Maha, a wonderful English teacher at the Ahliyyah College told me she could not even walk from her house to church because the main road was completely destroyed by the Israeli tanks. She sadly said: "Ramallah is not the Ramallah you know…there is a great deal of damage to the whole city."

Maha decided to go to church during the uplifting of the curfew to " just gather and pray…to ask God to protect us…at least we can talk to God…we can ask, where are you God? Why can't you stop these massacres? What have we done to be prisoners in our own homes? We started to think of our faith more … before I sleep I pray." Finally, Maha could talk on the phone today after being many days without phone service. She was one of the lucky ones because in her neighborhood she was only without electricity and water for the first four days. Eighteen days into the occupation and still there are actually people without water.

As more and more civilians continue to be punished without running water, electricity, phones and horrid house invasions that leave their property totally damaged, we continue the Christian legacy in the land where Christianity was born. We continue to pray and ask for God's mercy. We continue our Christian values in the midst of bloodshed and under Israeli guns. In Jerusalem this week another friend, Sister Maria Stephanopoulos was tonsured receiving the new name Mother Agapia. Thus, Christians continue to serve Christ. They continue to be witnesses in the land of Christ's birth and give glory to God with every breath they take. We shall speak the truth of the Israeli atrocities although some readers think these crimes against humanity are so awful they can't possibly be true and therefore must be "Palestinian propaganda." Maybe that is why God keeps us here to keep reminding the world the Holy Land is a sacred place and whether we are Christians, Muslims or Jews, we were given life to give glory to God. How easy it is for guns to help you forget that we were all made in the image and likeness of God.

Maha explained to me that the last two weeks have been full of terror for her family. "Not just the children are terrified, we are terrified too. We can't sleep at night. My husband and I take shifts because we are scared if the soldiers knock on the door and you don't open immediately they will bomb the door causing much damage and fire. You expect them to come and enter any time...the only sound you hear outside is the sound of tanks in the street all night and our heart just beats with terror...and no one is talking about going back to schools...there is nothing...and they terrify us how they steal everything valuable and damage and destroy property...only God can protect us."

Fr. Ibrahim listens to his parishioners with a heavy heart. The grounds keeper for the school and church, Abu Ghassen after having his home invaded by the Israeli soldiers and turned upside down was also robbed of all his wife's gold and valuables. Maha's brother was also robbed of all valuable and had his home damaged by the Israeli soldiers. When the soldiers searched the Latin convent and school grounds, Fr. Ibrahim asked them not to enter the church with weapons because it was a holy place.

One soldier insisted to enter the church so the priest tried to explain the Holy Sacrament was in the altar and the soldiers must show respect for Christian religious values and traditions. The soldier quickly stated that Jesus was himself Jewish so for sure he would be forgiven if he entered the church with his gun. Fr. Ibrahim reminded the soldier of a hard and cold reality that "Jesus was not behaving like the Jew of today."

Since the Israeli soldiers are simply out to get the "terrorists," I have such a hard time understanding why they steal and totally destroy people's homes as they did to the principal of the Friend's Girls School, Ms. Diana Abdel Noor. They just damaged anything and everything in their site. She is a member of the Greek Orthodox Church not of Hamas or of Islamic Jihad. Do you think these poor young soldiers have a hard time knowing the difference between a terrorist and a civilian or are they simply brainwashed that all Palestinians are terrorists. As the military destroys educational and cultural places along with homes, it seems the Israelis wish to wipe out the entire identity and culture of the Palestinian people. Little do they know that Palestine will forever exist in the heart of each and every Palestinian and cannot possibly be destroyed no matter how many homes are demolished and bombs are dropped. The will and the desire of the people to be free and seek their human rights can never be crushed with guns.

Ariel Sharon will only help create a new generation of "terrorists" because his military tactics are not the right and just solution to the conflict in the Middle East. The resistance will continue because the Palestinian people have a legitimate right to free their land from occupation. And for the time being they only have their life to use as a weapon. Although we condemn suicide bombers, we can't stop them because their daily life is full of suffering beyond the imagination of the average human being. Thus, we can only pray that this catastrophic cycle of violence stops and God delivers us from this evil. *"Preserve me, O God: for in thee do I put my trust."* (Psalm 16) *"O lord my God...save me from all them that persecute me, and deliver me"* (Psalm 7)

Remembering Christ's Visit to Taybeh
April 23, 2002

The Sunday before Palm Sunday, our village of Taybeh traditionally remembers Christ's retreat to Ephraim (the biblical name for Taybeh). The parishioners of the Latin Patriarch Church of the Redeemer were honored to have His Beatitude Patriarch Michel Sabbah officiate the Mass under what were impossible road conditions to reach the church. The roadblocks were many and the entrance to the village was closed with large rocks and piles of dirt in order to keep the Palestinians off of roads that only the Israeli settlers wish to access. The Palestinians should stay caged in and locked up in their towns and villages so the settlers can easily move around. It is such a cruel way to treat humankind.

While delivering his homily, the patriarch admitted he thought about turning around and going back to Jerusalem but the driver asked the patriarch to keep getting in and out of the car as he drove through various holes by the valley and managed to sneak into the village for the Mass. The patriarch told the faithful that during our current tragic situation the final hope we have is God. He urged the local people to be faithful to our country, faithful to our land, faithful to our people and to remember God at all times. Patriarch Sabbah said, above all, we as Christians must be like the example of Christ himself, a builder of peace among all kinds of people in the Holy Land.

These special encouraging words were offered to the congregation before the patriarch rushed off to Bethlehem to meet other Muslim, Jewish and Christian leaders for a peaceful demonstration and prayer for the Holy Nativity Church. The demonstrators were not allowed to go to the Nativity Church and pray as had been organized by the Greek Orthodox Patriarchate for solidarity with the Palestinians suck inside the church.

Fr. Ibrahim Shomali, the parish priest felt it was very important for the patriarch to be with the people of Taybeh during this special day in the village in remembering Christ's visit to the area more than two thousand years ago. Fr. Ibrahim felt the patriarch could offer encouraging words to the faithful and show support for this small diminishing Christian community. People are currently depressed over the economic situation and stressed with over 50% unemployment, more and more families are becoming poor and people in general are very nervous and anxious about their future. During the three weeks of occupation even rich people could not get money from the banks because they were closed. And people that were working could not receive their monthly salaries as usual due to the Israeli invasion.

Fr. David P. Khoury, the Orthodox priest also agrees that people are suffering. He said: "These were the worst days we have ever had in our whole life. It was horrible what the Israelis have done in Jenin, the massacres...we can't do anything just evoke God to settle the problem."

Fr. Jack Abed, the Melkite parish priest confirmed that "in our prayer to the Lord, we pray for God to save us from evil...during these days we need to be saved from Sharon but we are just a voice crying in the wilderness and no one's hearing us." Actually, I laughed because just the same day President Bush said Sharon is a man of peace but unfortunately he had to demolish 800 homes to get "the terrorists" and make 5,000 people homeless. I tend to think like Fr. Jack and thought about Psalm 140 *"Deliver me, O Lord, from the evil man; preserve me from the violent man...keep me, O Lord, from the hands of the wicked...I said unto the Lord, thou art my God; hear the voice of my supplications, O Lord."*

Fr. Ibrahim also confessed how difficult it is to preach the word of God during war times. "You can't preach Jesus Christ at the moment...everything turns into politics...about the Nativity Church, about where are the Christians in the world...the people just put you in a difficult situation...you can't deal with it because their questions are real...you can't say love your enemies easily because people do not accept these words of Christ and they respond that the Israelis are killing us, they are making us hungry, etc., how can we love them? It is not easy to explain loving your enemies...so instead, I say love one another, try to help each other, your families. In the moment we have only God to trust. It depends on God only... even on changing the mentality of President Bush and the American government...that's it.... it's up to God."

The regular Christian services continue in Taybeh with daily Mass at six o'clock and a special silent hour of prayer every Wednesday in adoration of the Holy Sacrament with beautiful music in the church. Christians are trying to live their values and traditions and embrace the faith during these difficult times. Fr. Ibrahim has a routine of individual prayer in the convent every morning to begin his day. "We must pray," he emphasizes. As he was speaking about prayer I remembered the words I had read that morning in

Psalm 57 *"Be merciful unto me, O God, be merciful unto me: for my soul trusts in thee: yea, in the shadow of thy winds will I make my refuge, until these calamities be over past."*

Even praying in the Holy Land has become difficult. Deacon Sami, Fr. Ibrahim's assistant told me how he got stuck in the Beit Sahour Church (one hour away) after he had gone to help out with the Western Easter services during Holy week because in Taybeh all Christians will celebrate Pascha with the Orthodox Calendar. The Israeli army invaded Bethlehem in the middle of Holy week and Deacon Sami could not return home. When the curfew was uplifted for three hours and he tried to leave the area he could not make it to Taybeh or back to the Beit Sahour Church thus ended up spending one more week at the Beit Jala theological seminary before the Red Cross helped him return to Taybeh recently.

Truly our life is in the hands of the Israeli army concerning everything with schools, work and church. When we are not prisoners in our own homes, we are prisons in whole open areas. It is currently not allowed for Palestinians to travel out of the Tel Aviv airport nor over the bridge to Jordan and these are the only two ways out of the country.

Ariel Sharon thinks his military aggression will stop suicide bombers but instead he is making average good people think about turning into suicide bombers because of the awful and harsh conditions he imposes on a whole nation. The humiliation is so vast, the frustration is so deep, the injustice is so great and the rage and the anger are so out of control. May our Dear Lord and Savior, show Mercy. *"For with God nothing shall be impossible."* (Luke 1:37).

The ruins of St. George Greek Orthodox Church, 4th century

Orthodox Holy Week in Ramallah
May 2, 2002

"Do thou, O merciful Master, look down from above, and bring us, Thy sinful and unworthy servants, the shadow of the Grace of the Holy Spirit, in this hour..." (Prayer, Holy Wednesday Evening). As Fr. Iacoub was praying before the third Gospel during the Holy Wednesday Evening Service at the Ramallah Orthodox Church of Transfiguration, the loud speakers in the neighborhood started blaring the Muslim call to prayer as they do everyday around 7 p.m. It was so noisy I lost my place in my English prayer book listening to the service in Arabic.

Hundreds of faithful Christians had packed the church and continued to pray as the loud speakers from the nearby Mosque blasted "God is great." This harsh noise bothered no one except me because Fr. Meletios, the Archimandrite of the Ramallah Convent read the third gospel so eloquently it was indeed as it is known in the Orthodox services, 'Heaven is on earth.' Meanwhile meters away from the Orthodox Church at Arafat's compound the Israeli soldiers were preparing to withdraw to the outskirts of Ramallah. The last two nights we heard so much shooting anywhere from 10 p.m. until 5 a.m. that no one could get any sleep. Especially on Holy Monday evening there was one huge big explosion in the middle of the night everyone was asking each other in the morning what in the world had gotten destroyed now. Children and teachers just came to school with fear and terror in their eyes. It was hard to concentrate on any lesson.

The Israelis have not left much in shape after traumatizing over one hundred thousand people for three weeks in Ramallah and keeping them as virtual prisoners in their own homes. All of the important civil affairs buildings were systematically destroyed not just by bombing the structures but by damaging their computers, printers, copiers, video and fax machines. A complete and total destruction of the Palestinian culture and people took place. I really find it hard to believe that getting "the terrorists" means destroying all the vital records on land and housing ownership at the municipalities and the educational transcripts and financial records of public and private organizations. In my own education office, we were very lucky during the three hours uplifting of the curfew, Abu Khalil removed all the computers and printers and stored them in the church until the army withdrew leaving the city upside down. Thus we only had a damaged door to replace.

Our orthodontist, Dr. Nabil was not so lucky not only did the Israelis blow his office door open, they blew the wall out as well. They shot at all of his office equipment and turned all of his files and important records upside down. Dr. Nabil was in good spirits when I went to make an appointment for my daughter and give him my good wishes for a blessed Easter. With a big smile he said: "This is the oasis of the Israeli democracy in the middle of the Arab non democratic region." It seems the Israelis can destroy everything but they cannot destroy the spirit and dreams of the people. Even Arafat was full of smiles today, his first day in public after many months. I actually shook his hand as I pushed my way by his guards before he gave a press conference. This man actually survived the war of terror not the war against terror.

People after church seem to have nothing else to share with each other except the experiences of the soldiers invading their homes and whether they were lucky enough not to have property damage. But, everyone always seems to finish their story with: "Thanks be to God" Many of my colleagues and friends in the Bethlehem area cannot attend Holy Week services because the city is still under siege. Just imagine in the Holy Land where Christianity established the first church and two thousand years later you can't even go to church. The Christian communities of the West Bank have made an informal decision following the Oslo Peace Agreement to promote Christian unity. All Christian denominations would celebrate Christmas with the Western Calendar and Easter with the Orthodox calendar. This was a wonderful understanding without changing the Church dogma of course just to facilitate the celebration of these joyous events in our lives at the same time. However, Jerusalem and Bethlehem being very tourist oriented cities do not follow this compromise and observe the Western and Orthodox calendar at all times.

During this Orthodox Holy Week, we ignore the mass destruction and devastation around us and no matter where we live we take the spiritual pilgrimage and walk with Christ during His passion, crucifixion, and holy glorious resurrection. From the land where the true light of Christ was revealed to guide and remove humanity from the darkness, we thank you for your prayers of solidarity and ask God to be with you. May all of your days be filled with the radiant light of our Savior's Resurrection. Let us pray together that as Christians, Muslims, and Jews we may share this precious land and give glory to God in peace and harmony. After all, one of the most important commandments is to love thy neighbor as thy self.

School Remains the Only Hope for Palestinian Children
May 4, 2002

As the sound of bullets and explosions are heard all through the night in Ramallah, not very many children could get enough sleep listening to shooting from ten in the evening until five in the morning. There is not much left in children's lives other than going to school and in the last three weeks all schools in Palestine were closed due to the Israeli military reoccupation. The Bethlehem schools continue to be closed into their fourth week due to the siege at the Holy Nativity Church.

The land of Christ's birth has totally been destroyed by apache helicopters, f-16 fighter jets and tanks that constantly shoot rockets into different neighborhoods, all in the name of security for Israel. But who cares about the security of Palestinian children? Who can stop the war that has robbed children from their childhood in this Holy Land? How can Palestinian children receive a basic education under military occupation?

Samuel Delou, the seventh grader at the Al-Ahliyyah College in Ramallah, one of the Latin Patriarchate Schools of Jerusalem, says he is not even scared of soldiers anymore because it is such a regular part of his life now to see soldiers and tanks in the streets. The Israeli army has reoccupied Ramallah so many times since the start of the Palestinian Uprising September 28, 2000 that no one keeps count anymore.

Yesterday I had to drive several miles myself with the Israeli jeep in front of me having soldiers hanging out from the back pointing their rifles with their fingers right on their triggers in front of our car. These soldiers are so busy getting "terrorists" that it is hard for them to distinguish even a mother and three children. The only words my children kept saying: "Mom, they're going to shoot us...mom stop the car...mom don't pass them up, they will think we are suicide bombers." I kept wondering the whole day what type of school day my children will have when their day begins with soldiers, guns, and armored jeeps. Is it possible for children in Palestine to concentrate and learn any academic subjects when their lives are constantly at risk?

"I'm not scared of the soldiers...it is usual," says Samuel. His little brother David, eight years of age feels totally different. David is so terrified and frightened that he always stands next to his mother and holds on to her. The psychological affects of war may take time to show up in some children but it is evident that all will be affected by the awful cycle of violence that has terrorized both sides of the Palestinian Israeli conflict. At the Al-Ahliyyah College, a western catholic school educating children from kindergarten to 12th grade, many children show immediate reactions to the military occupation by their lack of concentration in the classroom, lack of interest to complete work at home, constant fear and discussion of tanks and soldiers and many children report nightmares and seeing blood in their dreams.

Samuel loves his school so much that the only thing that scared him during the three weeks of total occupation and severe curfew is the thought that school would be canceled for rest of the academic year. "They stayed a long time, I thought there will be no more school…I just saw tanks and soldiers every day," says Samuel who insists he is not scared of soldiers but he thought they would permanently stay in his city. Samuel is actually the oldest boy out of six children. Three sisters are older than him, Nellie, Sana and Noora. His two younger brothers are David, the youngest in the family who is always frightened and Awad who is ten years of age.

The children usually stay home after school every day. There are no activities to participate as in the past. Samuel helps his father very often at the vegetable shop. "I go to help my father…if I don't have homework, if I have homework, I do it, after this I help my father because my father is selling fruits and vegetable."

After talking to Samuel that day, I actually noticed him taking boxes of vegetables out of a small truck next to the Ramallah Latin Church and handing them to another young boy to carry in the vegetable shop. I perceived that he was polite, kind and hardworking. When I asked his science teacher Ms. Ghada how Samuel behaved in school she mentioned: "Academically speaking he is weak, as his personality goes, he likes being a comic all the time, making fun of people. He doesn't concentrate when he studies, he comes from a non-educated family but his mother cares about him, she comes often to school."

The science teacher's comments were consistent with the math teacher Ms. Randa who said: "Samuel is good in math but moves too much, jokes in class, he is not serious… He is smart but he is not using his smartness… he is loud, his style is to be loud."

Samuel did not think the above teachers were his favorite anyway. He said he liked Mr. Nicola, the history teacher because he was a good teacher and explained many things. "I am going to the Al-Ahliyyah for two years now before I was at the Evangelical school…this is a good school, the teachers are very good when they explain and I like gym and art and English…my house is near the school," explains Samuel.

Ms. Ghada, as a teacher and mother of two boys, strongly feels here in the Holy Land it is different than any part of the world for children. "They don't live their childhood like any other children in the world. They are deprived from the basic requirements. We can't create social activities for students in Palestine because you don't feel safe keeping students late. I don't see that students have good choices to spend their afternoons or weekends. It's not safe to send your child anywhere," she admits. She feels most children like school and this is the only activity left to do in our country. Students, however, do not like the large overloads of homework and sometimes they don't even like the actual lessons. But, they love coming to school. Her children have nothing to do after school either. They stopped going to the theater, playing basketball at the local playground or visiting their grandmother in Jerusalem! There is absolutely nothing to do, thus attending school is more important than ever.

Fadi Theodory, another seventh grader in the Al-Ahliyyah also admits that everyday after school he only does his homework. The last month he had to evacuate his home with his family and go and live with his grandfather until the soldiers go away from Arafat's compound right next to his house. There were too many explosions and the neighborhood was the worst in Ramallah in terms of danger so many families left their homes including the vice-principal of the school, Ms. Rana.

Fadi said: "I didn't want to go to my grandfather's house, I feel so bored there, all my things are in my house but my father and mother made me go." Fadi is described as a highly intelligent student by all of his teachers and he has won several certificates in the past for his excellent writing in English. Ms. Ghada says: "He has straight A's, very serious, studies well and is one of the best in the class."

About the current situation Fadi says: "I don't like them (the Israelis)…I hate them because they say that we are all terrorists and they kill us." Fadi was particularly sad the day I spoke to him because it was the day after Palm Sunday according to the Orthodox Calendar and his mother had not colored red eggs, nor made sweets, nor did they visit family and friends, as is typical tradition in the parish. "Every year the Palm Sunday is better but his year we did nothing," confesses Fadi.

Fadi has three sisters at the school as well: Laura, ten years old, Maram, eight years old and Raneen, five years old. He has been attending the Latin School since kindergarten. The principal of the school, Fr. Ibrahim Hijazin says that many families that have kept their children at the school for many years are facing difficulties with the tuition this year: "Most of the families are not paying the tuition and I understand why because most of them can not carry on this responsibility because of the very bad economic situation. They come here because they believe in the school. I think because they know our philosophy, which is to educate the whole child. We have to love the child and they know also we try to build the human personality and Christian personality."

School children walking home under Israeli guns

Liturgy at the Fourth Century Ruins
May 8, 2002

In our small village of Taybeh this last Monday it was April 23rd on the Julian calendar, the official feast day of our patron saint of the village, St. George. Less than a hundred people gathered to celebrate the liturgy at the St. George Orthodox Church archeological ruins in the middle of the village. St. George's Church was built on a high hill in the village looking down at the Jordan valley. It sits in the middle of Biblical Judea and Samaria.

It is amazing that thousands of years later we can gather and pray at the same site in a sort of unbroken tradition of Christian heritage and value. Fr. David, our parish priest led the liturgy with the assistance of Fr. Tawfik, the retired priest in our village. And please don't confuse Fr. David P. Khoury with the famous founder of Taybeh beer, David C. Khoury, although they are first cousins. Everyone in the village almost has the same last name "Khoury." In some way or another all residents are related. The word "Kkoury" in Arabic means priest. And the true Khourys, not the ones that just changed their name to be called "Khoury" are the families that dedicate family members to serve the church as priests and nuns for many generations.

The village is currently suffering from being newly under a severe siege. Residents cannot take their cars out to any other city. It seems like we are sealed off from humanity. People try to walk by the mountains and the valley to get out because there is a limit to how much village arrest you can take. The Israeli army has newly closed the main roads with large dirt piles and because the Palestinians kept opening the road, the Israelis closed it off in three layers, one of dirt, one of thick cement blocks and another row of thinner cement blocks to discourage anyone from removing the blockade.

I have tried several times to take my car from the valley and severely damage it from the terrible holes and large stones in the road. In the mean time, the nearby settlements are enjoying every freedom of movement possible under the sun. I feel we are so caged up. I feel we are treated like animals. How can human beings do this to other human beings? How can the chosen people of God act this way?

It is not enough these Israeli settlers illegally built their settlements on Palestinian land now they want to completely just get rid of the Palestinian people as well. If they make our lives miserable each and every single day, if they continue to humiliate us, if they continue to treat us like last class citizens, if they continue to keep us as prisoners in our own village surely we will go anywhere else in the world to live. Many people need the city not just for work and school but also for medical care. It is so frustrating month after month just to find more and more roads blocked. Instead of the situation getting better it just gets worse and worse. Especially since the day Arafat was freed from his compound, our village particularly was sealed off from the world.

As Christian people in the village, we are peaceful and we have harmed no one. This collective punishment Israel is carrying out the last nineteen months is totally out of control and not to mention very brutal and cruel. The frustration, the anger and despair among the people cannot be explained in simple words.

This week following the Orthodox Easter is a totally frustrating and aggravating situation in our area. Just imagine how awful our life is that we hope they will take away the roadblocks and put back the four-hour checkpoints because at least it is a way to move around. Even if you walk out of the village by the mountainside there are no taxis available to take you anywhere just settlers fully armed to shoot people as they wish. We are not people to them actually. They treat us as sub-human. The international media just reports that the tanks have moved out of Ramallah and the situation on the ground is worse than ever.

The daily suffering and pain of Palestinians just keeps intensifying. It has been a cruel and devastating week for me. I wanted to write a pleasant story about receiving the holy light from Christ's tomb on Holy Saturday but rage and anger have taken over my spirit because we could not get the Holy light to our church from these roadblocks. The Easter celebrations came and went in deep mourning instead of joyous celebration for a new life in Christ.

My friends that are priests here have a difficult time teaching people to see Christ's light and to put their hope in God. Some people are just fed up. The anger and the rage just run so deep on both sides. Palestinians just can't seem to forget their loved ones killed in cold blood or the destruction that has devastated this country. It is not easy for people to embrace their enemies. It is easier said than done. And the bombs inside Israel are the worst of all. They accomplish nothing except more collective punishment.

It is shocking to me that across the Holy Land this week the centuries old traditions of celebrating the Holy Light could not take place as the usual joyous occasion. Our Christians forefathers became martyrs so our Christian faith can be preserved and their courage in Christ could help others. The values and traditions passed down from generation to generation are all of a sudden forbidden for us to carry out.

What is happening in the land of Christ's Birth? Are you aware of the total destruction and devastation that has taken place of an entire population with American tax dollars? How can Americans support a war of terror being fooled under the slogan that it is a war against terror? American tax dollars should not be used to ethnically clean the Holy Land.

We must work together, talk together, sit together, and negotiate a way to live together. Christians, Muslims and Jews must find a way to share this little sacred spot on the earth. As Christians, we seek the right to be witnesses for Christ in the land of His birth. We seek the right to preserve our centuries old customs and traditions that have Christ at the center. We seek the voices of our brothers and sisters across the world to help us maintain our Christian legacy in the Holy Land.

St. George Greek Orthodox Church, 4th century

The Remarkable Experience of the Holy Light
May 12, 2002

"O Gladsome Light, of the Holy Glory of the Immortal Father, heavenly Holy, blessed Jesus Christ! (Orthodox Holy Saturday Morning Prayer)

It was Orthodox Holy Saturday in this devastating year of terror 2002 where Christians across the Occupied Palestinian Territories could not carry out their centuries old traditions throughout their cities and villages. Either people were under strict curfew as in Bethlehem or collective punishment as in Taybeh (my husband's village) were residents were blocked in with concrete blocks and large dirt piles to prevent their movement anywhere.

As a Christian, I thought it was appalling to be so close to such a sacred place like the Holy Sepulchre and not be able to partake in the special Holy Week services. I was determined to make it into Jerusalem and have this unique lifetime experience of receiving the miraculous Holy Fire as it comes from the Tomb of Christ each year while the Greek Orthodox Patriarch prays at the very spot where Christ's Body was laid over two thousand years ago.

The Great Saturday of the Holy Fire has traditionally been the highlight of the Easter services in the Holy Land. The Greek Orthodox Patriarch of Jerusalem, Irineos I is the only one that can conduct the service of the Holy Light at the Tomb of Christ inside a tiny chapel in Greek called "Kouvouklion." The tomb itself is enclosed within a highly ornamented marble. The tomb is reached through a second doorway in the "Kouvouklion," which is very low that it forces one to enter bowing. Not too many people fit inside this small sacred spot at the same time (maybe up to four or five). Usually this is the reason pilgrims wait many hours to enter this sacred place found inside the Basilica of the Holy Sepulchre where many chapels exist for various Christian denominations. Constantine the Great and his mother Helen take credits for building this magnificent Church complex in the fourth century.

When I first came to live in the Holy Land after the Oslo Agreement, The Saturday of the Holy Light was the most glorious celebrated event of the year. Thousands of pilgrims and local Christians would flock to see the Holy Fire and experience the miracle of Christ in our midst. A designated representative of the Christian community from each city and village awaited the Holy Fire to appear and take the Holy Light from the Holy Sepulchre to their city or village accompanied by the local scouts in a long joyous procession with drums, music and singing. To show their unity, Christians from the Orthodox, Eastern Catholic and Western Catholic Churches along with their local priests marched together in the procession in cities like Ramallah and other Palestinian towns throughout the West Bank.

My two sons along with many other altar boys carried candles and crosses from their churches to the outskirts of our village awaiting the Holy Light to arrive from Jerusalem. Once the Holy Light arrived from the "Life Giving Tomb" everyone marched back to his or her particular church conducted another procession three times around the church and prepared to celebrate the midnight Resurrection service. Most people would carry the Holy Light with candles and small lanterns to their homes to receive God's blessings. The elders in the village would touch the flame of the candle from Jerusalem with both of their hands and wipe their hands on their faces. This was a ritual that allowed them to feel the Grace of God would be with them and to seek the Holy Light to guide them and protect them in their lifetime.

However, this year...nothing. The destruction and devastation in the Holy Land overshadowed this beautiful religious and cultural celebration. Hardly any Palestinian Christian outside Jerusalem could enter the city to partake in this glorious event. In order to preserve the beauty, the values and traditions as they were handed down to us from generation to generation, the patriarchate staff arranged for the Holy Light to be delivered by priests that had permission to travel to Bethlehem and Ramallah. The curfew was uplifted for a few hours to allow the faithful to pray. No parades. No drums. No altar boys. No singing. It was just the religious service of receiving the Holy Fire but in mourning because of the current situation in Palestine.

Other years I could not get anywhere near the area of the Holy Sepulchre. I would stand blocks away near the souvenir shops because people that had slept overnight inside the church were the only ones that could get inside. Unless of course you were a special government official like Mr. Petros Panagotopoulos, our Greek consul general in Jerusalem you would get a front row seat. After many checkpoints and by the Grace of God, I stood at the altar steps inside the Resurrection Church directly across from the first entrance to the Tomb of Christ. I noticed all of the vigil lamps in the church were extinguished. I looked up to see more than one bird flying very high. I heard Patriarch Irineos and everyone chanting "Lord have Mercy" in Greek. The loud church bells began to ring thirty-three times in a joyous sound that is very familiar to me. The Holy Fire rushed out of the Life Giving Tomb as thousands of people lit their bundle of thirty-three candles at the same time while the Greek patriarch stood in front of the entrance to the tomb. I am too short and I could not see him. I felt extremely hot as in burning. It was like being inside a hot oven. In seconds the entire area was illuminated very quickly by passing the Holy Light.

The Israeli policemen had small red cans of spray and they would put out many candles for "security." We have extraordinary things happening on this side of the world in the name of "security." But the little old ladies from Greece were very upset and they were franticly screaming "min mou ta svinis" (Don't blow them out). I found myself on the floor from all the pushing, shoving and blowing out of candles by the dozens of policemen in the church.

I didn't really mind so much that my candles were blown out because the true light of Christ can truly illuminate the soul and the candle itself is only the symbolism of this Light that wins over the darkness. But, I felt better when my son said: "Don't worry mom, I got it." He showed me his little red lantern with a candle lit inside that could not be blown out by the Israeli policemen. I thought it was so wonderful for my son to receive the Holy Light as his father had done so many times before growing up as a child in the minority Christian community of occupied Palestine.

This is a remarkable ritual with a long and complex history that adds to the tapestry of the Christian legacy in the Holy Land. I remember once when I asked a local priest does the Light really come miraculously from the Holy Tomb? He laughed and said that it is not something you only see with your eyes. It is something you also feel. It is something the soul knows. But some people like my friend Mother Agapia Stephanopoulos actually have seen the physical aspects of the Holy Light in three different years appear in the same bluish color. Mother Agapia said it was a very low-key service this year.

The faithful little Greek lady next to me that had spent the whole night inside the church said she has also seen the Holy Light in clouds of bluish color glowing all over the church three different years. She has been to the Holy Land ten times to venerate the Holy sites. I asked her how in the world did she not feel scared to be in Jerusalem this year. She told me we must always travel with the Grace of God. Little did she know this is especially very true for me with every breath I take.

What we see or don't see is totally based on our faith in God. There will always be believers and non-believers. As Christ said to Thomas blessed are the ones that have not seen and believe. To believe that Christ came into the world to save you is a very personal choice. To have faith that the Light of Christ can guide you, simply and clearly gives you hope. To have faith that the grace of God is with you can only move you to serve humanity. To believe in Christ is the way to gain a new life in the Kingdom of God. And, to believe we have a right to be witnesses for Christ in the land of His birth should be a basic freedom allowed to people in the Holy Land. *"Come ye and receive Light from the Unwaning Light, and glorify Christ, who a rose from the dead"* (Orthodox Easter Sunday Midnight Resurrection Service)

The Life-Giving Tomb of Christ

Going to School with Gunfire
May 16, 2002

The humiliation and daily suffering of Palestinian people continues throughout the Palestinian occupied territories. Until the occupation ends, most school children will be crossing dangerous checkpoints and putting their life at risk just to go to school every day. In the small village of Ein Arik, in the outskirts of Ramallah where our Ein Arik Latin Patriarchate School educates 160 children from preschool to grade sixth, it was a terrifying start for the school day. Some children were so frightened they returned home. The daily terror living under occupation does not stop.

A group of soldiers that have established a new checkpoint on top of the mountain at the north end of the village, opened fire on unarmed civilians as they were climbing down the mountain to make it to work and school. The residents from approximately thirty villages use Ein Arik to get to the city of Ramallah because all of the main roads are closed. People today were walking in the mud because it had just rained some falling and some hurting themselves. It was enough torture and difficulty to try to make it to school by the mountainside. These children did not need the soldiers to open fire without any reason and terrify them. The soldiers were shooting indiscriminately at the people reported Mr. Khalil Shaheen, the head of the village council in Ein Arik.

Mr. Shaheen heard the shooting from his home and later rushed to the Ramallah hospital to check on Jabril, a father of four girls and two boys who had been injured in the shooting. Mr. Shaheen said there is shooting every single day since seven Israeli soldiers were killed at the Ein Arik checkpoint in March. The army wants to have revenge on the residents of this area by blocking their roads, making it difficult for them to get to school, work, hospitals and doctors. Basically the Israeli army wants to make daily life so miserable for Palestinians that it becomes unlivable. The soldiers want to terrorize and make people frightened by opening firing whenever they wish.

Mr. Abdallah Fawadleh, the English teacher at the school confessed: "This is something abnormal no one can imagine what is happening, it is not right, there is no reason to shoot, this is just their mood, everyday they are shooting." The soldiers on the mountain happen to be in front of Abdallah's house. He sees people struggling to come down the mountain everyday where 10-15 taxis await to take passengers to their final destinations. Today he heard the shooting while he was still at home. "Every day they shoot but this time they shot more directly at the people...I was getting ready to go to school when I saw the taxi drivers running away from the shooting," said Abdallah.

On her way to school, the principal Ms. Mervat Shomali was confused to continue or return back to her home. "I was coming on my way to school...I saw all taxis rushing quickly and I stopped. I saw people running very quickly, some students went back to Betunia (nearby city) they were too scared to come to school...some teachers came to school going up the side roads that lead to our school...everyone was frightened. Every day we have shooting...when we come to school, it is our daily routine...soldiers and shooting." Mervat also feels that the shooting is to take revenge for the Israeli soldiers that died near their school.

The principal feels if the situation continues with the closure and blockade, many students will not register in her school for next year because it is so difficult to travel to the school due to the checkpoints. She is worried that 50-60 students that want to be at the Latin Patriarchate School will not return and this is a big number for a small school like Ein Arik. Currently, 37 students have been absent for over three months because they are locked up in their villages. Their mothers frequently call the principal and explain how the children miss their teachers; their friends and they miss their school terribly.

Mr. Nader Rahil, the area development program manager for the Patriarchate working in cooperation with World Vision Jerusalem to provide better education, income, health and basic services in the Ein Arik area has not been able to make it to his office in Ein Arik the last three months. "This is a horrible situation, it's horrific for the village and for everybody, it's depressing to know there was this shooting at eight in the morning...I called to talk to the head of the village council about a matter in the education sector and he told me he was in the hospital," reported Nader.

Nader has been working for the Latin Patriarchate the last fourteen months in the Program Development Department and he strongly feels this bizarre shooting can only have negative affects on children in the village. Such daily incidents end up having traumatic consequences. His long-term program to enhance services in the Ein Arik area is scheduled for 10-15 years. But, how can any development take place in Palestine when people are evacuating their homes. Some families feel their lives are in danger and have been forced to leave their homes where the shooting is intense and their houses receive bullets every day in Ein Arik. As Mervat, who is also a mother of two girls pleaded before she hung up the phone: "God helps us."

Gas bombs thrown on Palestinians students at Surda checkpoint as they protest for the Israeli army to open the road to Birzeit University

New Leadership for the Latin Schools of Jerusalem
May 25, 2002

Fr. Majdi Al-Siryani was given the impossible challenge when His Beatitude Michel Sabbah handed him the responsibilities of the thirteen Latin Patriarchate Schools of Jerusalem to oversee the Christian schools in Palestine starting with academic year 2001/02. Following the footsteps of Fr. Emil Salayta the previous general director of the schools who provided so many educational programs and activities by upgrading training for teachers was going to require a herculean effort.

To start the school year, Fr. Majdi could not even get to the education office in Ramallah due to the general siege in the Palestinian areas and the checkpoints that get worse each and every single day since September 2000. That problem was solved immediately by opening a new education office next to the new Beit Jala preschool facility, a few meters away from the Beit Jala Latin Patriarchate School. Then the Israeli invasion of Beit Jala in October 2001 and the Israeli reoccupation of the Bethlehem area happened during the siege on the Holy Nativity Church. The only ones going to Fr. Majdi's new office were the Israeli soldiers on patrol with their tanks and armored jeeps. Stuck for days on end in his Beit Sahour Convent it became impossible to run the schools that were closed for over forty days.

Fr. Majdi is also the main priest in the Beit Sahour Latin Church, Our Lady of Fatima assisted by Fr. Shawki Batrian the newly ordained priest. To top these responsibilities, Fr. Majdi continues to be the legal advisor for the patriarch and is director of the Patriarchate's legal department. The patriarchate's endowments also fall under Fr. Majdi's responsibilities. In addition, he is a member of the Holy See delegation for any negotiations with the Palestinian Authority. All these duties are required for the man who was born to Orthodox parents in Madaba, Jordan in 1961.

Fr. Majdi comes from a Syrian Orthodox background very much like the famous Christian warrior St. George. He comes from a very large family and his mother was born in a Jordanian Christian Bedouin tribe called the Azzizat. Fr. Majdi was ordained in 1985 following his studies at the Latin Seminary in Beit Jala. Fr. Majdi has studied civil and canon laws at the Pontifical Lateran University and received his doctorate degree in law in 1998. A very polite and kind individual who wants to create a new system in the Latin Schools and reorganize the entire staff, unfortunately leaving me completely out of it.

Fr. Majdi was the perfect choice for leading the schools because he had previously managed the schools during the first Intifada from 1987 to 1992. "It's not the first time I am in charge of the schools...I am very acquainted with the schools. I know the ends and outs of the schools," Fr. Majdi said in an interview in Beit Jala prior to the Israeli reoccupation of the Bethlehem area.

Why do you think the patriarch selected you for this job?

Fr. Majdi: "The schools are going through a difficult time and since I had previous experience running the schools during the first Intifada and experience with networking...maybe he thought I will do whatever it takes."

What is the major need of the schools right now?

Fr. Majdi: "There are lots of issues at the schools...lots of important issues such as the financial aspect. Administratively, we are working on fundraising. The teachers' salaries are not enough. This is a big problem in hiring and firing. From an academic point of view it is possible to think of many programs we need but we are facing a financial obstacle all the time. It is like having a car without gas. We must find resources."

What do you want to change in the schools?

Fr. Majdi: "The schools need updating, better facilities, inside the schools we need labs, computers, extra curriculum activities because we are sticking to the minimum, we are not able to provide lots of activities pertaining to education. We need better salaries for the teachers and training. The political instability does not allow for any normal planning. Even if we plan we can't implement. All of our plans are messed up."

How can you improve the schools?

Fr. Majdi: "I want to bring more resources to the schools. If we don't have money, we are short of the essentials. We are running with the minimum. What we are doing is basically just surviving. Yes, we are planning but there are lots of obstacles.   It is not planning that is lacking; it is the financial resources missing to implement the plans."

How has the occupation affected the schools?

Fr. Majdi: "The school days are affected, the teachers not being able to make it to school…traumatized students, traumatized teachers, traumatized parents, parents that can't pay tuition, all of types of problems. We can't go on school trips. We are in prison in our schools both by the political situation and the financial situation. Either way, we are handicapped. Even to sit down, as a school board is not possible. We can't have a meeting. We are cut off from each other. We changed our office three times…Jerusalem…Ramallah…Beit Jala. We are also losing our employees."

What do you think is the most positive aspect the schools offer?

Fr. Majdi: "Our schools mission is to first educate mostly Christians but also Muslims and to educate students how to co-exist. Our schools make it possible for every Christian, those that can't afford other private schools to get an education with us not available at a state school. The Latin Patriarchate Schools are in remote locations where Christian communities exist. Actually, we follow the people to remote places where other Christian schools do not go. But the villages and remote locations are the financial burden because of the low number of students and their inability to pay enough tuition fees. We teach catechism and this is how we provide our faithful with Christian education."

What do you see the future of the schools?

Fr. Majdi: "Our students can barely come to school. We must try to provide quality education for them and our main mission is they do not lose hope. The moment we are liberated, the law will rule. We don't have rule of law because of the occupation."

The Current Situation in Palestine
June 6, 2002

The current situation in Palestine is a pure disaster with barbaric and illegal measures taking place in the name of "security." The last two academic years 2000/01 and 2001/02 have been a dead lock catastrophic cycle of violence that have watered the Holy Land with Palestinian and Israeli blood. Since the Palestinian Uprising began September 28, 2000, over 1600 people have died with 450 children under eighteen. The number of injured people has exceeded beyond 40,000. The Gaza Strip was totally cut off from the West Bank. Gaza itself was split into three areas. West Bank towns and villages were cut off from each other with hundreds of roadblocks to the point of physical and psychological strangulation.

It is not humanly possible to live with the tortures imposed by the Israeli army. Yesterday when I complained about the illegal checkpoint and insisted to pass as a legal visitor of Israel on a foreign passport with a current visa, the soldier smashed my car window. The only thing that I could think of is that the legitimate aspirations of the Palestinian people for freedom and independence have never been more important than right now.

The total destruction of the economy has devastated families the most and increased the poverty rate. The official unemployment rate by the Palestinian Central Bureau of Statistics was reported at 36% this year before their office was completely destroyed by the Israeli army. People face daily dehumanization, humiliation, harassment and risk their lives to go to work and school. Most people face anywhere from two to five checkpoints going to work daily (in each direction) and hours on the road restricted from using cars to cross these nightmare checkpoints walking on bare foot through dirt roads, mountainsides and valleys to make it to school, work or the hospital. The walking is possible for the days that cities and towns are not under a total and strict curfew as was experienced by Bethlehem residents for over forty days.

This last week Ramallah has being tightly sealed off to everyone except diplomats. This closure has disrupted hundreds of children that could not get into Ramallah to take their final examinations for the end of the school year. Ambulances have often been denied access to where they are most needed and many medical personnel have been shot dead while they were trying to help the injured especially during the three-week period Ramallah was under total occupation. Hospitals have been hit by live ammunition not only resulting in injury and death but severe damage to vital medical equipment.

Israel continues to demolish homes especially in Jerusalem. The Israeli government is trying to limit Palestinian population growth in the occupied Palestinian City, claimed by both sides as a capital. Israel has demolished hundreds of Palestinian homes and uprooted over 500,000 acres of crops during the Palestinian Intifada, a flagrant violation of international law. The international Committee of the Red Cross cited they had to help over 5,000 homeless people due to Israeli operations of demolishing 655 houses since September 2000 and this is not counting the total destruction of the Jenin camp that left the additional 600 houses completely destroyed.

On January 10, 2002, in Rafa refugee camp in the Gaza strip, Israeli occupation forces destroyed 60 houses and left 600 people homeless all in one day. According to international human rights the demolitions and destruction of crops constitute collective punishment and are totally illegal but Israel gets away with it because the United States is willing to finance this mass destruction.

The situation can only improve if Israel ends the thirty-five year old Israeli occupation of Palestinian territory. It is not possible to have peace and occupation at the same time. The Palestinian Authority has recognized Israel on 78% of historic Palestine. It is Israel that refuses to acknowledge Palestine's right to exist on the remaining 22% of land occupied in 1967. The constant enlargement of illegal Israel settlements in the West Bank and Gaza will continue to be a great obstacle to peace. These 250,000 settlers demand the protection of the Israeli army on Palestinian territory that constantly flares up the violence.

America's position for Arafat to "stop the violence" falls short of addressing the root causes of that violence: denial of Palestinian freedom. Following Israeli's intense efforts to humiliate and weaken President Yasser Arafat, he continues to hold a symbolic importance as the patriarch of Palestine.

The harsh closure has brought the following results according to the Birzeit University Public opinion poll (February 18, 2002). It is however, necessary to have new opinion polls after the Israeli reoccupation of Palestinian territories because the destruction and catastrophe is beyond belief.

About 11% of Palestinian students were prevented from continuing their education as a result of the Israeli imposed closure.

66% reported that their children have suffered or still suffering from trauma and stress due to measures undertaken by the Israeli army or settlers; 75% in Gaza and 61% in the West Bank.

78% report that school-age children are unable to focus on (or complete) their homework as result of the current situation.

66% report an increase in the level of violence among children and young people as a result of the current situation.

67% are facing additional difficulties in accessing health services as result of the imposed closures.

42% of Palestinian wives had to sell their jewelry ("gold gifts-savings from dowry") to help their families cope with the rising poverty rates.

(Statistics for this article were specifically collected from B'Tselem Israeli Information Center for Human Right in the Occupied Territories, The Jerusalem Times, and Birzeit University Media Center)

The Israeli army demolishing another Palestinian home

The Patriarchal Visit to Taybeh
June 12, 2002

As I was seriously thinking of joining the Christian exodus from the Holy Land, two patriarchs full of grace showed up in my village to inspire and show their love towards the local faithful. His Beatitude Michel Sabbah arrived in Taybeh for the graduation ceremony at the Latin Patriarchate School and His Beatitude Irineos I, spent the whole day in Taybeh to congratulate this years graduating class at the Greek Orthodox School following the Divine Liturgy. It was a full day for a little village.

I was deeply moved by the words of the Greek patriarch during his sermon when he said that we must work together to maintain our roots in this land and if we lose even one soul from this little Christian village, the bones of our forefathers will ache and hurt. The Greek to Arabic translation probably had a message only for people like me who think about running away to middle-class America. I could not stop myself from crying because His Beatitude Irineos I, urged everyone to do their part to preserve and maintain our true faith that dates back two thousand years as a continuation of the work of the apostles. But it is becoming impossible to live and bear witness only to more and more bloodshed.

I don't worry about dying anymore, I worry that I am in fact alive and see the destruction and the atrocities that no one in the world seems to be able to stop. The Patriarch also said kind and generous words about the village of Taybeh mainly that it uplifts the image of Christianity in the Holy Land since the first bishop of Palestinian descent was from Taybeh, Bishop Symeon, God rest his soul. The patriarch emphasized there was a special relationship between Taybeh and the Greek Patriarchate and we must all work together to maintain our Christian roots and faith.

His Beatitude met with the parish members of St. George Greek Orthodox Church following the Liturgy in an open forum to listen to their problems and concerns. The most critical issue was the need to help parents pay school tuition during these very difficult times with many people out of work. The need to raise funds for the housing project to help thirty families build their first homes was expressed as well. The problems were many but the solutions were few. The Patriarch with his entourage of ten clergy and laity including two bishops had a tour of St. George Church ruins. Followed by a visit to the

Orthodox School were an extension is needed to help the overcrowded rooms. A short stop was made at the small chapel next to the main church that was build in the early 1980's over fourth century mosaics discovered by Fr. David, our parish priest. Following a pleasant luncheon with Fr. David, and the retired priest Fr. Tawfiq who has served the church for forty-five years, the Mayor Mr. Fuad Taye, members of the municipality, the teachers of the Orthodox School and some of us unworthy servants of God, His Beatitude was generous to answer the following questions:

How is your first year as Patriarch of Jerusalem?

His Beatitude: Difficult, many difficulties. We need much time and many people to work.

What should others know about Orthodox Christians in the Holy Land?

His Beatitude: What deep meaning the holy places have for the world in general and Christianity specifically, we must keep people updated and informed, people living in other countries don't necessarily know what is going on here unless someone tells them. We must tell them about the people, how many churches we have. People should know how meaningful the Holy Land is to Christianity because Christ was born here, lived, taught, was crucified for our sins and resurrected. We are the continuation of the Apostles. We are the Mother Church. Christianity started right here. The Orthodox Church is the Church of 2000 years. We care about the future and to keep our schools and churches…to have a presence.

What do you see as our future here?

His Beatitude: I can't foresee it, it is a difficult situation. We must think how to get people with authority and power to do whatever they can to bring peace, love and harmony.

Do you think the political situation will get better here?

His Beatitude: The situation can get better if people are willing to be humble.

What should we do as Orthodox Christians?

His Beatitude: Whatever we can to serve the one whom we love and follow. We are students of the one we serve. Christ taught humility. We must do without announcing our good works, we must listen to the word of Christ and practice His teachings.

Who is your favorite saint?

His Beatitude: The Panagia. Like all my other brothers in Christ that give their life here from the time they are young boys, I feel close to the Mother of God. She is our mother.

What do you see the role of women?

His Beatitude: From the time of Christ there are women that followed Christ and were the first to see the resurrection. We have the myrrh-bearers. The role of women is a very important role. The upbringing of children to become good human beings is an important role. Women are the strength behind their husbands, women make men stand strong. The women play a big role in the family, in the Church, and in the community. In the holy tradition we also have the Panagia. She is the extra honor and blessing...she is the women's voice. The Theotokos gave birth to Christ, lived the passions of Christ and her heart was wounded to see her own son crucified...which heart would not melt or break in front of such tragedy? But she shows us faith. This is an honor and exemplifies strength for females.

Tell me about the Holy Light? What should we tell people who ask if this is a miracle?

His Beatitude: It is the victory of life over death. We have many that witness. We can't teach people about the Holy Light, it takes belief. People should come and see. Let them come.

How did you feel for the first time that you did the service for the Holy Fire this year?

His Beatitude: Fear of God...the thought came to ask God as it is stated in one of the prayers that... please God do not prevent the miracle because of my sins...allow the Holy Light to appear aside from my sins, I prayed that

God will not prevent this miraculous gift because of me or something I had done.

How did you feel when the Holy Fire appeared?

His Beatitude: In that moment it is like you are not alive. You are in another world. I cannot find the appropriate words to express it. The brain stopped, everything stopped. I can't express it in words.

Did you get tiered?

His Beatitude: No, you don't feel tiered. You receive life.

After receiving the Holy Light what is the first thing that you thought about?

His Beatitude: I thanked God that He gave this gift.

When is the first time you had ever experienced the miracle of the Holy Fire?

His Beatitude: I was fourteen years old and I was standing outside the Holy Tomb and it is not just I that saw it but all that were with me. The flame swirled above us. I was shocked. I was shaking. I remember at that time Patriarch Benedictos coming out holding the candles of the Holy Light and a tall Russian archimandrite with a full long beard was standing and received the Holy Light right in front of him and it would not burn his beard. He was holding it up to his beard and it would not burn. It was amazing.

Did you see other miracles?

His Beatitude: That we are alive is a miracle, is it not? Don't you think it is a miracle that we are alive?

And truly believing that it is indeed a miracle to be alive in the land of Christ's birth after the Israeli army has destroyed just about anything and everything in site, I stopped asking the patriarch questions. He was very pleasant, kind and spoke with deep humility. I begged him to speak in simple Greek words that I could translate. It was a day filled with much spiritual strength and faith because when Christian leaders take time to express their love and concern for the faithful, they never know how many souls they can actually save.

Especially in the Holy Land we need to practice what Patriarch Sabbah urged the new graduates to do which is to see God in each and every human face we meet. Only then, possibly, can Christians, Muslims and Jews live in peace in this sacred land of our holy fathers.

His Beatitude Irineos next to Fr. David P. Khoury, Maria & David Canaan Khoury, and Mr. Odeh Abdallah at the 4th century ruins of St. George in the village of Taybeh

Fr. Tawfiq Nasser

Students Speak Out
June 24, 2002

It has been a difficult and devastating academic year to say the least for students and teachers in the Latin Patriarchate Schools throughout Palestine. Most students went to school daily while listening to bombing and shooting nightly. Many teachers reported lack of focus and concentration in their classrooms. It was a struggle to even physically make it to school. Some students were absent weeks in a row because they were not allowed to pass the checkpoints at all. Most students from villages suffered to go to schools in the city climbing down mountainsides and walking through dirt roads because towards the end of the school year the army imposed stricter closures than ever.

The worst thing of all is the frequent shooting at innocent people at checkpoints. It has become a pattern for soldiers just to open fire and shoot at anyone in site especially in the last few months. Many students and teachers were in the middle of gunfire for no reason at all other than to go to school or to return home from school. The Israeli army is becoming successful at robbing children of their education and their human rights but they have failed to steal the wishes of Palestinian students:

"My wish is to be a big journalist to tell the world about what's happening in Palestine." (**Hussam** Yousef, 6th grade, Ramallah). "My wish is to see my country free and has no troubles. My wish is to see no occupation and no bloodshed. I wish to see girls and boys go to their school safely and happily." (**Reham** Dahir, 6th grade, Taybeh)

"The Palestinians will fight until they achieve freedom because we have no other choice." (**Olfat** Khalil, 6th grade, Zababdeh). "I think that we live in very bad conditions because we live under Israeli occupation." (**Wala** Bassim, 6th grade, Zababdeh). "I don't feel that I am safe. I always feel that I live in fear and I'm disappointed because there is no stability. So I wish peace will be coming one day." (**Mary** Khalil Sayez, 6th grade, Birzeit). When I grow up I want to be a soldier to protect my land which is the most expensive thing we own. I want to carry my weapons to defend my country and protect it... The Israeli army took our land and destroyed it and killed my people...But with all our effort we'll defend our land. (**Luay** Awwad, 8th grade, Beit Sahour).

"We can't play and enjoy life like other children in the world, but always Israeli soldiers shoot us, bomb us, and kill the Palestinian people, even the children. And there are some children sleeping in tents after the Israelis destroyed their houses... I ask God to give us peace." (**Manawe**l Salameh, 6th grade, Jifna). "I wish that my three brothers one day live in a nation where they will not be judged by their passport but by their character." (**Nadia** Khatab, 6th grade, Ramallah). "I wish that peace will be born in the Middle East...and thanks to God for everything he gives to us." (**Ghadeer** Sayeen, 6th grade, Aboud)

"My wish is the wish of all the Palestinians, all the Arabs, all the Muslims, and the Christians. It's the freedom of Palestine." (**Nabih** Hanbali, 6th grade, Nablus). "I want the refugees to come back to Palestine." (**Rana** Awad, 6th grade, Ramallah). "I wish to raise our flag at the top of Jerusalem wall, at our capital and the sun rise again with peace in the land of peace." (**Wael** Aboudi, 6th grade, Ramallah)

If I had One Wish, I would say....
By Niveen Al-Masow, 9th grade, Beit Jala Latin Patriarchate School

My wish is "Peace." I choose this wish because I want to live in peace and everyone loves peace and wishes to live in it. There are many people who hate the peace very much. The peace will start in our hearts and then it spreads. When I speak about the peace, people, who hear me, will think about my speech. The peace and security, everyone needs peace especially my country. It needs peace. When we want to have peace, the first step we live it inside ourselves and persuade ourselves that the peace is essential for our life. Then we persuade the others.

The second step we pray to God to let these presidents to look forward for peace. The third step, we teach our small sisters and brothers the importance of having peace in our life. Finally we speak with all the people who don't believe that death and tragedy is worse than peace and war and hatred will lead to this tragedy. This means to me send a message to everyone in the world to live with others, to accept each other as we are, to forget jealousy, hatred and war. But think in love and peace.

So let's think seriously in the words of this song and try to live it:

I have a dream. You have a dream
We all have a dream, and they have a dream, too.
Peace, security and dignity
Peace, with justice for all
Me and you, they and us
We all have a dream

So let's dream until this dream becomes true. Finally, if I had one wish, I would ask everyone in this world to forget hatred, selfishness, and war and start a new life with love, respect in our hearts towards each other because by this only we will have peace.

A Poem
By Tamara Shomaly, 9th grade, Beit Sahour Latin Patriarchate School

Even if we are occupied
And not satisfied
I have a desire inside
A desire to dream
A desire to fly
To reach the sky
To pray for love
For peace, for
No more war
No more disease.

Tamara Shomaly

I'll pray
For children not to die
For mothers not to cry
I'll dream as long as I live
Of something to do.
Of something to give.
I'll take the wind and fly
Carrying my dream
I'll sleep on a cloud
And dream…..

Niveen Al-Masow

The Humanitarian Fund at a Critical Time
June 28, 2002

The humanitarian fund of the Latin Patriarchate was established from Rome by the Knights and Ladies of the Holy Sepulchre after the start of the Intifada last year. We are very grateful for this very generous fund that was used by the Latin Patriarchate to distribute to the different parishes for helping families in need especially the unemployed. Parishes received funds in three phases to help needy families especially during Christmas and Easter. The fund was shared with the Pontifical Mission to help people restore their damaged houses and shared with Caritas to help families with food and medicine.

The humanitarian fund could have not come at a better time with the suffering and distress families are experiencing in the Holy Land. Fr. William Shomali stated that "the humanitarian fund itself shows a big concern about our brothers and sisters and it is a solidarity fund…it is important to know it was given quickly…it is providential." Fr. William expressed how this fund filled a great gap in the society because of the outbreak of the Intifada and it is so useful in helping families in need.

All Latin parishes in the Holy Land helped people in need through the humanitarian fund. For example, Fr. Rick Water in the Jifna parish was able to help approximately seventy-five needy families that could not pay their tuition this year because of the heavy burden placed on parents of educating children under terrible economic conditions.

Fr. Rick feels in addition to food and medicine, certain families were in deep need to help pay for their children's education. He says: "We appreciate our brothers and sisters abroad who are aware of our needs and working with us to try to meet these needs and we ask our Lord to bless them and re-compensate them for all they have done."

In the Zababdeh community where approximately 500 Christian families live, Fr. Aktham used the fund in three different ways. He created temporary jobs for unemployed people especially fathers that have many children as dependents. He managed different groups of five workers at a time that lasted ten to fifteen days while changing the groups three or four times to allow the maximum opportunity for as many men to work as possible cleaning the cemetery for the community and building walls and a gate.

Another way Fr. Aktham used the fund was to help seven university students attending local institutions who were not able to pay for their own tuition. The third way the fund was used to help extremely poor families in Zababdeh from the Latin, Anglican and Orthodox churches. Some families were instructed to purchase items that they need by themselves at the supermarket while the church paid the bill.

Other families were given cash money directly to help pay rent, electricity, water and other utility bills. Fr. Aktham reports that among the three churches at least fifty families are in deep need of help especially since the head of household lost their jobs as workers with Israeli companies. Fr. Aktham is very grateful to help his parishioners with this generous fund but he says: "It's good, it's not resolving the problem, it is not enough to give them food each month, we have to find a way to help them have a steady income."

As the economy continues to decline in the Holy Land and as the general siege and closure on Palestinian towns and villages prevent people from moving around, every parish priest continues to make the list of poor families longer and longer. In the Taybeh Community the list that included fifteen needy families prior to September 28, 2000 has now climbed up to about one hundred and fifty families at three different categories of need.

I can't remember if it is a Greek saying or a Chinese saying but the Church in the Holy Land now faces a new challenge not to just give people fish to eat but to teach them to go fishing themselves.

Job creation in Taybeh working on beautifying church grounds, Latin Convent

Shooting at Children and Teachers at the Checkpoint
June 29, 2002

Even when the Israeli army closes the roads, it is not humanly possible to stay home for long periods of time without having the need to get out. It is almost impossible to live without the city. Even if it means walking through checkpoints with soldiers shooting at you or above your head, people need to move around and are risking their lives every day to do simple things in life that others across the world take for granted. It is an absolute torture to be cut off from all community services including schools, hospitals, and banks.

On a regular Thursday morning and another school day, things are not so regular going to school from the village to the city. As Ramallah is declared a military zone for the one hundredth time, Dr. Grace, a business professor at Birzeit University felt obligated to teach her classes at the university and get her two girls to St. Joseph's School in Ramallah as part of the usual daily routine. Never did she image that the Israeli soldiers would shoot at a mother and two little girls clearly dressed in catholic school uniforms.

"Luba (her 6th grade daughter) had an exam and I made them walk almost two kilometers before reaching the second point where we have to take a taxi and walk more and they were sweating because it was hot so early in the morning. I saw many people putting handkerchiefs on their mouths and they warned us to go back because the soldiers where throwing gas bombs to stop people from going to work and school. But I felt frustrated that I had made the girls get up and dressed and we had already walked so much, it was better to continue and try to make it to school. I hate for them to miss school. We didn't imagine that they will shoot at children and women," says Dr. Grace. "It's becoming so dangerous just to go to school. I can't believe we have reached this level, it's really dangerous to move around," she explains.

Dr. Grace remembers after she began walking the checkpoint, an armored jeep quickly pulled up close to them and five soldiers jumped out pointing their guns directly at them and shouting something in Hebrew. The soldiers started shooting at them.

She says: "I remember hearing at least seven shots. We felt we are in danger but if we go back it is still dangerous, they are shooting and if we go forward, the danger is still there but forward was better because I saw a large wheat field so I started screaming for the girls to drop to the ground and hide between the wheat. We began to crawl and we hurt ourselves among the thorns. My feet are still blue and bruised from the ground. The only thing that kept going through my mind is that one of them will be shot in front of me and it would be my fault for making them wake up and go to school. They have began to hate school because of the terrible way to school...because of the terrible roads to school, although they are straight "A" students and they love their teachers and their friends but they hate the way to school. It has seriously become dangerous to go to school these days."

There was a young man in front of Dr. Grace and he broke his arm as he fell to the ground so he needed transportation to the hospital. She remembers the girls' faces being pale and yellow. They were terrorized. She crawled for many minutes while the soldiers continue to shoot at them. When she finally got in a taxi to make it into the city she could hardly breathe from fear. Someone in the taxi had ventalin (the medicine) due to their asthma condition so they gave her some of this medicine to help her breath.

"For the first time in my life I felt I was risking their lives to make them go to school.... I should have not insisted on crossing the checkpoint but they do this to us everyday, we can't go anywhere. The roads are always closed and people need to get to school and work," says Dr. Grace who stayed trembling several hours following the shooting.

Other people need to get to the bank like Rawand, an excellent teacher at the Birzeit Latin Patariachate School who needs to travel from Birzeit to Ramallah not only to finish her graduate classes for a master's degree in education but to also make deposits in the bank for the school. After having walked down the mountainside at the checkpoint as the only way to pass, she suddenly heard shooting from the valley below and the bullet from the M-16 rifle passed from the right to the left in front of her eyes, only a hair away from her forehead.

She was walking with a young man named George and another student at Birzeit University and as they dropped down to the ground, George scrapped his hand on the rocks with severe bleeding. They had nowhere to hide and Rawand thought that George was shot when she saw the blood, but they were very lucky to make into Ramallah alive.

"I could not take a breath, we were scared because there was no place to hide, no big rocks, no trees or anything to go behind, just open space, I was scared they shot George. I looked down and saw his hand full of blood but it was not from the bullets, it was a wound from the ground and falling and sliding in a hard way. There was no telephone, there was no ambulance if we needed one, all the taxis just drove away fast when they heard the shooting and they left many people behind. I had scheduled to quickly get to the bank and return to school to finish calculating the grades with the other teachers but I left the school at 11 am and now it's 4 pm and I don't know how I am getting back to Birzeit since they are shooting at the checkpoint. There is another longer way back but we must walk for two hours to use that road," Rawand said in Arabic. And sure enough that very evening after seeing Rawand at the old education office in Ramallah it took her many hours to return home safe.

I suggested it is not a good idea crossing these checkpoints because they are becoming more and more dangerous. She responded by saying: "It is always curfew, we can't get anything done, we must use the city, we must finish our work, we need the city, now the soldiers started to know all the side roads and they find us. God willing this will finish, it must finish."

The daily shooting at the checkpoints and speaking to people immediately after they have been terrorized by gunfire just makes me feel like running away. But a wise seventh grade student in the Aboud Latin School certainly does not think like me, Bnan Khalaf writes:

"We are staying on our land Palestine to learn and struggle against the occupation until we get our freedom and independence. Everyday they kill children, men, women, arrest people and put them in prison. But we are very determined to liberate our country...The Israelis have the weapons, but we will win the battle at the end because we have the will...Israel seized this land by force...I want the Israelis to get our of my country and give the refugees their right of return to their homeland. I'd like to ask you all to pray with me for peace in the Holy Land."

Greek Women in Ramallah
October 12, 2002

"It should not be worse than April," announced the new General Consul of Greece to Jerusalem, Ms. Eleni Sourani speaking to the Greek Women's Association in Ramallah this week as Greek women married to Palestinians gathered to greet her in the new post and arrange for emotional support and solidarity during crisis times. The new consul general is very worried about a major panic and fear that might occur in the Holy Land if the United States initiates a war with Iraq. Her major concern is not that Greek citizens would want to leave the Holy Land and the Greek government would not help them instead she is extremely worried about a major siege and curfew that would leave mothers and children of all ethnic groups starving in their homes if curfew is prolonged in Palestinian communities that are difficult to reach under military occupation. A war on Iraq would be very tragic for all of us already living under horrible military conditions.

I had just finished spending seventeen days of curfew in Taybeh myself because Ramallah was completely closed during the Jewish holidays. Completely closed means people stuck at home without being able to leave the house and in Nablus the curfew has reached over 100 days. It is so unfair and unjust that one group in the land celebrates holidays and continues life as normal while the other group is totally locked up like animals. The children are constantly missing school and this is a way that the Israeli army steals the rights of students to have education. I was completely overwhelmed with my father-laws funeral, Mr. Canaan Khoury, officiated by the Greek Orthodox Patriarch His Beatitude Patriach Irineos that curfew meant very little this time.

All European countries are cooperating to have the same plans for a war emergency but each country is responsible for negotiating safety for their particular citizens. The tragic news is that if Greek citizens receive help from the Greek government to leave under war conditions they will not have a right of return just as in 1948 and 1967. Thus, Sharon is really going to take advantage of any attack on Iraq and empty out the land of Christ's birth. People of Jewish heritage have a right to return to Israel even if they have never lived here before. But, someone like my husband who was born in Jerusalem, his father and grandfather were born in Palestine and have personal and business properties has no rights whatsoever. During the twenty three years my husband spent outside Palestine, he returned each and every single year to always renew his Palestinian identity card or else he would not have a right to return to his birthplace. Not every Palestinian can afford to go through this procedure. Thus, it is truly a miracle that some Christians even continue to live in the Land of Christ's birth. This might not be true fifty years from now if Sharon continues his state terrorism against the Palestinian people who seek their basic human rights.

The Greek government with the help of the Greek Women's Association headed by Margarita Kapetanea will help prepare a list of Greek citizens throughout Palestine believed to be about 250 individuals to facilitate evacuating them in case Sharon is planning another Sabra and Shatila massacre. May God have mercy upon us and can you please pray for our world leaders to use peaceful methods and non violent resolutions to solve international problems. War is not the answer.

The Greek Consul appeared to be a very kind hearted human being with the intention to help the local people and to honestly serve the Greek community in the Holy Land. Immediately I asked her for help for the housing project of St. George Greek Orthodox Church in Taybeh to support Christians stay in the village by having affordable housing and she mentioned the awful circumstances with the new Beit Sahour housing project built by the church that the Israelis want to demolish in the Bethlehem area. It is so difficult to do any productive work in the Holy Land for any few steps forward, the Israelis send us backwards with their military policies. We are surrounded by illegal Israeli settlements that continue to grow by the hundreds and the Israelis want to knock down one little housing unit built by the church. Where is justice in this land...I go crazy thinking of the discrimination and suffering Palestinians experience to survive as a nation.

How to you feel about your new post in Jerusalem?

Greek Consul: It is quite challenging and interesting.

What do you think of the Christians in the Holy Land?

Greek Consul: The Christian presence is the balancing factor between the two major conflicting sides. I find the Christian community very soothing, it balances the extreme.

How important is a Christian presence in the Holy Land?

Greek Consul: Extremely important. How can you have Holy Land without Christians, without life, without heart? It is not enough to have churches, shrines and monasteries. Of course we need the Christians to stay here.

How can we keep Christians here with the terrible economic conditions?

Greek Consul: By having projects that would support them, keep them in their land. It is the necessity that makes them leave; no one wants to be an immigrant. People usually want to live with their families, their relatives in their own land.

Following a wonderful gathering with a dozen Greek women, the general consul reassured us that she cared about us very much and wanted to support us with projects that would keep the Greek language alive in the Ramallah area by having classes on Thursdays and Saturdays and also by promoting music events and programs that provided humanitarian aid to all people under these difficult economic conditions where so many families suffer from basic needs.

The Greek Women's Association was established in 1999 in Ramallah but actively began to work with the Palestinian Uprising in the Fall of 2000. The first goal is to provide support and cooperation among Greek women in the area to further pursue Greek values and traditions and function as a solidarity group. However, it also works with The Greek Caravan of Solidarity to help orphans by fundraising 50 euros each month for Palestinian children that do not have a father. In addition, the group cooperates with many Greek organizations to help families having unemployed parents that need tuition money for their children's education.

Currently, schools in Palestine are being matched up with schools in Greece to have greater cooperation and cultural understanding not just financial support through non-government educational organizations. Also, Margarita and Maria Vekou keep in touch with isolated Orthodox monasteries in the Holy Land like the one at Jacob's Well in Nablus where Fr. Ioustinos has had seventeen assassinations attempts on his life. The previous abbot was assassinated in the 1970's.

Christian Village Under Curfew
November 18, 2002

Rarely does a little peaceful Christian village like Taybeh in the Holy Land go under curfew. Since Ariel Sharon sparked the Palestinian Uprising, the village has only been under curfew twice and the second time we begged the soldiers to uplift the curfew so we could carry on the planned Greek Orthodox engagement party that was scheduled at the Church Center for a young man named Mohib and his fiancée Doris. The soldiers kindly agreed and the curfew was uplifted so a traditional parade took place with clapping and singing from the family home to the church. But even when the village is not directly under curfew, the two main entrances to the village are technically blocked off by the Israeli army thus you can't get very far. It is like being a prisoner in an open space.

You can imagine there is not much available in a little village in the middle of the wilderness of Judea and Samaria. Sometimes I go to all five little mini markets and can't find a simple item like yogurt. And you wonder why I would even want yogurt but many traditional Arabic rice meals need to be eaten with yogurt thus the children refuse to eat the main course if they can't have it with yogurt.

I learned of the curfew because I have been waiting for my airline ticket to be delivered from Jerusalem in order to attend the one-day symposium about Christians in the Holy Land scheduled on November 23, 2002 in Chicago. The driver made it all the way to the outskirts of the village but could not enter to deliver the ticket and I could not go to the checkpoint to pick up the ticket either. I am stuck at home one more time as the Israeli army jeep patrols Taybeh announcing curfew.

A few hours earlier Palestinian militants attacked an Israeli settler on the road right next to our village. House to house searches will be made until someone is found to pay the price for the killing of this Israeli settler. Why do innocent people have to die daily on both sides? Just yesterday, an innocent Palestinian young lady of twenty-one died in her home from an Israeli tank shell. It is most likely that you will never hear about the Palestinian woman having a tragic death but surely the international news will announce that the so called terrorists have attacked the Israeli women and we will see on the evening news a human side to her life story.

Doesn't anyone ask, the Palestinians that die daily, are they not human? Last week twenty-five Palestinians were killed in one week alone, does not any one wonder if any were brothers, fathers, grandfathers, children, infants, do they all wear the label of "terrorists?" A two-year-old child bled to death in his father's arms shot by the Israeli army, doesn't anyone in the international community question the definition of terror in this new millennium?

As the bloody violence goes on and the Israeli army bombs and destroys people and places in Palestine and Muslim freedom fighters continue the suicide bombs and attacks on settlers it looks like a hopeless situation. The fanatics on both sides are destroying a life for the regular folks. A whole nation of people must pay a price for their actions with severe collective punishment.

Christians with their non-violent voices are just stuck between two extremes. Christians do not believe in being martyred for their country. This is sometimes held against them because they are pacifists. It is difficult to be a teenager in Palestine and on top of it to be Christian because you will be the minority and you will have pressure to join the mainstream and fight for your country but how do you respond when Christ says turn the other cheek and love your enemies.

We desperately cry out unto the Lord and ask for a peaceful resolution to a problem since 1948. How can the world continue to ignore that Palestinian Christians and Muslims do not have some very basic human rights in the land of their birth and in the land of their forefathers. It is an outright injustice and crime to be treated sub human on a daily basis. Since the president of the United States, the Pope, the United Nations, the European Union and Russia could not get Sharon to stop the occupation let us put our hope and our faith unto Christ our God.

Express your solidarity with Palestinian Christians by praying daily for justice to come in the land of Christ's birth. "I cried unto thee, O Lord: I said, Thou art my refuge and my portion in the land of the living. Attend unto my cry; for I am brought very low: deliver me from my persecutors; for they are stronger than I." (Psalm 142)

Chicago Symposium on Christianity in the Holy Land
The Divine Light Still Burns sponsored by HCEF
November 23, 2002

"By the grace of God the small Christian community will keep the torch of faith burning in the land of Christ and live in the strength and comfort of his words *"do not be afraid, little flock, for it is your Father's good pleasure to give you the kingdom."* (Luke 12:32)

This quote is from a fellow Christian in Palestine Naim Ateek of Sabeel Theological Institute in Rev. Dr. Don Wagner's book *Dying in the Land of Promise*. People have been dying in Palestine not just during this current uprising against the occupation but since 1948 and the world continue to ignore the Palestinian struggle for a homeland and the Palestinian Christians just continue to suffer and dwindle in lower numbers as a result. Our situation is so tragic it can only be reflected by a poor joke I know. Sir Rateb Rabie may never invite me to another conference by starting with this joke but it is meant with good intention to show our desperate situation that goes answered for what seems eternity. A group of Palestinian refugees were massacred and when their souls went to heaven of course they met St. Peter at the gates of heaven because every joke about heaven has St. Peter in it. These people begged St. Peter to get into heaven because the refugees said "you know St. Peter our whole life we have suffered under Israeli occupation, surely you must let us have our reward in heaven for all this suffering on earth." So St. Peter responded and said " Well I have bad news and good news for you…The bad news is that heaven is completely filled up and I can't let you in, but the good news is that hell is completely filled up so I can't let you in there either.

"But St. Peter, what are we suppose to do after a lifetime of suffering and pain, what do you mean we can't get into heaven, what are we suppose to do? St. Peter thought for a moment and responded, "I don't know, sometimes there just aren't any answers but I don't mind if you put up a few tents and hang out here for a while." So these poor Palestinians displaced for eternity. This is how helpless we feel in the Holy Land…that we must live with injustice forever.

Eight years ago when I moved to the Holy Land I realized that the Palestinian Christians are the ones that kept the flame alive for two thousand years in

Christ's birthplace. I moved to Palestine during a very promising time when the Oslo Peace Agreement offered Palestinians in the Diaspora to return to their homeland for a promising future living side by side to the Israelis in a two state solution that had so many loop holes it made the map of West Bank look like Swiss cheese. The Israelis gave Palestinians the center of towns to control but no roads to the towns. But we ignored the negatives and wished for the positives to come true where Palestinians and Israelis would live in peace with one another if only justice would take place by allowing Palestinians to have their independent state and their basic human rights on the West Bank which has been occupied since 1967 when my father in law put a white flag on top of his house and refused to leave after having built his home in Taybeh, the only all-Christian village that I always mention in my articles and after having fled the massacres in Haifa in 1948 to restart a new life he accepted to live and raise his children as Palestinian Orthodox Christians under military occupation.

As I was growing up very Greek in Denver Colorado, I didn't even know Palestinian Christians existed. I was born in Tripoli Greece but my parents immigrated for the same reasons all immigrants leave their homeland for better economic and educational opportunities. I grew up learning Greeks were good and everyone else was a "Xenos" a foreigner that was not good. I was suppose to live at home and go to college but I begged my father to let me attend the only Greek-American college that existed in the Western hemisphere, Hellenic College, and since it was a Greek college and everything Greek is good, I convinced him to let me go to Boston.

It was my luck to meet the only non Greek at the college, my husband a Palestinian Eastern Orthodox Christian who had also come to study theology because he come from a very devout family that had a whole line of priests serving the church. His grandfather was a priest in the village, his two uncles were priests, his aunt was a nun at the Russian Convent in Gethsemane and his cousin that brought him to Hellenic College finally became a bishop in the Antiochian church. The name "Khoury" in Arabic means "Priest." The priest right now at St. George's Greek Orthodox Church in Taybeh is Fr. David Khoury but it is not my husband but rather his first cousin. After debating for five years to be married or not since David my husband did not marry a nice girl from his village, His Beatitude Diodoros I officiated our wedding ceremony at his private residents in the Mt. of Olives where Christ's

Ascension took place. It was the commitment I made on that day that was about to change my life.

My husband spent 25 years in Boston but always had the dream to return back home and especially to please his late father who had the dream of every Palestinian Dad. To see his son receive the skills and knowledge and money from the West and bring it home. With the family unit breaking in America, I was convinced, if the military occupation stops and there is peace, it would be a wonderful place for my children to grow up with their grandparents and their aunts and uncles and have a real sense of the love and support of the extended family and at the same time my husband David and my brother in law Nadim Khoury would boost the economy by establishing the only microbrewery not just in Palestine but in the entire middle east region. It was truly a dream come true for them. Immediately more than 100 newspaper stories were written internationally about Taybeh Beer because people wanted to know who was going to be making beer in a 98% Muslim population where the Koran forbids drinking of alcoholic beverages. Strange titles came out such as "Dead man walking." My husband wanted to be a prime example to others that if Palestinians abroad would pick up their skills, talents and money and return to their homeland surely the State of Palestine could be built.

Then came Ariel Sharon and September 28, 2000 and all the dreams of the Palestinian people that had returned to their homeland were shattered by a new terror that had not taken place in the Holy Land since 1967 and 1948. Only now, more American money and more American weapons were available to crush the Palestinian civilians that went to the streets to protest Sharon's military visit to the Islamic Holy Site.

The first week of October 2000 was the worst week I have spent on earth. Seeing children shot to death on Palestinian TV (live coverage) and bloody scenes day after day, I immediately wanted to pick up my children and return to my home in Boston which of course I fought to keep empty in case of an emergency like this one. Of course life as normal had stopped, there was no work, there was no school, there was a complete closure and everyone was staying home glued to the news to see what would happen next. Especially when the first bombs dropped in Ramallah on the police station next to my children's school the Friends Boys School and eight classroom's were damaged I knew the Holy Land was not the place for me. I packed my bags,

I gathered any money that I had, I made reservations and I wanted to leave so desperately.

There was only one problem. My husband did not want to go with me. People that left in 1948 did not have a right to return; people that left in 1967 lost their identification card controlled by the Israelis. My husband had traveled every year since he was a student in college to maintain his Palestinian identification, something a bid costly that not everyone can do. After such a major investment like his microbrewery and five years waiting for our huge home to be built in the village, like his father in 1967, he was not about to leave his possession behind nor his father and mother nor the whole extended family. I sort of knew that in the Arabic tradition you kind of marry the whole family not just the guy but this was just too evident and frightening that I could not go anywhere unless they went with me and of course they are patriots they will not leave. I am a foreigner it was so easy to leave. My heart was just torn to pieces because I did not know what to do.

All my life I have been an obedient wife but now it was endangering my children's life. I put up such a fight to leave because at nights for several weeks I could not sleep thinking of the violence and killings. I just could not close my eyes. When I did sleep I would dream of bloody scenes and death and soldiers and guns. When the schools started up again at the end of October 2000, I would drive with the children to school and literally my feet would shake and my hands would shake with fear that someone would shoot us at any moment. In the beginning of the uprising we had so many incidents of Palestinians killing settlers and the next day settlers attacking innocent Palestinians on their way to school or work.

We went several months with these tragic killings back and forth and driving the same roads where people died every day I could not stand myself being alive and seeing these things happening around me. When I did make it to work at the Latin Patriarchate Schools in the Ramallah Education office I just could not be productive because you spent so much effort and time making it to work you were mentally and physically exhausted. And in 2000 most of the times, there was a call to evacuate the city of Ramallah because the Israelis would start bombing. So you have hundreds of people trying to pick up their children from school at the same time and desperately go to their houses or leave the city. There was such a chaos and panic in the streets it is hard to find the right words to describe the fear and terror that was in the air and running in terror as I try to collect my children and pass four sometimes five checkpoints to make it home to the village. And every day it would be a different side road because more and more roads were closed up as the situation continued to deteriorate.

The checkpoints are the other problem because the Israeli army can put up checkpoints anywhere it well pleases. So we have major checkpoints that never go away and extra ones that might not be there in the morning when you went to school but will be there in the afternoon when you returned home. And you might be five minutes away from your house at the entrance of the village and the soldier might say an absurd remark like, you can't pass, go back, and you think, go back where, my house if five minutes away straight on this road, and he does not care where you go or do not go because these checkpoints are not to prevent the so called terrorists from entering Israeli cities because these are checkpoints going from Palestinian villages to Palestinians cities. They are set up to humiliate, degrade, frustrate, and make the Palestinian people suffer daily for the most basic things like going to work, school, the hospital or the bank. It is such a torture just moving around. Most days we are just at the mercy of these soldiers that do or do not let you pass depending on their personal mood and disposition.

There is no logic to the checkpoints because on Holy Saturday traveling from Ramallah to Jerusalem with only three cars in front of me at the Qalandia checkpoint, another nightmare checkpoint that in July it was taking me six hours to drive through it from Ramallah to the village of Taybeh, which is normally a ten minute drive without checkpoints, these three cars took one hour and half to pass. We were so happy to drive to the checkpoint and not find hundreds of cars as usual but only three cars and we said thank God we will pass without waiting but the soldiers intentionally just keep you waiting and delaying. So these checkpoints are such a problem because they are not practical it is so difficult to estimate what time you will get anywhere. On Holy Saturday I made sure to leave my house at 7:00 am to make sure I make it there by noon.

The Christian holidays were celebrated in a larger scale before September 2000. For example on Holy Saturday you would have many villages all around Ramallah waiting for the Holy Light to come from Christ's tomb and as soon as it was distributed in Ramallah it would travel to the surrounding villages. All of the Christian denominations would march in a parade with the boy scouts and the girls scouts and other Christian youth groups to receive the Holy light and take it first to the Orthodox church of the Transfiguration in Ramallah and than their individual parishes, and it was such a joyous and festive occasion and also it was just so lovely to participate in traditions and customs that have been carried out for centuries in the Christian community in the Holy Land. The tradition and the celebration of the Holy Light on Holy Saturday is one of the most important events and the biggest event that takes place in the Holy Land. Last year during this time, the city of Ramallah was under 21 days of total curfew during holy lent and the city of Bethlehem was under siege for 39 days during the Lenten period. The Israeli army had the courtesy to uplift the curfew for a few hours in Bethlehem so people can pray at church for this holy day and not at midnight where it is customary but at a time that the Israeli army decided. But no parades, no music, no marching, no patriarchal procession, nothing festive and joyous. It was almost like receiving the Holy Light in mourning.

Each and every one of us must find the way to keep the divine light burning in our world. When we have taken on Christ in baptism we must follow Christ and honor His commandments to love one another, thus we take on the responsibility to keep the divine light burning because as Christians it exists in our hearts and it must shine as we go out in this dark world that contains evil. God's love and grace must over power evil. What have I personally done do keep the divine light burning?

Ask yourselves this in prayer today, because certainly we must seek God's hand in all of our problems in all of our difficulties in all of our sufferings. We must come close to God from our experiences here on earth. I believe whatever gifts God gave us, they are meant to give Glory to Him whom gives us eternal life. Thus if God gave you "knowledge" help others understand, if God gave you "power and authority" make a difference in the world by bringing justice, if God gave you "wealth and money" give to the poor." I truly believe that if God gives us blessings when we are sharing them with others we are keeping the divine light burning no matter where we live.

To find a purpose in life and to find a way to contribute to maintaining my faith was very important to me very early in life and this is why I wanted to study at a Greek Orthodox college and know more about myself and my heritage. I found a way to preserve these values and traditions with the books that I write for young children. Because I do believe that faith is like a little seed if we plant it and nurture it, our spirituality is enriched and we grow closer to God, we develop spiritually.

The first book I ever printed *Christina Goes to Church* is just a simple explanation of all the why's in the church. Sometimes as Orthodox Christians we look so strange to outsiders and little children should know the symbolism and the traditions of the church to deepen their understanding of our customs, like why do we light candles, why do we kiss the priest's hand, why do we kiss the icon, why do we receive holy bread at the end of the service. I have had many adults tell me that they have benefited from reading my children's books.

Christina Learns the Sacraments is another educational book that I have published that explains in children's language why some people get married, why some people become priests, why do we take communion or go to confession. Again an effort to document traditions and values of the Christian faith and why they are practiced as a way to preserve these traditions and maintain them for generations to come by reading about them as bedtime stories.

The other two books I have published are a counting book and an alphabet book in relationship to faith and the church because it is a reflection that faith is natural as children learn their abc's or 123's, they also learn values from their faith that are meaningful. These books are meant to reflect that we are Christian every day; we are not Christian when we go to church on Sunday. We are Christian when someone curses at us, how do we respond, we are Christian when the car in front of us cuts us off, how do we respond with anger or with understanding. We have been baptized unto Christ thus we need the Christian response to everything that happens to us in life as Christ teaches us through the commandments and the gospels. To live a Christ centered life is my interpretation of keeping the Divine Light burning.

The last book I printed *Christina's Favorite Saints* is to help children become familiar with people that have worked very hard in their lifetime to preserve the Christian faith and to live a Christ centered life. One of these saints tremendously helped me feel at peace with my situation. Because I was always complaining about living in the Holy Land even before the bombings and the shootings and the violence, I was bothered by the lack of hot water in the winter, no central heat 24 hours a day, no central air conditioning during hot days, no laws on smoking, 99% of the population smokes everywhere, the wilderness and living in the middle of nowhere in Judea just bothered me after having been in a cosmopolitan city like Boston for twenty years.

I was totally shocked to find out St. Herman left his home in Russian and stayed his whole life in Alaska preaching the gospel and teaching the local people about Christ. I was surprised he never went back to Russia and he never wanted to go back to Russia. He made his new home in Alaska preaching the good news. Thus my life took on a new meaning of being a small voice in the wilderness promoting a Christian presence in the Holy Land. I am trying to find a publisher to print this collection of over sixty articles that are more like a diary since September 2000 for people who are interested in knowing more about the Christian presence in the Holy Land.

The terrible siege and general closure has greatly affected my life because for three years I have been working in the education office in Ramallah for the Christian schools under the Latin Patriarchate and it was devastating for me when my new boss Fr. Majdi Siryanni opened a new office in Beit Jala that under the current checkpoints I just cannot physically get to it every day so I lost my job that had given great meaning and purpose to my life because I was helping teachers and students in the Christian schools work with modern teaching methods and strategies and get away from the traditional Palestinian education that had passive learning.

I was excited to be making a difference in the English language learning in the schools by introducing critical thinking skills and many activities that here in the West you just take for granted. And the funny thing is that Fr. Majdi opened the new office in Beit Jala because he simply could not pass the checkpoints and could not come to the Ramallah office. And after his office in Beit Jala was completed with office furniture and computers the only people going to his office where the tanks and the Israeli soldiers because he was stuck in his convent under curfew that went on and off for many months last year in the Bethlehem area.

It is so hard to move ahead because the Israelis keep putting us years behind especially now with the total destruction and devastation of almost everything in the West Bank. Day after day it just does not stop the frustrating checkpoints, the invasions and reinvasions into Palestinian towns, the house to house searches, the detentions, and the constant shootings and bombings.

As Christians of the Holy Land, we are in God's hands. The Israelis and the Muslims continue attacking each other and we are just stuck in between. We believe and we promote non violent resolutions to the current crisis. The occupation has gone on for so long that it is a surprise the spirit of the Palestinian people has not been crushed because everything else in the land has been destroyed. I truly believe the Christian presence has to survive the violence and the bloodbath by people staying in the land of Christ's birth and bearing witness to Christ our Lord and Savior under these harsh conditions.

However, The Holy Land is not just for the Palestinian Christians to keep the Divine Light Burning but it is for all Christians everywhere to show their solidarity to their brothers and sisters in Christ by adopting the Holy Land as their spiritual homeland. We must all pray and work together to keep the eternal flame glowing in our hearts. The Holy Land does not only need financial support but needs Christians to make the pilgrimage of a lifetime and take the spiritual journey through the land of Christ's birth. I thank HCEF for their efforts to support a Christian presence in the Holy Land. I especially thank Sir Rateb Rabie and the board for the great blessing to be with you today and I invite all of you to be living candles that shine on earth with Christ's love and grace by coming to the Holy Land and rejuvenating yourselves with Christ's spirit and feel the spiritual beauty of where the word become flesh and dwelled among mankind. And of course while you are in the Holy Land ask for the one and only Palestinian beer, "Taybeh Beer."

Since I opened with a terrible joke I must close with a meaningful prayer that I read in my church each Sunday and also I suffer reading in English while everyone else is praying in Arabic but it goes to prove how we are all part of one body because no matter what language we speak or what cultural customs we follow it is just important to give glory to God and feel the strength and love that comes from being brothers and sisters in Christ. Let us pray together *"Illumine our hearts, merciful Master, with the pure light of our knowledge of You, open the eyes of our minds to comprehend fully the message of your Gospel. Instill in us also deep respect for your blessed commandments so that, having conquered the desire of the flesh, we may pursue a spiritual life, thinking and doing all those things that are pleasing to you: for, You, O Christ our Lord, are the light of our souls and bodies."*

The divine light still burns because for over two thousand years our brothers and sisters in the Holy Land have suffered and died to give witness to Christ, our God. Pray for me to have such a blessing.

Taybeh Glorifies Christ's Birth
December 26, 2002

"For unto you is born this day in the city of David a Saviour, which is Christ the Lord."
(Luke 2:11)

The Angelic voices of the twenty-five member choir filled the Latin Church on Christmas Eve in the small village of Taybeh where songs giving glory to Christ's birth were sang for several hours during an evening service in Arabic led by our beloved Fr. Raed Abusahlia spending his first Christmas with us as the parish priest. Much credit should be given to Mr. Suhail Nazal who generously works with the student choir on a weekly basis to train and challenge the students to give their outmost to the church. Our volunteer Seminarian from France, Stefan, was also very active in directing the choir. We have such amazing talent existing all in one little village. Listening to this beautiful Christmas service was my proof that it is the soul that prays to God regardless of what language we use for communication.

The Latin Church was packed as standing room only especially with some extra people like me who have to wait another thirteen days until it becomes December 25th on the Julian Calendar so that the Orthodox Church can hold the Christmas liturgy. To promote Christian unity on a social level following the Oslo Agreement all of the West Bank towns and village agreed among the people to celebrate Christmas together on the Western Calendar and to celebrate Easter on the Orthodox Calendar. However, the Orthodox Church services technically have not changed, this agreement was only to facilitate the social occasion of wishing each other a blessed Christmas on the same day.

However, the last two years we have not had Christmas lights in the streets, nor Christmas carols, nor Christmas murals painted everywhere depicting Christ's birth as was customary in the village in the past. The boy scouts have not marched for any holiday since September 2000. The festive part of Christmas in the Holy Land has disappeared but as Christians, of course, deep in our heart we rejoice in the birth of our Savior, Christ our Lord. *"He came unto his own, and his own received him not. But as many as received him, to them gave he power to become the sons of God, even to them that believe on his name."* (John 1:11-12).

This spiritual joy in our hearts can not be expressed in a cultural or social level because violence and death continue to swallow us up. Daily destruction and oppression overwhelm our lives. For about a month now, the two main entrances to our village have been sealed off. Begging the American Consul and the local Israeli District coordinating office to help us open the road has been in vain. We are basically locked up in an open prison. The way the security walls and the tall cement blocks are going up all over the West Bank is exactly like creating ghettos so the Israelis do not have to see the Palestinians or deal with them. Palestinians are denied all basic human rights and are literally being chocked up emotionally, physically psychologically, and spiritually.

As Christians we will promote peaceful resolutions and seek non violent ways to this terrible oppression. During this holy season we thank you for praying for the people of the Holy Land who suffer this terrible oppression. Christ is Born! Glorify Him!

IC XC
NI KA

Orthodox Christmas Silently Passed
January 7, 2003

The Sun has just set in the beautiful hills of Judea marking the end of the Orthodox Christmas Day celebration on the old Julian calendar in the Land of Christ's birth. The words of a nasty email keeping ringing in my head "Judea is for Jews," "Arabia is for Arabs" as part of recent hate mail I received for promoting human rights for Palestinians and an end to the Israeli occupation in the West Bank and Gaza. I keep thinking of the words of Christ Himself in Acts 1 "...*and you shall be witnesses unto me both in Jerusalem, and in all Judea, and in Samaria, and unto the uttermost part of the earth.*"

Does this not indicate that Christ calls upon to practice our Christianity no matter where we live? Should Christians disappear from the Land of Christ's birth just because Israelis make their life miserable each and every single day? I can't understand why the Jewish race is above all laws. They have Israel created in 1948 by the United Nations why can't they live inside Israel and get out of the West Bank and Gaza and let the Palestinians have their own independent state? Why must they have illegal Israeli settlements in Judea and Samaria too?

Palestinian children die each and every single day on their way to school and from school. Palestinian homes continue to be demolished every single day leaving hundreds homeless and helpless. Palestinian land continues to be confiscated for security walls and illegal settlements daily. The only time the world hears about Palestinians is when the Israelis want the international world to know about suicide bombers blowing themselves to pieces killing innocent people that no Christian, Jew or Muslim should condone.

The desperate circumstances of these people that have had their human rights neglected for over 54 years should not give them permission to harm innocent victims. However, all the money and weapons from the United States goes to Israel thus the Palestinians are left to fight with only their bodies because they do not own f-16's, tanks, and armored jeeps paid by American tax dollars. Palestinians are seeking freedom and independence, they are not terrorists.

Since I live in the middle of the wilderness I can't claim to know much but if the United States stops sending so much military aid to Israel maybe the

Israelis wouldn't carry out so much destruction which so far has including blowing up the historic and archeological cave chapel of St. Barbara from the fourth century in the village of Aboud, damaging the back door and parts of the Nativity Church in Bethlehem, firing unto St. Nicholas Church in Beit Jala, damaging the Orthodox Church in Nablus and firing missiles on the Orthodox Club in Beit Jala.

If the United States wanted peace in the Middle East it could achieve it in one week by asking the Israeli government to stop the cruel occupation and torture of the Palestinian people. But instead the United States is preparing for war in Iraq and announcing a possible 18 month occupation of Iraq. The Bush government should seek diplomatic and peaceful resolutions not war. I am so confused as how America thinks as one nation under God and resorts to war as the answer. The God I grew up knowing from my Sunday school teachers and my parents is the God of love and the God of peace. Is this not the God that created all humans equal as Christians, Muslims and Jews to give glory to Him and to do unto others as we wish others to do unto us?

On Orthodox Christmas every year I drive to Bethlehem to attend the midnight service at the Nativity Church giving glory for Christ's birth. This year I am blocked in my little village by large cement blocks on both main entrances and the Israeli army is keeping Bethlehem under curfew. The Orthodox Christmas services took place as usual but local Christians outside Bethlehem found it difficult and impossible to attend.

I spent this Orthodox Christmas Day listening to shooting and gun fire not knowing who was shooting who. We are all currently prisons in our individual towns and villages and peace seems more distant than ever. The fanatics on both sides of the Israeli-Palestinian conflict continue to ruin life for the average people that are willing to live in coexistence. Please know that the terrorists are not the Palestinians which the media continues to overemphasize but a greater terror is taking place with American money and weapons that you should be aware and contact your government officials to vote for diplomatic and peaceful resolutions not more military aid to Israel.

In closing I hope I am not what another email stated " a disgrace, an embarrassment to even be called Greek," instead I hope in all humility you find me as a witness for Christ and a small voice crying in the wilderness and speaking the truth from the occupied Palestinian territories where Jews and

Muslims are slaughtering each other daily and Christians are just disappearing in this Ethnic Cleansing campaign that started September 28, 2000 by Ariel Sharon. May Christ our true God Who selected this Holy Land to reveal His glory bring inner peace where peace does not exist among the people. *"Glory to God in the highest, and on earth peace, good will toward men."* (Luke 2:14)

St. George Greek Orthodox Church of Taybeh re-built 1931
Taybeh, Ramallah District, Palestine

Fr. David P. Khoury
Parish Priest

Preparing for War in the Holy Land
February 13, 2003

While the Israeli public is busy buying "duck tape" and purchasing water and food supplies enough for at least three days, it is totally impossible for Palestinians both Christian and Muslim to prepare for anything or even have gas masks ready to save their lives as the Israeli civilians. We have lived in a war of terror into the third year now with daily killings, political assassinations, medical personnel shot dead on duty, homes being demolished, people being detained without charges, home invasions, checkpoints, road blocks, closures, total siege and a total devastation and destruction of the economy, education and social life in general.

When Palestinian families have suffered without jobs and trying to meet their daily needs where in the world would anyone get enough money to stock up for a war? Some curfews or if you prefer the word "house arrest" go over 21 days in our area and certainly families run out of basic needs like bread, milk and needed medicine when the army confines them to their homes. In the city of Nablus, Palestinians were confined to their homes for over 100 days in the summer. It is sometimes difficult to conceive of such cruelties and harsh conditions. With over two thousand people dead since September 2000 and over forty thousand injured, we know and have experienced the brutality of war. Innocent civilians are bound to suffer and be killed if America decides to bomb Iraq. Let us pray for God's mercy and enlightenment.

No reason to write stories anymore because the world has forgotten that Israel continues to deny Palestinians their human rights for over 55 years and not only refuse to give them independence but the Israeli army makes their daily life so miserable, so awful and full of struggle and agony that possibly they could flee over the bridge into Jordan. Thereby Israel could rejoice at this ethnic cleansing and claim a 100% Jewish homeland.

Where is our voice as Christians in this land? Our roots were established by Christ Himself with the Mother church in Jerusalem. This is the sacred land that Christ chose to be born in and to create His Holy Church. Why should the American money and weapons destroy the most significant heritage and legacy of Christianity? It is the "living stones," the local Christians that have kept the torch of faith burning for over two thousand years. Palestine has Christians and Muslims living in the Holy Land and peaceful solutions need to be found to coexist with Jews. However, the unjust policies of the United States in the Middle East are affecting the dwindling Christian Community in Palestine. It is time that Christians in the West questions their leadership. Blind support to Israel must stop sooner or later. It is totally out of control.

As Christians we do not only belong to this world alone but are called to seek God's kingdom. I would suggest preparing for war by fasting and praying. Preparing for war might mean going to confession so that we can beg for God's forgiveness and remission of sins. As Christians we are sent on earth to give glory to God with every breath that we take and to see God in others. Truly we must live each day as if it is the last day in our life. While your government is asking you to purchase certain items and be on a high alert also consider seeking God's kingdom and flock the church to take communion. Christ died on the cross so that we may have eternal life.

God gave us a brain so we can think thus possibly stock up on some bread if we can afford it but God also gave us a soul so that we may give glory to Him. *"I am the bread of life; he that cometh to me shall never hunger; and he that believeth shall never thirst."* (John 6:35)

We are preparing for war in the Holy Land by the only method that we know: to be witnesses for Christ. We must confess love for our neighbor and to turn the other check to our enemies by seeking peaceful solutions to our conflicts. As Christ Ascended into Heaven while the disciples watched, He said: *"...you will be my witnesses in Jerusalem and in Judea and Samaria and throughout all the earth."* (Acts 1:8)

The altar boys at St. George Greek Orthodox Church

The Holy Land Buries Christina
March 28, 2003

I have a special connection to the name "Christina" because it is the ideal Orthodox character in my books for children that promote the symbolism and beauty of the Orthodox Christian faith. "Christina" is used to help children grow closer to God by helping them be knowledgeable about the faith. Thus, I was heart broken to hear that a beautiful young Orthodox Christian girl named Christina was killed instantly after being shot by the Israeli occupation army in Bethlehem on Greek Independence Day March 25th and on the very holy day of the Annunciation according to the Western calendar.

This innocent ten year old child was a victim to Israel's cruel and unlawful assassination policies of political activists as her family was driving by the Shepherd's Hotel near the Cinema area. This is a tragic example of the "democracy" that Israel practices. The Israeli army also killed three men in the car in front of Christina's family. Over two thousand Palestinians have been killed since September 2000 with over four hundred being children.

Christina, a good student at St. Joseph's School in Bethlehem and who often prayed at the Nativity Church was in the car with her parents and older sister Marianne when the Israeli soldiers opened fire and shot her sister in the knee and father in the back and side. Christina was shot in the head and believed to have died on the spot thus was not taken to the hospital like her fifteen year old sister and parents. Christina's father, Mr. George Sa'ada is the principal of the Orthodox School in Beit Sahour.

Rev. Sandra Olewine, the United Methodist Liaison in Jerusalem actually heard the gunfire around 7 p.m. in Bethlehem. She states: "I was on the phone to a friend in the US, when gunfire erupted nearby. It was loud enough that my friend on the other end of the line could hear it. A few seconds later another loud round went off. Moments later I could hear the sound of an ambulance approaching. The local television station was soon showing a group of Palestinian medics trying to carry away someone who had been killed, a car with the entire back window blasted out and the trunk riddled with bullet holes, and a few Israeli soldiers in uniform keeping watch on everything. The scene was on the hill just four houses up the street from my own."

Today (March 28th), the Holy Land buries Christina with her father and sister not being able to attend the funeral services because they are still in the hospital. One can not help but wonder why the Israeli army opens fire in a residential neighborhood? Why does the Israeli army continue to kill innocent civilians every day under the slogan "they are getting the terrorists?"

When will the world realize that under these awful and horrible living conditions created by the occupation we are all turning into terrorists? May God give us the strength to follow our Christian values and principles and seek peaceful ways to live together as Christians, Muslims and Jews. We need to follow the words of Christ and not only forgive our enemies but love our enemies. Please help children in your church know about our tragic situation in the Land of Christ's Birth so that Christina's death will not be in vain. Let the children pray for peace in the Holy Land.

The Holy Nativity Church built over the birthplace of Jesus was Christina's home parish

Mr. Canaan David Khoury
December 25, 1926 - September 13, 2002
Founder of the Taybeh Orthodox Housing Project

Fundraising in the Middle of the Wilderness
March 30, 2003

As the Christian population continues to fall below 2% of the three million Palestinians that live in the West Bank, Gaza and inside Israel we are probably looking at a future that might not include Christians living in the land of Christ's birth. How sad for such a sacred land where Jews, Muslims and Christians should practice co-existing instead of slaughtering each other. Actually living in the Holy Land, I see the Jews and the Muslims killing each other and the Christians just disappearing to other countries.

The fight we endure is not just physical but also an entire economic occupation and strangulation of the Palestinian territories due to checkpoints, closures and complete siege on towns and villages under Israeli military control in the West Bank. Palestinians are prisoners in open areas blocked by cement blocks and walls the Israelis are constantly putting up for security. I don't see how the Apartheid walls will ever bring security to Israel. It is so frustrating and aggravating getting around these walls to go to work and school daily.

As a Greek-American of Orthodox Christian faith living in the middle of Judea on top of one of the highest mountain ranges in Palestine surrounded by hundreds of illegal Israeli settlements, I overlook Jerusalem from my living room window and grateful to be alive each and every day the Lord grants me in the middle of the bloodshed.

My husband's village of Taybeh is one of the only all-Christian villages left in Palestine. As members of the St. George Greek Orthodox Church of Taybeh we want to work very hard to maintain this Christian presence that has been here since the time of Christ. At least we want to keep the 1300 residents that live in the village because today there are more people from Taybeh that live in Detroit, Michigan than this little Christian village itself.

I am volunteering my time at St. George Church to help fundraise for a critical housing project to help minimize the Christian immigration to other countries. We want to help young married couples have their own home at a reduced cost and at the same time to help create temporary jobs--much needed due to economic hardship from the siege and closures. Such a project would help maintain an Orthodox Christian population and encourage local residents to stay with the Orthodox Church instead of converting for housing opportunities.

In 1998, the Greek Orthodox Patriarch allocated land to the Taybeh Church in order to help thirty families build their homes by providing the land without cost. A committee was formed by my late father-in-law, Mr. Canaan D. Khoury, the founder of the housing project to search for funds and manage the project licensed under the Orthodox Youth Club of St. George's Greek Orthodox Church registered with the Palestinian Authority. The funds are managed by the six member housing committee approved by the late Patriarch Diodoros I of Jerusalem and include *Fr. Daoud P.Khoury (Jerusalem Patriarchate Representative);* Dr. Grace C. Muaddi (Administration); *Mr. Naseem Fqier (Treasurer).*

Sub Deacon Nicholas and Nancy Tentzeras are helping us construct a website for the church and bring awareness to the housing project and the fact that there are Palestinian Orthodox Christians living in the Holy Land that trace their roots back two thousand years. Although our site still needs a lot of work and corrections it exists (www.saintgeorgetaybeh.org).

The housing project hopes to help thirty families, all members of St. George Church acquire their first homes at a low cost if they meet a strict financial need requirement. Each family must agree that they will not sell their unit except through the church to another needy family or leave it to their own children. In addition, each family must contribute monthly to a building fund toward the total cost of the project. Our fundraising at least hopes to cover building the skeleton structure of the thirty housing units and is estimated at over one million dollars.

The first phase of the housing project will be to build twelve houses as soon as at least $350,000 are raised. All funds currently raised will equally help only the first twelve families. However, due to the tragic situation in the Holy Land, we have more than 60% of the people currently without work. None of the members have made payments since September 2000.

We are seeking twelve churches, organizations or private donors that would like to help the twelve families build their first homes. Raising money has been difficult. So far we have only fundraised $18,000.

We are praying to find 12 parishes or private donors that would sponsor the twelve families at $50,000 each home. Without such help we can not go forward with this desperately needed project.

Will you help? Could your parish assist us? Could you seek support on your parish for a special collection, or series of collections, so that young Orthodox Christian couples in Taybeh can obtain their first home? We would be so grateful!

Ideally, cooperating parishes would have one year to conduct fundraising through bake sales, Sunday school projects, car washes, philotopchos or ladies society activities, youth activities, etc and can express their solidarity by collecting funds within one year.

Please also tell your parish about the $1.00 Campaign for the Holy Land Housing specifically helping Taybeh for the Lenten Season. Each member of a cooperating parish is asked to contribute just $1.00 to Orthodox Christians in Taybeh during the Lenten season. It would be a tremendous help to the housing project if 100 parishes responded by sending $1,000 each parish even if two Lenten Seasons were used to participate in the $1.00 Campaign which will be in progress from Lent 2003 to the Lenten Season 2006.

Contributions will be managed by the housing committee in Taybeh and held in an account at the Arab Bank-Ramallah, Al Balad Branch. Your help is greatly needed. Donations may be sent by check to **Taybeh O.C. Housing Project, P.O. Box 867, Taybeh, Ramallah, Palestine VIA ISRAEL.** Or by electronic transfer to Arab Bank-Ramallah, Swift code ARABPS 22090, Al Balad Branch Account # 9090-662656/4/510 Taybeh Orthodox Club Housing Project, Via the Arab Bank New York, swift code US33. Please notify by email if there is a check in the mail/money transfer for better tracking: Khourymaria@hotmail.com or drmariakhoury@yahoo.com

Don't forget your fellow Christians living in the sacred land of Christ's birth. Get your church involved with this important housing project to express your solidarity and support to Orthodox Christians in the Holy Land. One day you may have the gift of visiting the Holy sites and it would be rewarding to meet the living stones, the local Palestinian Christians, who have maintained the Mother Church for over two thousands years in the land that was made holy by Christ himself.

General Information About the Holy Land

Christ is Born in Bethlehem when Herod is King of Judea

33   Christ celebrates Passover in Jerusalem, is arrested, tried, crucified under the Governorship of Pontius Pilate

34   The first bishop in Jerusalem, James, leads the Christian community following the resurrection and ascension of Christ

66   The Jewish revolt against the Roman Empire

70   The Romans defeat the Jewish rebels and destroy the Second Temple except for the Western Wall

132   Jews fight Romans to stop Emperor Hadrian from making Jerusalem a city for many gods

135   Hadrian defeats Jews and builds a pagan city for the gods, Jerusalem now called Aelia Capitolina, and Judea known as Palestina. Jews banished

213   Bishop Alexander establishes first Christian library and Christian School in Jerusalem

290   First monastic community established in Palestine near Gaza

325   Emperor Constantine makes Jerusalem Christian and part of the Byzantine Empire; with his mother Helen builds many churches including the Holy Nativity Church and Holy Sepulchre

614   Persian invasion of Jerusalem. Many churches destroyed

622   Muhammad's flight from Mecca to Medina. Islamic religion is born and a Muslim empire grows

628　Persians defeated. Byzantines again rule in Jerusalem

632　Death of Prophet Muhammad. Muslim Arab Empire now ruled by religious, political, and military leader known as the caliph

638　Byzantine Jerusalem taken over by Muslim Caliph Omar

691　Caliph Abed el-Malik builds Dome of the Rock in Jerusalem

775-1071　Jerusalem ruled by three different Muslim empires

1099　The First Crusade takes over Jerusalem. Many Jews and Muslims massacred

1187　Christian armies of Second Crusade defeated by Muslim leader Salahadin. Crusaders leave the Holy Land

1191　Third Crusade arrives and Christians gain some land but do not totally control Jerusalem

1270　The seventh and last Crusade in the Holy Land

1291　Muslim Egyptian Mamluks conquer Palestine and take over Jerusalem

1516　Jewish community in Palestine starts to appear again while the Ottoman Empire controls Jerusalem into the 20th century (1517-1917)

1538　Suleiman the Magnificent rebuilds walls of Jerusalem

1832　Ibrahim Pasha, an Egyptian Muslim, takes control of Palestine

1840　Egyptians pushed out of Palestine by Turkey with the help of France and Great Britain

1882 Arrival of first modern Jewish settlers in Palestine

1918 Jerusalem taken over by the British at the end of the World War I

1948 The creation of the State of Israel in Palestine but the Old City of
      Jerusalem is under Muslim control by Jordan

1967 Israel occupies East Jerusalem and the West Bank in the
      Six Day War

1987 The First Palestinian Uprising (Intifada)

1993 The acceptance of the Oslo Peace Agreement
      The Israelis and the Palestinians agree for a two state solution

2000 The outbreak of the Second Palestinian Uprising
      Al Aqsa Intifada

References for above dates are the Encyclopedia Encarta (2003) and the Arabic version of
Khoury, Shehadeh (1924) *Summary of the History of the Jerusalem Orthodox Church*,
Jerusalem Press. The dates are approximate and are arbitrarily selected to give basic
background in understanding many groups sought to gain control in Jerusalem based on
feelings of historical, political, and religious rights.